Environment and the nation state

Issues in Environmental Politics
series editors Tim O'Riordan, Arild Underdal *and* Albert Weale

As the millennium approaches, the environment has come to stay as a central concern of global politics. This series takes key problems for environmental policy and examines the politics behind their cause and possible resolution. Accessible and eloquent, the books make available for a non-specialist readership some of the best research and most provocative thinking on humanity's relationship with the planet.

already published in the series

Environment and development in Latin America: the politics of sustainability   *David Goodman and Michael Redclift editors*

The greening of British party politics   *Mike Robinson*

The politics of radioactive waste disposal   *Ray Kemp*

The new politics of pollution   *Albert Weale*

Animals, politics and morality   *Robert Garner*

Realism in Green politics   *Helmut Wiesenthal (editor John Ferris)*

Governance by green taxes: making pollution prevention pay
Mikael Skou Andersen

Life on a modern planet: a manifesto for progress   *Richard North*

The politics of global atmospheric change   *Ian H. Rowlands*

Valuing the environment   *Raino Malnes*

Environment and the nation state

The Netherlands, the EU and acid rain

Duncan Liefferink

Manchester University Press

Manchester and New York

Distributed exclusively in the USA by St. Martin's Press

Copyright © Duncan Liefferink 1996

Published by Manchester University Press
Oxford Road, Manchester M13 9NR, UK
and Room 400, 175 Fifth Avenue, New York, NY 10010, USA

Distributed exclusively in the USA
by St. Martin's Press, Inc., 175 Fifth Avenue, New York,
NY 10010, USA

British Library Cataloguing-in-Publication Data
A catalogue record for this book is available from the British Library

Library of Congress Cataloging-in-Publication Data
Liefferink, Duncan.
Environment and the nation state: the Netherlands, the
European Union and acid rain / Duncan Liefferink.
    p. cm – (Issues in environmental politics)
Based in part on the author's dissertation, Wageningen
Agricultural University, 1995.
Includes bibliographical references.
ISBN 0-7190-4924-5
    1. Air–Pollution–Government policy–Netherlands. 2. Acid rain–
Government policy–Netherlands. 3. Air–Pollution–Government
policy–European Union countries. 4. Acid rain–Government policy–
European Union countries. I. Title. II. Series.
HC39.5.A4L54
369.73'92'09492–dc20   96-28199
                                                              CIP

ISBN   0 7190 4924 5   *hardback*

First published 1996

00 99 98 97 96   10 9 8 7 6 5 4 3 2 1

Printed by Biddles Ltd, Guildford and King's Lynn

Contents

Part II   Case study: acidification policy

Part III Analysis and conclusions

Preface

Why does someone decide to embark upon a research project in social science? Why does one seriously want to sit down in a red and brown painted room for several years of one's life, to struggle through piles of books and articles (while realising there are so many more books and articles one should read), and to spend months thinking over, writing down and interpreting the outcomes of a couple of conversations? Why does one do such a thing?

That is an interesting question, but it will not be answered here. I can however think of some reasons why I never regretted the decision. One of those reasons is the fascination of the subject – the thrill of seeing how people try to cope with a complex and pressing problem like environmental degradation and how their ideas and actions gradually take the form of organisations, negotiations and rules, and start to play a game of their own.

Another reason was the help I received from many people who were involved in the project. This book started as a dissertation, presented at Wageningen Agricultural University in the spring of 1995. I have appreciated the freedom Wim Brussaard and Ad Nooij, my promoters, gave me to develop my own approach to the project, but also their critical and often stimulating comments on my draft chapters. Graham Bennett, Willem Kakebeeke and Ekko van Ierland followed the work at some distance and saved me from losing direction. Twenty-three people in The Hague, Brussels and elsewhere were prepared to talk to me about their ideas and experiences. Their kindness and openness was an uplift to me.

A major factor was the presence and support of the people sitting in the red and brown painted rooms nextdoor. Tuur Mol was both an adviser and a companion. Working with him was a great pleasure in many senses. Our collaboration on the precursors of chapter 2 gave a new impulse to my work. Without Gert Spaargaren the book would not have existed. He showed me how to study environmental policy and laid the foundations for the research proposal. As colleagues and friends, Frans van der Zee, Hilkka Vihinen, Jan van Tatenhove, Kris van Koppen, Joris Hogenboom, Viviane Ampt and Menno van der Velde were always prepared to share their views with me. A number of MSc students accompanied and inspired me during parts of the work. Hélène Grijseels was the first of them. It is difficult to say if it was her preparatory work on the negotiations over outputs from large combustion plants or her infectious enthusiasm that was most valuable to me. Corry Rothuizen and Ciska de Harder performed innumerable organisational and administrative tasks and contributed much to making me really feel at home in the corridors of sociology.

Outside the university buildings the world appeared to have more colours than just red and brown. Colleagues abroad, particularly Philip Lowe, Mikael Skou Andersen and Henning Arp, were sources of new ideas and inspiration. Katharina Holzinger kindly permitted me to make use of considerable parts of her dissertation on the 'clean' car process before it was published. The help and advice of Albert Weale were indispensable in the final stage of preparing this book. Many friends – Mark van Berkel perhaps most of all – were patient enough to listen to my stories and to encourage me when necessary. My parents did so from the very beginning.

Although writing a dissertation is not unlike a period of courting Science, crowned with a wedding in the Sacred Halls of the University, it did not prevent Riet and me from getting married in the same period. I even think that our adultery with Chemistry and Political Science, respectively, added a new dimension to our relationship.

I wish to thank here all the people who have, in one way or another, contributed to this book.

Wageningen
August 1995

Persons interviewed

All interviews were conducted between December 1992 and June 1993.

Mr L. C. van Beckhoven, Noordwijk (formerly Ministry of VROM, The Hague)

Mr A. P. M. Blom, Ministry of VROM, The Hague

Mr E. J. Borst, Ministry of VROM, The Hague

Mr F. Christophe, Volvo Car Corporation, Helmond

Mr C. Dekkers, Ministry of VROM, The Hague

Mr S. Depla, Ministry of VROM, The Hague

Mr R. H. Donkers, Commission of the EC, DG XI, Brussels (formerly Ministry of VROM, The Hague)

Mr W. F. van Eijkelenburg, RAI Vereniging, Amsterdam

Mr J. T. J. Fransen, SNM, Utrecht

Mr J. Gerritsen, Landbouwschap (Agricultural Board), The Hague

Mr H. J. Haanstra, Ministry of VROM, The Hague

Mr H. Henssler, Commission of the EC, DG III, Brussels

Mrs B. Humphreys, Secretariat-General of the Council of Ministers of the EC, Brussels

Mr V. G. Keizer, Ministry of VROM, The Hague

Mr E. R. Klatte, Commission of the EC, DG XI, Brussels (formerly Ministry of VROM, The Hague; EEB, Brussels; Greenpeace EC Unit, Brussels)

Mr J. van der Kooij, SEP, Arnhem

Mr N. Marsman, KW, Amersfoort

Mr D. Pietermaat, Ministry of EZ, The Hague

Mr N. J. Stenstra, Spijkenisse (former Vice-President of OCC, The Hague)

Mr P. Stief-Tauch, Commission of the EC, DG XI, Brussels

Mr A. van Straaten, Ministry of LNV, The Hague

Mr G. H. Vonkeman, Zeist (former Director of SNM, Utrecht; former Vice-President of EEB, Brussels)

Mr W. M. Zijlstra, VNO, The Hague

Abbreviations

ACEA	Association des Constructeurs Européens d'Automobiles
ACP	African, Carribean and Pacific [States] (former colonies of the EC Member States)
bat(neec)	best available technology (not entailing excessive costs)
BEES	Besluit emissie-eisen stookinstallaties (Decree Emission Requirements Combustion Installations)
BEUC	Bureau Européen des Unions de Consommateurs
CCMC	Comité des Constructeurs d'Automobiles du Marché Commun
CDU	Christlich Demokratische Union
CEC	Commission of the European Communities
CEFIC	Conseil Européen des Fédérations de l'Industrie Chimique
CIM	Coördinatiecommissie Internationale Milieuvraagstukken (Co-ordination Commission for International Environmental Affairs)
CLCA	Comité de Liaison de la Construction Automobile
CoCo	Coördinatiecommissie voor Europese integratie- en associatievraagstukken (Co-ordination Commission for European Integration and Association Problems)
CONCAWE	Oil Companies' European Organisation for Environmental and Health Protection
COPA	Comité des Organisations Professionelles Agricoles
COREPER	Committee of Permanent Representatives
CSU	Christlich Soziale Union
DG	Directorate-General (in the EC Commission)
DG III	Directorate-General for Internal Market and Industrial Affairs
DG IV	Directorate-General for Competition

DG VI	Directorate-General for Agriculture
DG VII	Directorate-General for Transport
DG XI	Directorate-General for Environment, Consumer Protection and Nuclear Safety (since 1990: Environment, Nuclear Safety and Civil Protection)
DG XVII	Directorate-General for Energy
EAP	Environmental Action Programme
EC	European Community
ECE	Economic Commission for Europe (United Nations)
ECSC	European Coal and Steel Community
EEB	European Environmental Bureau
EEC	European Economic Community
EFIEC	European Federation of Industrial Energy Consumers
EFTA	European Free Trade Association
EMEP	Co-operative Programme for the Monitoring and Evaluation of Long-Range Transmission of Air Pollutants in Europe
EP	European Parliament
ERGA	Evolution of Regulations, Global Approach
ESC	Economic and Social Committee
EU	European Union
Euratom	European Atomic Energy Community
EZ	[Ministerie van] Economische Zaken ([Ministry of] Economic Affairs)
FDP	Freie Demokratische Partei
FRG	Federal Republic of Germany
GATT	General Agreement on Tariffs and Trade
GFAV	Grossfeuerungsanlagenverordnung
GNP	gross national product
IMP	Indicatief Meerjaren Programma (Indicative Multi-Year Programme)
KW	[Vereniging] Krachtwerktuigen (organisation of Dutch industries in the field of energy and environment)
LNV	[Ministerie van] Landbouw, Natuurbeheer en Visserij ([Ministry of] Agriculture, Nature Conservation and Fisheries)
MVEG	Motor Vehicle Emissions Group
MW	megawatt
NCW	Nederlands Christelijk Werkgeversverbond (Association of Dutch Christian Employers)

NMP	Nationaal Milieubeleidsplan (National Environmental Policy Plan)
OCC	Olie Contact Commissie (Oil Contact Commission)
OECD	Organisation for Economic Co-operation and Development
OPEC	Organisation of Petrol Exporting Countries
RAI	Rijwiel- en Automobielindustrie [Vereniging] ([Association of the] Bicycle and Automobile Industry)
RIVM	Rijksinstituut voor Volksgezondheid en Milieuhygiëne (National Institute of Public Health and Environmental Protection)
SEP	Samenwerkende Elektriciteits-Produktiebedrijven (Dutch Electricity Generating Board)
SNM	Stichting Natuur en Milieu (The Netherlands Society for Nature and Environment)
UK	United Kingdom
UN	United Nations
UNICE	Union of Industrial and Employers' Associations
UNIPEDE	International Union of Producers and Distributors of Electrical Energy
US(A)	United States (of America)
V&W	[Ministerie van] Verkeer en Waterstaat ([Ministry of] Transport and Public Works)
VDA	Verband der deutschen Automobilindustrie (Association of the German Automobile Industry)
VDEN	Vereniging van Directeuren van Elektriciteitsbedrijven in Nederland (Association of Directors of Electricity Companies in the Netherlands)
VNO	Verbond van Nederlandse Ondernemingen (Association of Dutch Employers)
VOCs	volatile organic compounds
VoMil	[Ministerie van] Volksgezondheid en Milieuhygiëne ([Ministry of] Public Health and Environmental Hygiene)
VROM	[Ministerie van] Volkshuisvesting, Ruimtelijke Ordening en Milieubeheer ([Ministry of] Housing, Physical Planning and Environment)
WHO	World Health Organisation
WWF	Worldwide Fund for Nature (formerly World Wildlife Fund)

1

Introduction: environmental policy in the EC

Introduction

When this study was conceived, at the end of the 1980s, the European Community (EC)[1] was in the heyday of the '1992' internal market project. Finally, after thirty years of tiresome efforts, the Community was to remove the last remaining barriers to the free movement of persons, capital and goods. The prospect of half a continent unimpeded by internal borders was alluring and further steps such as co-operation in the political and the monetary field were discussed. The Community seemed to be 'taking over' more and more important political powers from its Member States. What was about to happen was broadly regarded as a decisive new step in the process of European integration, if not as the prelude to the United States of Europe.

At the beginning of the 1990s, the shift of competences from the nation state to the Community was still being debated, but the perspective had gradually changed. Both the full removal of trade barriers and border controls and entry into new fields of co-operation had proved to be more difficult than anticipated. The 'Maastricht' Treaty on European Union had met with little enthusiasm, not only in traditionally 'Euro-sceptical' countries such as Denmark and the UK, but also for instance in France, Germany and the Netherlands. The 'Europeanisation' of policy, in other words, was now seen as a threat to national autonomy, rather than as an adequate response to the challenges of the increasingly global society. Every curtailment of the Member States' room for manoeuvre by 'Brussels' was looked upon critically and much of the dynamism of the preceding years had evaporated.

Environmental policy played a significant role in the ups and downs of this period. As the number and effect of environmental measures at the Member State level had sharply increased in the last two decades, the harmonisation of those measures became one of the major concerns in the Community's internal market project. The pursuance of environmental policies at the EC level was further stimulated by the growing recognition of the transboundary character of many environmental problems. In this specific field as in the general debate on the transfer of powers, however, both positive and negative voices could be heard. On the one hand, EC involvement in environmental policy was welcomed as an important step towards a common approach to the causes and effects of the degradation of the global environment. On the other hand, it was feared that common efforts would lead to 'lowest common denominator' policies, unable to accommodate specific national or local circumstances and objectives. Adherents of the former view argued that still more environmental policy competences should be transferred to the Community, whereas the others questioned even the present degree of co-operation.

There are, in short, two good reasons for considering in more detail what is actually going on in EC environmental policy. Is the Community really in the process of 'taking over' the environmental policy field from the Member States or are the basic decisions still made at the national level? What forces are behind any such take-over and under what circumstances do they operate? Answers to those questions can, first, add to the understanding of the EC's increasing role in environmental policy making, which is one of the crucial trends in the policy field. Secondly, insight into this matter is relevant to the study of the broader process of European integration. As environmental policy is one of the most dynamic and fastest growing areas in the Community (cf. Liefferink *et al.*, 1993b), its emergence and development may shed light on how and why Member States co-operate in a more general sense. While the public and political perception of integration can obviously turn rapidly from one extreme to the other, focusing on a longer period of, for instance, one or two decades will probably help to highlight the more fundamental tendencies.

When talking about the Community 'taking over' the environmental policy field from the Member States, I refer not only to formal competences but to the policy process as a whole. This includes legal rights and obligations, but also the establishment of general policy objectives, the articulation of various societal interests and the making of basic and follow-up decisions. In the context of the questions raised in this study, it is particularly interesting where the various aspects of policy making actually take place, where the margins for concrete policy measures are essentially established, where interest groups are granted access and where their views are taken into account, and – most importantly – to what extent shifts in the 'centre of gravity' of environmental decision making can be observed. On that basis it will be possible to assess whether environmental policy is indeed 'on the way to Brussels': if it is really moving house or only paying occasional working visits to the EC capital.

Summarising the argument, this study will be guided by the following basic questions. To what extent and in what way did the increasing involvement of the EC in environmental policy making lead to increasing inter-relation and interaction between environmental policy making at the EC level and the Member State level? To what extent did such changes lead to a shift of policy making from the national to the EC level? Which forces stimulated or hampered this development?

In the next chapter these questions will be further worked out, theoretically buttressed and operationalised for empirical investigation. The remainder of the present chapter will be devoted to an initial exploration of the subject. In the next section a short historical account of environmental policy making in the Community will be given. This will enable a first sharpening of the research question and the formulation of a number of general, substantive expectations about the way in which EC environmental policy is built up. Finally, an outline of the rest of the book will be given.

A concise history of EC environmental policy

In this section the emergence and development of EC environmental policy will be reviewed. After sketching the international context of the growing interest in environmental problems in the 1960s and early 1970s, three phases in the history of environmental policy in the Community will be distinguished. They will be based primarily on the evolving relationship between the environmental policy field and the dynamics of the process of European integration in a broader sense, with an obvious emphasis on economic issues. In addition, developments in environmental policy globally will be taken into account.

The international context: the emergence of the environmental issues

During the 1960s public concern about the deterioration of the environment rapidly spread in Western countries. Efforts to preserve nature and wildlife, at both the national and the international level, had been made since the nineteenth century, but now the emphasis shifted to stresses on ecosystems and natural resources. Water pollution, air pollution, the diffusion of dangerous chemicals and other problems typical of modern industrial society were gradually taken up by policy makers. In many countries the first genuinely environmental laws were enacted in the second half of the decade.

Apart from national experience with environmental policy making, according to Caldwell, the broad perception of 'the interactive, life-sustaining processes of the biosphere ... as a concern common to all mankind' was a prerequisite for international environmental co-operation to come about (Caldwell, 1990: 23). The seed for this was also sown in the 1960s, culminating in 1972 in the United Nations Conference on the Human Environment in Stockholm. One of the dominant themes during this conference was the link between environmental issues on the one hand and international economic relations and problems of underdevelopment on the other (Caldwell, 1990: 41ff.). It was still to be the main theme at the follow-up conference in Rio de Janeiro twenty years later.

The present study, however, will deal with environmental co-operation between the rich, industrialised countries in Western Europe. Here also, the importance of the economic aspect was evident from the beginning. This is probably best illustrated by the fact that three economic organisations soon emerged as the focal points for international environmental co-operation in this region: the United Nations Economic Commission for Europe (ECE), the Organisation for Economic Co-operation and Development (OECD) and the EC.

The ECE, comprising most East and West European states as well as the United States and Canada, took up environmental problems in the mid-1960s. Although the ideological tension permanently underlying the activities of the ECE prevented far-reaching work on the socio-economic implications of environmental issues, the ECE did manage to produce a number of notable framework agreements, starting in 1979 with the Convention on Long-Range Transboundary Air Pollution. The ECE was thus able to play a significant initiating role in environmental co-operation in Europe (see further: Bishop and Munro, 1972; Füllenbach, 1981: 167–175).

The OECD started its environmental activities in the same period as the ECE. As the OECD had a rather homogeneous membership of Western industrialised countries, strong ideological differences were absent here. Being a high-level study group rather than a decision-making body, the OECD never acted as the arena for the negotiation of international agreements. It did however issue a number of influential recommendations and background reports, often dealing with fundamental aspects of the relationship between economic activities and environmental problems. Well known examples are the propagation of the 'polluter-pays principle' (OECD, 1975) and the more recent work on economic instruments in environmental policy (OECD 1989) (about the OECD in general, see: Bungarten, 1978: 250ff.; OECD, 1986; Caldwell, 1990: 98–100).

Compared with the ECE and the OECD, the EC's involvement in environmental issues started more indirectly and more hesitantly. The Community's first steps in the environmental field were aimed primarily at removing trade barriers caused by national environmental standards (for an excellent and detailed discussion, see Bungarten, 1978: 128ff.). Only in 1971, preparations for the United Nations Conference on the Human Environment being already three years under way, was the preoccupation with the economic and trade effects of environmental regulation seriously called into question. This eventually led to a declaration at the European Council[2] meeting in Paris in 1972. Here, the Heads of State and Government acknowledged that economic expansion should be accompanied by environmental protection so as to achieve a genuine improvement in quality of life. The institutions of the Community were invited to lay the basis for an environmental policy in the form of an Environmental Action Programme. The Paris summit is usually regarded as the birth of Community policy with regard to the environment (cf., among others: Bungarten, 1978; Koppen, 1988a; Johnson and Corcelle, 1989: 1–2; Liefferink *et al.*, 1993b: 3).

Modest beginnings: the 1970s

Although deeply rooted in the military-strategic situation in Europe after the Second World War, the Community – and particularly its core, the European Economic Community (EEC) – was basically an economic organisation.[3] As laid down in the Treaty of Rome of 1957, its main goal was the establishment of a common market between the six founding members: Belgium, the Federal Republic of Germany, France, Italy, Luxembourg and the Netherlands. The necessary shift of substantial economic powers from the Member States to the Community, however, turned out to be a continuous source of controversy. A major crisis in 1965–1966 could be solved only by accepting a right to a veto in the Council of Ministers[4] in cases where 'very important' interests of a Member State were at stake. For many years, unanimous voting remained the rule in practice in the Council (Kapteyn and VerLoren van Themaat, 1987: 174–177), particularly after the accession in 1973 of Denmark, Ireland and the UK, who were all not particularly eager to share too many of their national powers.

Against this background, the content of the Paris declaration was fairly radical. It implied the development of a wholly new set of policy goals at the Community level, as it were amending the original common market objective, and a further broadening of the Community's claims on national competences. It may be argued that it took about ten years to attain any sort of balance with regard to this question.

One of the first illustrations of the problem at stake was the debate about the First Environmental Action Programme, drafted by the Commission in 1973 (COM(73)530).[5] It was used by France to raise formal objections against the Community's competence to develop common environmental policies. Despite general consensus about the content of the Programme, France insisted that its juridical basis was too weak to adopt it as a decision of the EC Council as such. The document was eventually adopted as the Declaration of the Council of the European Communities and of the representatives of the Governments of the Member States meeting in the Council (EAP 1973–1976; cf. Bungarten, 1978: 147ff.). In the preamble it was stressed that actions included in the Programme were to be taken partly at the Community level and partly at the level of the Member States. The Programme did not bind the Member States and could not be submitted to the Court of Justice in Luxembourg (see Koppen,

1988a: 4–8). Significantly, the mixed status of the First Action Programme was preserved in all the following ones, despite repeated efforts by the Commission to use the more usual construction of a Council Resolution (with regard to the Fourth Programme, see Jachtenfuchs, 1989).[6]

A better record is provided by the policies actually initiated in the first years of EC environmental policy. The environmental directives[7] that saw light in this period can be broadly divided into two types on the basis both of their character and the treaty basis chosen for their enactment.

The first category includes directives that are directly related to the functioning of the common market. They were usually designed to remove trade barriers that had resulted from diverging national environmental requirements, such as the emissions from motor vehicles (Directive 70/220/EEC and several updates), the composition of detergents (73/404/EEC) or the sulphur content of gas oil (75/716/EEC). An uncontested legal basis for this type of measure could be found in Article 100 of the EEC Treaty (Rehbinder and Stewart, 1985: 21–26). Contrary to what might be expected, however, the number of this kind of directive adopted in the 1970s was fairly small. Moreover, they were either optional and not very strict (the car directives, see further chapter 6) or rather limited in scope (the directives regarding gas oil and detergents). This suggests that harmonisation of environmental product standards was very limited in this period. The failure of attempts to regulate the sulphur content of more types of fuels in the second half of the decade (cf. chapter 5) illustrates the fact that Member States halted proposals for product harmonisation that they saw as going too far.

The second category was much larger in scope as well as in number and comprises all directives that were not exclusively or primarily motivated by the logic of the common market. As a result, they could not be based on Article 100 alone. In most cases, therefore, the broad Article 235 was used (see Rehbinder and Stewart, 1985: 15ff.; Sevenster, 1992). Most directives in this group contained either environmental quality standards, for instance regarding surface water and air (76/160/EEC, 78/659/EEC, 79/923/EEC; 80/779/EEC), or framework provisions, primarily in the fields of water pollution and waste (76/464/EEC; 75/442/EEC; 78/319/EEC). In principle, it is right to observe that the directives, in particular those that referred to Article 235, were 'a matter of creating new policy' (Johnson and Corcelle, 1989: 4). Nevertheless, most of them, while intended to be far-reaching, required hardly any direct action. The Member States' reluctance to adopt such policies was further underlined by the slow adoption of specific emission values necessary to effect the surface water directive (the first 'daughter directive' being adopted more than five years later, 82/176/ EEC) and the poor implementation of the other framework directives and the quality directives (Haigh *et al.*, 1986; Bennett, 1991).

The double basis of many environmental directives was possible in practice because both articles prescribed the same decision-making procedure, which was in fact the usual one after the crisis of 1965–1966. Decisions were taken by the Council of Ministers by unanimity upon a proposal by the Commission, who had the exclusive right of initiative. The European Parliament (EP) and the Economic and Social Committee (ESC)[8] were only consulted; that is, they could formulate comments and amendments but did not have the formal power to make or change the final decision. Once Community legislation had been established, the room for divergent national measures was usually limited and had to be judged case by case on the basis of the exact wording of the directive in question (Sevenster, 1989: 35–37).

In conclusion, the first decade of EC environmental policy may be characterised by the combination of ambitious intentions and very modest concrete steps. Common policies were either directly related to trade interests or restricted to general provisions at a considerable distance from the actual polluting activities, even if they were properly implemented. Member States were reluctant to transfer substantial environmental competences to the Community and the requirement of unanimous decision making in the Council enabled them to be hesitant.

New initiatives: the early 1980s

The first signs of a change became visible in the early 1980s. It may be argued that earlier developments no longer met the needs created by the continuous increase in the number and impact of environmental problems, the growing national environmental policy responses, and the unflagging process of interweaving of the economies of the Member States in general. The perception of these shortcomings was strongly stimulated by the alarmist reaction to the problem of acidification in Germany and some other countries in this period. At the same time, as some authors argue, each piece of legislation that had been adopted in the EC had contributed to the step-by-step construction of a Community competence in the field of the environment. Every directive, however modest it might be by itself, facilitated the acceptance of a further extension of the Community's activities in the field (Bungarten, 1978). This complex of factors helped to prepare the ground for the Third Environmental Action Programme, which marked a shift in degree in the conception of EC environmental policy making, and the European Council meeting in Stuttgart, 1983.

The Third Environmental Action Programme, adopted in February 1983 (EAP 1982–1986), was the first to be something more than a detailed 'shopping list'. Instead, it emphasised two strategic aspects of environmental policy making: prevention of pollution and the integration of environmental considerations into other fields of Community policy. The latter element is particularly interesting as it seeks to close the gap between the group of strongly market-oriented product standards and the directives containing quality objectives and general provisions that were still relatively detached from economic and commercial activities.

A further impetus to EC environmental policy was given by the European summit held in Stuttgart in June 1983. It was the first European Council meeting to address environmental policy since the Paris summit. It underlined 'the urgent necessity of accelerating and reinforcing action at national, Community and international level aimed at combating the pollution of the environment' (Johnson and Corcelle, 1989: 20). This statement was strongly inspired by Germany and particularly by the problem of acidification, which had reached an unprecedented pitch on the political agenda in Bonn.

The new impulses were of course not immediately transformed into forceful new policies. In particular, penetration of environmental considerations into other, sometimes long-established policy fields turned out to be a difficult task (see EAP 1987–1992: 10ff.; EAP 1993–2000, *passim*; see also, for instance, Brinkhorst, 1989: 72–76; Kamminga and Klatte, 1994). The first half of the 1980s, however, did see the opening of some new, important sub-fields of environmental policy, notably air pollution. Moreover, some common emission standards were adopted, finally, under the framework directive for water pollution (76/464/EEC, see above, and its 'daughters' 82/176/EEC, 83/513/EEC, 84/156/EEC, 84/491/EEC and

86/280/EEC) and serious discussions about formulating such standards for some major stationary sources of acidification were started (see chapter 7). This step was significant, as emission standards were related to conditions of competition in a much broader sense than the earlier product norms and implied a considerably more far-reaching Community interference with industrial production than the quality norms decided in the 1970s. In addition, the instrument of environmental impact assessment was introduced in 1985 (85/337/EEC).

The institutional affirmation: the Single European Act and further
In 1985, the first major amendment to the Treaty of Rome, known as the Single European Act, was signed. In 1987 it came into force. The main idea behind the Single Act was the revitalisation of the project of European integration by completing the 'Single European Market' in 1992. Part of the '1992' programme was the strengthening of 'flanking' policies in a number of related fields, including environmental protection.

Until 1987, environmental policy had had no formal treaty basis. As the policy field had gradually evolved as one of the most dynamic ones in the Community, assigning a formal status to it was an obvious step, which had in fact been discussed for many years (Bungarten, 1978: 228ff.). The revision of the Treaty in connection with '1992' then was a suitable, almost inevitable opportunity to do so. From that angle, the sections on environment in the Single Act were mainly a formal confirmation of politically established practices (Koppen, 1988b: 624; Scheuing, 1989; Brinkhorst, 1989: 64; Johnson and Corcelle, 1989: 342). At the same time, however, they reflected the increased value attached to the integration of environmental considerations into a project as typically economic as '1992'.

Two parts of the Single Act were directly relevant to environmental policy. First, a separate environmental section was included (Article 130R–T). It laid down the Community's competence to act in order 'to preserve, protect and improve the quality of the environment' as far as these objectives could be better attained at the Community level than at the level of the individual Member States. The latter formulation was the first formal reference to the subsidiarity principle (Brinkhorst, 1992). It was combined with an explicit authorisation for Member States to maintain or introduce stricter measures than those adopted by the EC. The environment section empowered the Council to take the necessary decisions by unanimous vote (i.e. following the existing procedure). Secondly, the 'old' Article 100 was amended by Article 100A, prescribing a new co-operation procedure for all decisions aimed at the establishment and functioning of the internal market. This procedure was characterised by the principle of qualified majority voting in the Council[9] and limited formal powers for the EP. The EP's amendments, if adopted by the Commission, could be adopted by the Council by qualified majority, but rejected only unanimously. Article 130R–T thus offered a much more explicit and unambiguous basis for genuinely 'environmental' measures than Article 235, while Article 100A succeeded Article 100 for legislation more directly related to the functioning of the internal market (see further the extensive juridical literature on this subject, for instance: Krämer, 1987; Koppen, 1988b, 1993; Sevenster, 1989, 1992).

Apart from these formal and procedural changes, the generally strong motivation to progress with the '1992' programme for the removal of trade barriers, a number of them relating to the environment, and the widespread confidence in this programme conveyed a sense of co-operation between the Member States. Although the number of items did not dramatically increase in the years after the coming into force of the Single Act, some notorious issues were eventually brought to a conclusion in this period, such as the 'clean' car and the large combustion plants (see chapters 6 and 7). In addition, some major new environmental policy initiatives were launched. The most ambitious was no doubt the proposal for a 'greenhouse' tax on energy around 1990. The proposal introduced once again a new policy instrument and implied significant impacts in so far predominantly national fields such as energy policy and fiscal policy. As such it reflected an optimistic perception of the latitude for the penetration of other policy areas and for the transfer of substantial competences from the Member States to 'Brussels'. The later history of the proposal shows that this view was indeed too optimistic, notwithstanding the considerable efforts by the Commission to have the Community play a leading role in this field at the United Nations Conference on Environment and Development in Rio de Janeiro in 1992 (Jachtenfuchs and Huber, 1993).

A fourth, and at the time of writing the last, phase in the history of EC environmental policy was inaugurated by the 'Maastricht' Treaty on European Union, in force since the end of 1993. It set out a scheme for the establishment of monetary and political union by the end of the century. Environmental policies under Article 130R–T, with some exceptions, were now to be decided under the co-operation procedure (qualified majority and co-operation with the EP). Article 100A was to be governed by the new co-decision procedure, which again slightly extended the powers of the Parliament. In the same period, the Fifth Environmental Action Programme (EAP 1993–2000) was published, and this represented a renewed and ambitious attempt to bring about, eventually, a more integrated approach to environmental problems. More significantly, however, the 'Maastricht' Treaty, and the difficulties encountered in the ratification procedure in some countries, gave rise to a fundamental discussion about the subsidiarity principle and the desirability of (further) transfer of national competences to the Community. Although the period after 'Maastricht' could not be included in the empirical part of this study, the findings will be evaluated in the light of the recent developments in the last chapter of this book.

Framing the research question: environmental policy as a case of continuous 'Europeanisation'?

From its very beginnings in the 1960s to the Single European Act and the '1992' project, the evolution of EC environmental policy suggests a very intimate relationship between economic and environmental issues. In fact there appear to be two basic motivations for the internationalisation of environmental policy. One is the perception that environmental problems themselves cannot be solved at the national level because of their transboundary character. The other is the wish to avoid the negative economic consequences that would result from environmental policies being followed only at the national level. Examples are barriers to international trade caused by national product norms, or costs incurred by environmental requirements that would endanger the competitiveness of national industries. In practice, of course, both motivations often go together, but there is room for a considerable variation in emphasis.

This dual motivation was reflected in the early years of EC environmental policy. There was a considerable gap between a group of trade-related harmonisation measures and a larger, more diffuse group of general environmental provisions with limited economic ramifications.

At the beginning of the 1980s this gap started to close, owing to a gradual broadening of the range of policy measures. New themes were explored and new instruments were introduced, notably emission standards. The result was a growing influence of environmental policy on economic life, not only on conditions of trade, but also on conditions of production. With considerable difficulty, some links were also established with other policy sectors, such as energy and agriculture.

The process of broadening policy in the 1980s gave expression to the increasing perception of an interrelationship between economic activities and environmental protection *at the international level*. At the domestic level of industrialised States, this interrelationship had been recognised much earlier and it had been reflected at least to some extent in the first wave of national environmental laws around 1970. Now it became increasingly clear, however, that some isolated measures mitigating the environmental consequences of some areas of trade and some rather open-ended attempts to formulate common environmental policy goals of a fairly general kind were not sufficient to deal with the international aspects of the problem. The international co-ordination of a larger part of environmental policy was required, for instance at the Stuttgart summit in 1983.

This development was further stimulated by processes of internationalisation both in the environmental and in the economic field. In the West European context, the emergence of the issue of acidification appears to have played a major role in the recognition of the truly international character of environmental problems. The rise of global issues such as the depletion of the ozone layer and the 'greenhouse' effect some years later added to this trend. Policy efforts in the EC were in two of the three cases part of a broader network of international negotiations and agreements. The continuous increase of economic interdependence was of course not limited to the EC, but there can be no doubt that things proceeded particularly rapidly and conspicuously there. In spite of crises and delays in European political integration, the economies of the Member States had become increasingly intertwined and formerly 'national' industries were competing more and more at the European level. This underlined the need not only to remove trade barriers, but also to equalise, for instance, environmental costs.

The perception of changing circumstances was followed by institutional change. As argued, there are reasons to assume that this in turn facilitated the further development of the Community's environmental policy. By introducing qualified majority voting for an important proportion of decisions in the environmental field, the Single Act took away the possibility for a single Member State to block the adoption of common policies. At the same time, the explicit legal basis for environmental policy largely ruled out further questioning of the Community's competence in this field. Finally, the more firmly established permission for Member States to pursue stricter national policies under certain conditions probably reduced some of the resistance to common standards, at least in the environmentally more progressive countries.

This chapter opened with the question of whether the EC was gradually 'taking over' the environmental policy field from the Member States. The above assessment of the development of EC environmental policy from the early 1970s to the early 1990s seems to support a positive answer to this question. It outlined a process of steady growth, both in terms of substance (i.e. the number and scope of policy measures) and regarding the extent to which decisions taken in Brussels interfere with national policy. Does this imply that the Member States' sovereign powers are continuously 'leaking' to the Community, as is so often argued? Does it entail a constant reduction of national policy competences and an increasingly sharp curbing of national sovereignty by 'supranational' policies? It is tempting to consider the relationship between national powers and Community powers as a zero-sum game: the addition at one side would then be equal to the diminution at the other side. This is however too simple: it should not be forgotten that the principal motivation for dealing with certain environmental problems at the international level was that it was felt that they could not be adequately dealt with at the national level. Powers were shared, in other words, in response to the perception of an increasing loss of power at the domestic level, and this was supposed to lead in the end to *more* control of the problems involved.

The question if and to what extent powers and competences shifted from the nation state to the Community should therefore be accompanied by the more intriguing questions of why an increasing number of environmental issues were made subject to EC policy making and how exactly environmental goals, market forces and economic interests were related in this process. On the basis of the above account, the following general expectations may be formulated:

(i) a sharp distinction between 'environmental' and 'economic' motivations behind the development of EC environmental policy, particularly in the 1970s;

(ii) the introduction of more substantial environmental policy measures at the EC level from the early 1980s, interfering more directly with policies and conditions of industrial production at the domestic level and stimulated firstly by the emergence of some new, essentially international environmental problems, notably acidification, and secondly by the continuous process of further interweaving of the Member States' economies;

(iii) a reinforcement of such measures by the Single European Act and the '1992' project;

(iv) a very limited impact of developments in other specific policy fields in the EC, such as agriculture or energy, on the evolution of environmental policy, as well as vice versa;

(v) a close relationship between the development of EC environmental policy and the broader international environmental policy debate, at least as far as general themes and principles are concerned.

At this point, what may be called the 'pre-theoretical' exploration of the phenomenon of the Europeanisation of environmental policy should be concluded. The appropriate next step is to translate the questions and observations put forward so far into terms that allow both theoretical reflection and empirical investigation. Before doing so in Part I of the book, however, the next section briefly explains the order and logic of what is to follow.

The outline of the study

The Europeanisation of environmental policy basically entails the shift of competences and policy making in a specific policy field from the nation state to an international organisation. In order to analyse this process it is necessary first to understand the specific character of both the policy field and the organisation under consideration in the broader context of international politics. This in turn can provide the starting point for more specific questions and hypotheses regarding the process and its driving forces. For that reason, the theoretical foundations of this study will be sought primarily in international relations theory. On the basis of an investigation into the nature of sovereignty, chapter 2 attempts to position EC environmental policy in relation to other fields and other platforms of international policy. This will lead to a short evaluation of the merits of integration theory for the study of the extraordinarily broad and intensive co-operation in the framework of the EC. As an operational basis for the empirical investigation of day-to-day policy making in this half-way house between an habitual international organisation and a federation, however, chapter 3 will draw upon theoretical notions originally developed in a national context. Using the theory of power dependence and policy networks, a set of sensitising concepts will be developed with the help of which the evolution of the interaction between various actors at the national and the EC level in environmental policy making can be empirically characterised.

The second part of the book gives the results of the empirical study of the interrelation between policy processes in the Netherlands and in the EC in the field of air pollution and acidification between 1970 and the early 1990s. In chapter 4 the considerations leading to the selection of the case study area as well as the empirical methods applied will be explicated. In addition, the problem of acidification and the broad lines of the policies in this field in the Netherlands and the EC will be introduced. Chapters 5–8 will describe in considerable detail the decision making around specific policy issues that relate to acidification. They include the relatively well known issues of the introduction of the 'clean' car (chapter 6) and the control of emissions from large combustion plants (chapter 7), but also older processes that have attracted less public and scholarly attention, such as the establishment of EC-wide air quality standards and norms for the sulphur content of fuels (chapter 5). Finally, a case of a lack of policy at the EC level will be dealt with: the contribution to acidification by ammonia, a substance mainly emitted from agricultural sources (chapter 8). Both for the sake of clarity and in order to retain the documentary value of the material, I have chosen to separate as much as possible the reconstruction of the policy making from its theoretically informed analysis. The second part of the book will therefore remain at a rather descriptive level.

The interpretation of the case study in theoretical terms will take place in the third and final part of the book (chapter 9). The evolution of the interaction between domestic and Community policy making will be assessed in terms of the build-up of policy networks encompassing both levels of governance. This will provide the basis for a concluding analysis of the consequences of the Europeanisation of environmental policy for the sovereignty of states vis-à-vis the Community. An epilogue (chapter 10), finally, will evaluate some of the crucial choices made in the course of this study and put forward suggestions for further research. It will also, from the findings of this study and the present situation, outline some possible developments of EC environmental policy.

Notes

1   As this study investigates the evolution of environmental policy in the EC before the 'Maastricht' Treaty on European Union, signed in February 1992 and entering into force in November 1993, it will be generally referred to the European *Community* (EC) here. Only in the last chapter, where the implications of the findings for the future development of the policy field will be discussed, will the name 'European *Union*' (EU) be used.

2   The European Council is the meeting of the Heads of State and Government of the EC Member States, taking place at least twice a year. It acquired a formal status only in the 'Maastricht' Treaty on European Union in 1993 (see below). For further details about the institutional structure of the EC, see, for instance: Nugent (1991), Lasok and Bridge (1991), Kapteyn and VerLoren van Themaat (1987, 1989).

3   The details of the early history of the European Coal and Steel Community (ECSC) and the European Economic Community (EEC) will not be discussed here, but are given by, for instance, Jansen and De Vree (1985), Lasok and Bridge (1991), and Wallace (1990). The habitual reference to the organisation as 'European Communities' or – more commonly – 'European Community' was introduced in 1965 by the so-called Merger Treaty, which drew together the ECSC, the EEC and the European Atomic Energy Community (Euratom). In this study it will be referred to the EEC only if the EEC Treaty proper, for instance as the formal basis for Community legislation, is at stake.

4   The Council of Ministers is the highest decision-making body of the Community. The so-called General Council consists of the Ministers of Foreign Affairs of all Member States. In addition, almost all other ministers of the Member States regularly meet, for instance as the Agriculture Council or

the Environment Council, to discuss matters and take decisions in their respective fields of competence.

5 COM documents are policy documents prepared by the EC Commission. They are referred to in the text by their official numbers. See also section II.B of the list of references at the end of this book. Other official documents from the EC are also listed there. The Commission may be regarded as the EC's executive. The Commissioners are appointed by the Member States but are expected to work independently. They are supported by some twenty-three Directorates-General (DGs), together employing several thousands of officials. In 1981 the unit for Environment and Consumer Protection, which previously had an independent position within the Commission, was incorporated into the existing DG XI, which was then named 'Environment, Consumer Protection and Nuclear Safety'. In 1990 it was renamed 'Environment, Nuclear Safety and Civil Protection'.

6 It should be added that there may be a direct connection between the ambiguous and non-binding status of the Programmes and their persistently ambitious contents: partly *because* of this status the Commission may have been able to include often rather far-reaching plans and proposals, which in turn would explain the preference of some of the Member States for continuation of the mixed legal character.

7 Directives are the most common type of Community legislation in the environmental field. 'A directive shall be binding, as to the result to be achieved, upon each Member State to which it is addressed, but shall leave to the national authorities the choice of form and methods' (Article 189 of the EEC Treaty) (see further Kapteyn and VerLoren van Themaat (1987, 1989). Directives are referred to in the text by their official numbers, for instance 70/220/EEC. The first number refers to the year in which the directive was adopted; the second is a serial number. The addition 'EEC' indicates that the directive was legally based on the EEC Treaty. Directives referred to in this book can be found in section I.B of the list of references.

8 After the accession of Spain and Portugal in 1986 the EP had 518 members. After German unification, this number was extended to 567. Since 1979 the members of the EP are elected directly by the people of the Member States. The ESC is an advisory body consisting of representatives of organisations of employers, workers and other interest groups.

9 A qualified majority consisted of fifty-four votes out of a total of seventy-six; the votes of the twelve Member States were weighted according to their size. See further Articles 148 and 149 of the EEC Treaty (note that the 'Maastricht' Treaty on European Union replaced Article 149 with Article 189A–C).

Part I
Theoretical framework

2

Theories of sovereignty and European integration

Introduction[1]

Among international organisations the EC is unique. In the first place, the scope and detail of the Community's activities are unprecedented in international relations: they range from the regulation of wheat prices to the right to parental leave, and from attempts to bring peace to former Yugoslavia to the control of the quality of bathing water. Secondly, the profoundness of the co-operation between the now fifteen Member States is remarkable. Considerable political powers, such as the right of initiative for new legislation, are delegated to a common institution, the Commission. Although the final decisions about new policies are still taken by the Member State governments in the Council of Ministers, individual States can be outvoted by a majority in an increasing number of policy fields. The legislation thus adopted, moreover, is binding all over the Community's territory. In case of non-compliance, Member States can be convicted (and since the 'Maastricht' Treaty even fined) by the European Court of Justice. It is the combination of both aspects – the scope and force of the Community's tentacles, so to speak – which raises the possibility of the gradual transfer of sub-stantial parts of a policy field from the Member States to Brussels.

How can this intriguing process be described and interpreted? Which theoretical notions are available to analyse the emergence and development of the EC and the increasing interpenetration of policy making at the national and the EC level? This book will be mainly devoted to the empirical investigation of the Europeanisation of environmental policy. The present chapter has a double purpose. First, it aims to explore and characterise the broader context of the process of Europeanisation. By discussing the notions of sovereignty, supranationalism and integration, it will provide a basis for the following, more empirically focused chapters. Secondly, the concepts and insights introduced here will be considered with an eye to the central issue of this book, the shifting relationship between national and EC environmental policy making. Some theoretical notions can then be selected that may help in analysing and understanding the process and consequences of the Europeanisation of the environmental policy field in the context of increasing international co-operation and integration.

The shift of policy-making powers from the national to the international level will first be viewed as a response to increased international interdependence. At the core of this discussion will be the concept of sovereignty, four different dimensions of which will be distinguished. On the basis of that the special status of the EC as a particularly intense, allegedly 'supranational' specimen of interstate co-operation will be explored. The section on supranationalism will be followed by a concise review of the literature on the process of European integration, paying special attention to the notions of issue linkage and spill-over and to the treatment of domestic factors in integration theory. Some evaluative remarks will conclude the chapter.

International interdependence and sovereignty

Unique as it is in its intensity, it should be realised that the 'Europeanisation' of policies is in fact part of a considerably broader process. Economies become more and more intertwined, political, scientific, social, and cultural relations across boundaries steadily grow and increasingly serious environmental problems do not respect national borders. Classical theories of international relations are hardly adequate to cope with this multidimensional process of globalisation (for more detail see Mol and Liefferink, 1993). The theory of realism in the tradition of Morgenthau (1948) and others, on the one hand, is too strongly preoccupied with military power and security problems and offers no basis on which to analyse the relatively autonomous dynamics of international politics, for instance in the economic or the environmental field. Neo-Marxist approaches such as Dependencia theory (Frank, 1967; Dos Santos, 1973) and Wallerstein's world-system perspective (Wallerstein, 1979, 1984), on the other hand, fail to accommodate international political processes that cannot be entirely reduced to economic development and power.

So far the most suitable theoretical model to start the analysis of processes of globalisation is that of complex interdependence as developed by Keohane and Nye (1977, 1987). They do not contest the realist assumption that military power and security interests ultimately dominate international relations but they claim that there are interests and sources of power below this level that are relevant in their own right. Because of increasing international inter-dependencies and worldwide crises, they argue, there is a growing need for peaceful co-operation between States on issues such as security, but also economic prosperity, social welfare and environ-mental degradation, which leads to continuous negotiation in these policy areas. A situation of complex interdependence has three basic characteristics:

(i) societies are connected through multiple channels, ranging from high-level intergovernmental relations and so-called transgovernmental relations between sub-units of governments to transnational relations between non-governmental actors;
(ii) the agenda of inter-State relations consists of various issues that are not arranged in a clear, stable hierarchy;
(iii) the use of military force is considered too costly and therefore even the threat of it is irrelevant between the States involved.

As an ideal type of international relations and an alternative particularly to the realist approach, the model of complex inter-dependence fairly well approximates the relationship between the EC Member States, and also, for instance, between the USA and Canada.

Sovereignty and environmental problems
Growing interdependence and increasing international co-operation pose a continuous challenge to the sovereignty of the nation state. This is particularly true in the EC, where 'supranational' institutions and procedures have started to interfere with powers that used to be exercised exclusively at the national level. In order to understand this process, it is useful to pay some attention to the concept of

sovereignty and to what happens to it in situations of complex interdependence. If not taken in a strictly juridical but rather in a political sense, the concept of sovereignty can be associated with such notions as autonomy of independence. According to Anthony Giddens:

> A sovereign State is a political organisation that has the capacity, within a delimited territory or territories, to make laws and effectively sanction their upkeep; exert a monopoly over the disposal of the means of violence; control basic policies relating to the internal political or administrative form of government; and dispose of the fruits of a national economy that are the basis of its revenue.
>
> (Giddens, 1985: 282)

The sovereignty of states can be challenged by different, partly independent processes of modernisation in the world system. Giddens distinguishes four dimensions of modernity, three of which are directly relevant for the study of international relations:

  (i) processes of growing interdependence of the world capitalist economy;
 (ii) processes associated with the political State system and the increase of international organisations;
(iii) processes concerning the world military order.

When talking about changes in the sovereignty of States, one should be clear about which dimension is at stake. Giddens himself, for instance, defines sovereignty in basically political/military terms. On this basis he is sceptical about any decline in sovereignty. Wallerstein, on the contrary, focuses on the emergence of the single economic world system and observes a growing interdependence of core, semiperiphery and periphery. The two interpretations are not necessarily in conflict, however. Although global capitalism undoubt-edly influences the international State system and the military dimension, there is no one-to-one relation between them. Growing economic interdependence does not need to be paralleled by de-creasing sovereignty of the nation State over political and military issues. Sovereignty, in short, is a multidimensional concept.

   Giddens (1990: 59) distinguishes an additional, fourth, dimension of modernity: the transformation of nature by industrialism. This dimension is particularly pertinent to the study of international relations and the environment. One implication is that the sovereignty of States can be challenged along this dimension as well – for instance, through transboundary pollution or through trade in environmentally harmful products. Another implication of viewing the transformation of nature as a distinct dimension of modernity is that international environmental relations cannot be reduced entirely to the economic, political or military dimensions. This is not to say that there is no relationship with these dimensions, but rather that international environmental relations have a certain autonomy governed by their own ecological rationality, different from military, political or economic rationalities.

Although the introduction of an 'ecological' dimension of sovereignty may at first glance look somewhat adventurous, the essence of the idea has long been firmly established in international law. In fact, the three traditional characteristics that make a sovereign State are a permanent population, a defined territory, and effective government (Holsti, 1983: 65; Cassese, 1986: 77ff.; Brownlie, 1990: 69ff.; Kooijmans, 1990: 31). The criterion of territory, which also figures in Giddens's definition above, and particularly the sovereign (unimpaired) control that states are supposed to have over this territory, is directly related to transboundary environmental effects. This was already explicitly recognised in Principle 21 of the Stockholm Declaration, adopted at the United Nations Conference on the Human Environment in 1972:

> States have, in accordance with ... the principles of international law, the sovereign right to exploit their own resources pursuant to their own environmental policies, and the responsibility to ensure that activities within their jurisdiction or control do not cause damage to the environment of other states or areas beyond the limits of their jurisdiction.[2]

This formula unambiguously states the dilemma between sovereignty in the sense of a State's absolute freedom to act on its own territory on the one hand, and the requirement to respect the territorial integrity of other States on the other. The conflict is obvious: whereas the first part of the principle seems to allow a State to develop every possible polluting activity, the second part seriously restricts this freedom, as illustrated for instance by the case of long-range transport of air pollutants. Principle 21 merely poses the dilemma; its solution is left to legal and political practice.

The increase of interdependence in the ecological dimension can thus be regarded as a challenge to the capacity of States to control not actually the borders but rather the quality or what may be called the 'ecological sustenance base' or 'eco-capacity' (Opschoor and van der Ploeg, 1990: 84ff.) of their territories. Whereas the challenge of sovereignty in the military dimension can (in principle) be requited with military means, however, it is hard to imagine an 'ecological' response to environmental impacts caused by another State. Problems of this kind have to be solved either in the economic dimension (for instance by import restrictions on polluting products), or in the political dimension (by internationally agreed policy measures, leading for instance to the installation of antipollution equipment). In the last instance even military power may be called upon to help. This partial reliance of one dimension on another is nothing new, to be sure: problems of economic interdependence can be dealt with in the political or even the military arena.

As environmental impacts are closely related to processes of production and consumption, it can be argued that the increase of ecological interdependence, at least since the industrial revolution, has gone hand in hand with the development of the world economy. Discussion and – to some extent – regulation of ecological problems in international political institutions, however, started much later than international co-operation in the economic dimension. More-over, when it started, this happened largely in the framework of institutions originally designed to deal with economic matters (cf. chapter 1). This observation is important to the study of the rise of environmental issues in organisations such as the EC.

The EC: supranationalism, or the shift of sovereignty

One aspect of increasing worldwide interdependence is a growing number of international organisations. Stressing the increase of interdependence and the importance of international organisations often goes together with the idea of a shift of sovereignty from the nation state to these institutions. This assertion is too simple, however, as these processes are related to each other only indirectly. As argued, growing interdependence in any of the four dimensions of modernity can challenge a State's sovereign powers, for instance its capacity to influence inflation or stocks of natural resources. On the basis of their perception of this challenge, actors may attempt to share their powers across borders in order to deal with the problem more effectively. That this in turn will lead to the actual transfer of sovereign powers to international organisations is by no means certain. State policies are shaped by a large variety of governmental and non-governmental actors. Complex interactions between those actors, at both the national and the international level, will eventually determine the political response to the problem. The shift of sovereignty from the nation state to international institutions can thus be viewed more precisely as the possible outcome of the political process between various (State and non-State) actors in response to a perceived situation of interdependence.

It is the aim of this book to investigate in more detail the nature of this response with regard to environmental problems and in the context of the EC. For that purpose it is useful to realise that the EC is indeed a special case among international organisations, as pointed out in the introduction to this chapter. Generally speaking, Giddens (1985) may be right to assert that growing interdependence has so far failed to provoke a substantial shift of sovereignty. Compared with the nation state, he claims, most international organisations, such as those of the United Nations, have little ability to affect economic, political, military or ecological issues. However, this observation seems to miss the essential point of what is going on in the EC. The shifting balance of political and decision-making powers between Member States and the Community shows that the perception of growing interdependence in certain dimensions can indeed lead to significant sharing or 'division' (Wallace, 1983a: 65) of some sovereign powers.

Supranationalism

Since the 1950s, analysts have tried to capture the special character of the EC. Whereas most writers agree that it is neither a traditional international organisation nor a fully fledged federation (for example Haas, 1958; Wallace, 1983b; Keohane and Hoffmann, 1991), it is much more difficult to get hold of the ambiguous status of the Community in more positive terms. The debate about this question, and more particularly about the future development of the organisation, obviously has a strong political and ideological aspect. At the same time, however, the question has an important academic interest, as our understanding of the nature of the Community is directly relevant to the choice and use of theories for the analysis of the making of common policies. A central element in the scholarly attempts to bridge the gap between an international organisation and a federal State has been the notion of supranationalism (or supranationality). The concept of supranationalism can basically be regarded as a counterpart to the concept of sovereignty. It seeks to pin down the result of the sharing or pooling of political powers in the context of the EC, or, in other words, the transfer of sovereign powers from the Member States to the Community. As argued in chapter 1, this process should not necessarily be viewed as a zero-sum game, but there can be no doubt that it entails a 're-balancing' of sovereignty between the nation state and a higher, common level of governance. Although long and intensive use has tended to stretch the concept of supranationalism to the point where it is in danger of becoming meaningless, it may still provide a starting point for a closer consideration of the peculiarities of the 're-balancing' of sovereign powers in the framework of the Community.

In the conventional sense of 'over and above individual States', supranationalism refers to a situation in which sovereign powers have been transferred from the nation state to a higher level of governance. In an article about the 'dual' character of supra-nationalism in the period before the Single European Act, Joseph Weiler (1982; further developed in Weiler, 1991) argues that this kind of definition of the concept is too general and too static. In his view, the concept in fact evades definition, first because of the danger of circularity implied by the fact that the EC would be both the exclusive basis and the exclusive subject of such a definition and secondly because of the dynamic nature of the EC. Instead, he concentrates on measuring 'progress or retrogression of supra-nationalism and integration' and distinguishes two axes along which sovereignty can shift from the Member States to the Community system, the normative and the decisional. His approach, which deals only with the institutional structure and process of the EC and does not address substantive policy fields, can be regarded as a further analytical elaboration of the political dimension of sovereignty.

Normative supranationalism refers to the relationships and hier-archy between Community policies and legal processes on the one hand and those of the Member States on the other. Weiler is certainly not the first to observe a profound deepening ('*approfondissement*') of the juridical aspects of the integration process, expressing itself in the doctrines of direct effect and the supremacy of EC law and the principle of pre-emption, that is, the exclusivity of Community competences in a given policy field (Weiler, 1982: 273–279, and references given there). Those three principles, brought to maturity in a series of judgements by the Court of Justice, are also key elements in the legal systems of federal States. They result, among other things, in what Weiler denotes as the 'all-or-nothing-effect': selective application of EC law on a structural basis or partial retreat from common policies already decided is almost impossible. Only total, unilateral withdrawal from the EC is an option, and a theoretical one at that (Weiler, 1982: 296–297; 1991: 2412). In view of this, Weiler speaks of the process of centralisation in the normative dimension and even of 'constitutionalisation', that is, the gradual interpretation of the Treaty as the constitution of a federal State.

Decisional supranationalism relates to the institutional framework and the decision-making processes in the EC. In contrast to the normative dimension, decisional supranationalism has not steadily increased over the years. Particularly in the 1970s and early 1980s, a decline of the political role of the Commission vis-à-vis the Member States, for instance in the shape of the European Council and the Committee of Permanent Representatives (COREPER), could be observed. At the same time, virtually all decisions in the Council of Ministers were taken by unanimous vote. Weiler, writing in 1982, interprets this as an increase of, or even a retreat to, inter-governmentalism in the Community (Weiler, 1982: 280–292).

Combining the two aspects, Weiler argues that in this period the diminution of decisional supranationalism and the normative deepening together constituted an equilibrium through 'a cyclical interaction of the judicial-normative process with the political one' (1982: 292). On the one hand, in reaction to the increasing impact of EC law on their national legal systems, Member States felt the need to consolidate their control of the making of this law. On the other hand, it was precisely the key role of the Member States in decision making in the EC that allowed for the active 'integrationist' approach of the Court of Justice (in contrast to many federal States where the members' interests have to be 'defended' against federal decisions). According to Weiler this balance was an important factor in the overall stability of the system and in the acceptance by the Member

States of 'a normative evolution unprecedented in other international organizations' (1982: 292–293).

In the second half of the 1980s, however, the '1992' project and the Single European Act reasserted the role of the Commission and brought back majority voting in some crucial policy areas. In a later article, extending his earlier analysis in somewhat different terms, Weiler argues that this indeed constituted 'an eruption of significant proportions' (Weiler, 1991: 2455). While the attainments of normative supranationalism remained intact, a number of pre-cautions included in the text of the Single Act turned out to be either ill-conceived or impracticable. As a result, Member States could now be forced to accept binding legislation against their will (Weiler, 1991: 2459–2463). Weiler even goes as far as to conclude that this change so profoundly shattered the equilibrium between normative and decisional supranationalism that it 'puts the Community and its Member States in a new "defining" situation' (Weiler, 1991: 2462). A few years and one Treaty revision later, this conclusion seems questionable. The complications of the 'Maastricht' Treaty and the increased emphasis on national decision-making powers and subsidiarity in fact suggest that Weiler's original equilibrium is considerably more robust than it seemed to be in 1991.[3]

Weiler's assessment of supranationalism throws light on the consequences of European integration. It shows that the evaluation of the shift of political sovereignty in response to the perception of increasing interdependence in the context of the EC is by no means unequivocal, but on the contrary highly dependent on the point of departure. In essence it entails a distinction between a genuinely political and a juridical perspective on (the shift of) political sovereignty. The present book focuses on the decisional aspect and thus adopts the former perspective.

However valuable, Weiler's refinement does not solve the basic problem of which kind of theories to use for the analysis of EC policy making. For that purpose it might be useful to turn to the analysis of the political *process* rather than the outcomes of European integration. In the past decades, regional integration theory has produced various conceptualisations of the forces behind and unleashed by the creation of a 'supranational' Community. As the next section will show, the erratic development of integration theory to some extent reflects the continual confusion about the ambiguous status of the EC. Nevertheless, it may help to set the scene and provide some clues for the study of day-to-day policy processes between the Member States and the Community.

Integration theory

Regional integration theory is closely associated with the complex-interdependence school of thought. According to Haas (1971: 61), it attempts to explain how and why the sovereignty of States is under pressure and how and why it is voluntarily mingled, merged and mixed with neighbouring countries, so as to acquire new techniques for resolving conflicts. Although integration theory has been applied to other geographically limited areas such as North America or Latin America, its main focus has always been Western Europe.

Neo-functional integration theory

Undoubtedly the most influential school of thought in integration theory has been the neo-functional approach, as developed by Haas (1958, 1964) and Lindberg and Scheingold (1970, 1971) (cf. Haas, 1971). Although neo-functionalism is based on the assumption of economic interdependencies between States, political aspects are also incorporated into its conceptualisation of the integration process. It departs from the self-interest of actors by highlighting the primacy of incremental decision making. According to neo-functionalism, the interconnectedness of economic relations and problems will facilitate common action on other political issues – the process of so-called 'spill-over' in sector integration (Haas, 1958). As soon as it becomes clear that supranational agencies are the increasingly dominant problem-solving institutions, relevant interest groups will shift their attention, and ultimately their loyalties, from the nation state to the supranational level. This will in turn further stimulate the spill-over effect. Among neo-functionalist theorists there has always been discussion on what was called the 'dependent variable' of integration (what should be explained or predicted) and which phenomena could be seen as causes and which as consequences of regional integration, despite considerable efforts by Haas (1971), Lindberg (1971), Nye (1971) and Schmitter (1971), among others, to outline one or a set of such variables.

Regional integration theory turned out to have a serious shortcoming. Having been developed from the late 1950s until the early

1970s, the theory may have provided valuable insights into the early development of European integration, but it was not able to cope with the major crises in the process in later years. It was Ernst Haas himself, the main initiator and advocate of the approach, who in 1975 declared that although integration studies still had some relevance, they were no longer 'a good investment of our time and ingenuity' (Haas, 1975). Crisis and stagnation, rather than the predicted ongoing process of economic and political integration, had not discredited integration theory, Haas argued, but it had simply been overtaken by changing conditions (see also Keohane and Hoffmann, 1990). Three things in particular had changed to make integration theory less useful for analysing international relations in Western Europe.

Most visibly, the EC's institutional development had lagged behind expectation. While neo-functional theory continued to cling to the early intentions of the founding fathers of the Community to build a highly supranational or even federal institution, actors in practice failed to do so. Although the growing importance of the EC could not be denied, the organisation itself had evolved to a 'huge regional bureaucratic appendage to an intergovernmental conference in permanent session' rather than to a federation (Haas, 1975: 6). This anomaly in neo-functionalist terms could be explained, according to Haas, on the one hand by a process of re-evaluation of the Member States' national interests in the post-war period. On the other hand, it could be related to a second, more fundamental factor: external influences.

According to Haas, the history of the EC in the 1960s and early 1970s had shown that neo-functionalist theory had underestimated the impact of relations and commitments beyond the Community and ignored the possibility of different Member States having different interests in such relations. For instance, the 1975 Lomé Convention with the African, Caribbean and Pacific (ACP) States could not be explained in terms of the internal dynamics of the EC (Haas, 1975: 11). Generally speaking, the position of the EC as a channel for the Member States to cope with the consequences of growing international interdependence turned out to be not as privileged as theorists expected.

The third and most important factor identified by Haas was the gradual departure from the simple logic of the establishment of a customs union. In the course of the 1960s, a number of new objectives, related notably to redistribution and quality of life, were introduced into Community policy making. As many of those 'post-industrial' objectives conflicted in one way or another with the original orientation of the EC on free trade and industrial development, this challenged the incremental decision mode and the spill-over processes that formed the very basis of neo-functional integration theory (Haas, 1975: 21ff.). They were replaced by what Haas called fragmented linkage of issues, based on a more diffuse and variable perception of reciprocity (Haas, 1975: 24–39; further developed in Haas, 1980; see also below).

Although Haas's argument is basically convincing, two comments can be made here. First, redistributive issues were not as new as Haas suggests. As Nau observes, 'some intervention in competitive markets and hence in the automaticity of functional linkage was always foreseen in the European integration process' (Nau, 1979: 126). Secondly, it can be argued that the introduction of the 'new' objectives themselves is an example of spill-over at a more aggregated level. While the increased attention to post-industrial issues in Western countries since the 1960s, including prominently the issue of environmental deterioration, of course has to be linked to broader changes in society, the fact that they were raised *also* at the Community level is immediately related to the EC's original, economic core activities. Many of the redistributive and environmental demands put forward in Brussels were ultimately motivated by the wish to mitigate the consequences of unrestricted free trade and competition. It can thus be asserted that with the 'new' objectives, which themselves took away the conditions for spill-over on an issue-by-issue basis, the limits of spill-over on the basis of the original 'agreement' about the basic motives of the EC (Haas, 1975: 15) had been reached.

The regime approach

One of the consequences of the passing of regional integration theory was a denial of the uniqueness of Community or integration politics as a special form of international organisation. During the 1970s and 1980s, regional integration was increasingly seen as just 'a special case of response to interdependence through institutionalised mechanisms' (Nau, 1979: 138). At that time, the rising general concept for this kind of mechanism was that of the international regime. It was also applied to the Community.

Building upon the work by Keohane and Nye (1977) on complex interdependence, Krasner (1983) defined international regimes as 'sets of implicit or explicit principles, rules, norms, and decision-making procedures around which actors' expectations converge in a given area of international relations'. One of the most powerful advocates of the regime approach in relation to the EC in those years was Stanley Hoffmann. In his view, the EC functioned largely as an extension of the Member States to facilitate the pursuance of essentially national policy goals. The regime was stable because of the perception of long-term reciprocity and the high 'issue density', allowing for extensive 'inter-issue bargaining' (Hoffmann, 1983: 33–35). Others, for instance Carole Webb (1983), proposed the application of the regime concept at a sectoral level within the EC.

Conceiving of the Community or its sectoral policies as international regimes has one major advantage: it conceptually connects them to related international policies. In particular, the idea of connected and 'nested' regimes dealing with various, broader or alternatively more restricted issue areas gives room for investigating linkages between issues within the EC framework and for assessing the position of EC sectoral policies, such as environmental policy, in the context of international relations and international co-operation at large (Mol and Liefferink, 1993). For the analysis of how the Community actually works in specific policy areas, however, the regime approach turned out not to be particularly helpful. Whereas the broad and encompassing character of regime theory made it very attractive for the study of co-operative arrangements under complex interdependence in general, the concept proved to be too unspecific to be able to generate meaningful conclusions about the intricate political processes inside the multi-level institutional context of the EC (Nau, 1979). Apart from that, as also recognised by Keohane and Nye (1987) and Young (1986), among others, the lack of conceptual precision and theoretical backing in regime theory seriously hindered a fruitful operationalisation of the concept.

Integration theory revisited
It was not until the Community had recaptured some of its old dynamism in the second half of the 1980s that a revival of neo-functionalist integration theories began to emerge. This in fact nicely illustrates how trends in the basic theoretical approach to the EC follow rather than explain the ups and down of the integration

process at large. Keohane and Hoffmann (1990, 1991), for instance, argued for a more careful analysis of the conditions under which neo-functionalist propositions would apply. In particular, they claimed that successful spill-over was still possible, but only within the limits of an encompassing intergovernmental bargain. In their view, the Single European Act brought back basic programmatic agreement among the EC governments and thus re-established the conditions for spill-over to operate.

Keohane and Hoffmann's plea for a re-appreciation of the idea of spill-over can easily be related to – and to some extent underpinned by – Haas's own attempts to develop a more modest alternative to the spill-over concept. In his remarkable 1975 essay, he first introduced the notion of fragmented linkage, which later came to be included in a more systematic treatment of the phenomenon of linkage in international relations (Haas, 1980).

Haas distinguished three basic types of linkage: substantive, tactical and fragmented linkage. Substantive linkage can, but will not necessarily, take place when actors perceive an intellectual coherence between issues, for instance in terms of common causes or common effects. In the case of tactical linkage no such coherence exists and no perception of interconnectedness is needed; the objective is merely 'to obtain additional bargaining leverage' (Haas, 1980: 372). Fragmented linkage, finally, is based on the combination of commitment to some overriding goal on the one hand, and uncertainty about the exact nature of the interrelatedness of the issues involved and the ways to achieve the overall goal on the other. Issues are nevertheless linked in the interest of maintaining collective bargaining strength in prospect of anticipated gains. If applied to the EC as a whole, it can be argued that the Member States have committed themselves to the principal economic goals of the Community. In doing so, they obviously expected to be better off, in spite of recurrent disagreement about the means to attain those goals and considerable uncertainty regarding both overall effects and distributional impacts. This strong conviction about the long-term gains implied by EC membership results in relatively high willingness, when compared with other international fora, to make concessions, to accept short-term losses in specific cases and to avoid escalation of conflicts.

Spill-over is in fact a form of substantive linkage with the relatively dramatic effect of 'pulling' a new policy issue to the EC level. According to Haas (1975), as well as Keohane and Hoffmann (1990, 1991), this is likely to occur only if sustained by a strong perception of general, long-term reciprocity. The notion of fragmented linkage can now be used as a concept to pin down the variations in the perception of general reciprocity and commitment to the EC. A situation of strong fragmented linkage would facilitate both the construction of political compromises and the occurrence of substantive linkage. Spill-over may be expected only in a situation of genuine programmatic agreement, as it existed in the 1960s and, following Keohane and Hoffmann, in the period of the Single European Act and the launching of the '1992' project.

The domestic link

Integration theory, quite naturally, focuses on the political process of integration at the EC level. It examines, among other things, the roles of various types of actors in this process, but mainly as far as they have a direct input in Brussels. The analysis usually involves the roles of Community institutions (Commission, European Parliament, etc.), the Member States' governments in their capacity as members of the Council and its extensive sub-structure, and transnational interest groups. Despite the acknowledgement of the very close ties between the Community and the national level, however, the interrelation between domestic political processes and those in Brussels is hardly systematically treated (Huelshoff, 1994). This is even more the case for the regime approach. Although this approach has its roots in the interdependence school of thought, which puts considerable emphasis on the role of transgovernmental and transnational relations, domestic processes are in practice largely neglected by regime theorists. Particularly in integration theory, however, there are some exceptions.

One of the first and best known attempts to link domestic and EC policy making was made by Simon Bulmer on the basis of his research on Germany and the EC (Bulmer, 1983). His basic aim was to explain how domestic politics 'may have a vital impact on the policy-making output of the EC' (Bulmer, 1983: 350). He first distinguished between the domestic policy-making 'structures' and the 'attitudes' held with regard to the EC[4] and then applied the concept of policy style (Richardson, 1982) to draw together the impact of both dimensions on the Member State's behaviour in the Community. More recently, Michael Huelshoff (1994) focused on

domestic party politics to explain the strength of national governments in international negotiations.

The studies by Bulmer, Huelshoff and some others (e.g. Van den
Bos, 1991; Garrett, 1992; outside the EC context, see also Allison,
1971; Katzenstein, 1978; Krasner, 1978) have undoubtedly contributed significantly to our understanding of the domestic basis of the
international behaviour of States and, in some cases, non-State
actors. It should be noted, however, that in the end all of them treat
the two levels as separated: the domestic process creates the input
into the international process, which is mediated essentially by the
national government. The aim of the present study, by contrast, is to
investigate to what extent national and EC environmental policies
are becoming increasingly interrelated and what consequences this
may have for national sovereignty. For that purpose the 'domestic
politics' studies referred to above can provide some useful clues, but
not the basic conceptual starting point.[5]

Conclusion

The first purpose of this chapter was to provide a concise,
theoretically informed overview of the broader international context
of the phenomenon of the Europeanisation of environmental policy.
The discussion focused on three basic concepts which together may
be regarded as cornerstones of the analysis of processes of
globalisation and increasing international co-operation. The multidimensional interpretation of the concept of sovereignty has been
useful to give a clearer picture of the nature of the growing
interdependence between States. Particularly in relation to the EC,
which covers so many different issue areas, it is essential to realise
that the perception of different types of interdependence can lead to
different responses and, thus, to different levels of international co-
operation. Although environmental problems are in many cases
strongly related to the economic dimension, it was argued that the
specific characteristics of the challenges to a State's ecological
sovereignty justify their treatment in a separate dimension.

With regard to the EC as a framework for common policy
making, it can be observed that the complex and dynamic character
of the organisation is in a sense reflected in a continuous, sometimes

slightly confused scholarly debate. The notion of supranationalism and some of the achievements of regional integration theory certainly do highlight a number of crucial features of the evolution and status of the Community. They include Weiler's distinction between the normative and the decisional aspect of supranationalism as well as the idea of spill-over, if used with caution, and its relationship to the more generally applicable notion of linkage. Turning to the second aim of this chapter, the 'extraction' of conceptual notions for the empirical analysis in the following chapters, however, it has to be concluded that the conceptual fog around the basic character of the Community has tended to obscure, at least from a theoretical point of view, the actual, down-to-earth policy-making process in Brussels (cf. Liefferink and Mol, 1993). A considerable gap still exists between the relatively abstract discussions in this chapter and the empirical analysis of the interactions between the national and the Community level in day-to-day policy making. The next chapter, therefore, develops a more operational analytical framework for dealing with the question of Europeanisation and thus to close at least a small portion of that gap.

Notes

1   This chapter has its basis in two older articles (Mol and Liefferink, 1993; Liefferink and Mol, 1993). I would like to thank my co-author, Arthur Mol, for many inspiring discussions and for his kind permission to reprocess some of his ideas.

2   Source: UN Document A/CONF.48/14/REV.1, reprinted in *International Legal Materials* 1972: 1416–1419.

3   It may be argued, however, that the strengthening of decisional supranationality in the Single Act and in the 'Maastricht' Treaty was largely responded to *within* the political domain. The parallel reduction of normative supranationalism logically following from Weiler's equilibrium thesis, in other words, did not necessarily follow, because the effect of qualified majority voting was largely outdone by a greater reluctance on the part of the Member States to engage in common policies.

4   It is interesting to note that Bulmer's notion of 'attitude' towards EC integration in fact constitutes the domestic counterpart of the idea of fragmented linkage, introduced above.

5   In a sense, the 'two-level games' metaphor introduced by Robert Putnam (1988) comes closer to the central question of this book, as it deals with the entanglement of political processes at the national and the

international level. Putnam's approach, however, is strongly oriented towards the strategic games played by actors at both levels simultaneously. While the politico-institutional setting and its consequences for the division of power and sovereignty are taken as given in that kind of analysis (and actually hardly referred to in the article in question), they are precisely the focus of the present study.

3

Towards an analytical framework: power dependence in the EC policy system

Introduction

It is clear that the Europeanisation of policy is not a straightforward phenomenon: policy-making powers are not simply vanishing to 'Brussels' without leaving a trace at the national level. As pointed out in the previous chapter, the Europeanisation of policy is to be regarded as the political and institutional response to the perception of growing interdependence between the Member States. Both this perception and the response to it may vary across issue areas, issues and aspects of issues. The result is an intricate and, what is more, moving pattern of policy-making powers, some of them (still) located predominantly in the realm of national sovereignty and others 'shared' to a greater or lesser extent in the framework of the EC. The process of Europeanisation, then, is not a matter of transfer of entire policy areas or issues from one level to another, but rather of increasing interwovenness between policy making at the national and the Community level. In order to study this process empirically, a coherent set of concepts at a more 'practical' level or what may be called a middle-range or meso-theory is needed.

In this chapter, the notions of power dependence and policy networks are used for this purpose. As will be demonstrated in the next section, these notions may offer an empirically 'tangible' starting point for the analysis of relationships between various types of actors in complex decision-making processes. This will be followed by a discussion in more detail of a number of dimensions along which relations of power dependence in policy networks can be analysed; these dimensions are then linked to some of the findings of the previous chapter. A final section will summarise the conclusions.

Power dependence and policy networks

Middle-range theories of policy making are usually connected in one way or another to more general, macro-level theories of the relation and interaction between State and society. The two standing rival bodies of theory of the State in capitalist societies are pluralism and corporatism. Both have been elaborated in several sub-streams, such as clientelism, iron triangles, corporate pluralism or State corporatism. Several of those aimed to reconcile elements from both schools of thought. Most of them, moreover, provided starting points for valuable empirical research in the context of single nation states or in a comparative perspective (Williamson, 1989; Van Waarden, 1992; Smith, 1993). Before plunging into the seemingly endless scholarly debate between advocates of the various streams, however, it is good to consider the basic tenets of pluralism and corporatism and to see to what extent they can actually accommodate the specific features of political processes at the EC level.

The basic premise of the pluralist approach is the existence of a large number of societal interest groups, competing with each other for influence over policy making by a State which is in itself 'neutral', that is, reflecting the forces within society (Dahl, 1961; Schmitter, 1974). This implies that power is widely, but not necessarily equally, dispersed among interest groups. The most fundamental critique against pluralism, as Williamson (1989: 56ff.) points out, is that this concept of power is too simple and too narrow. Institutional and ideological factors can profoundly affect the availability and exercise of power (Smith, 1993: 25ff.). This point is particularly relevant to the political context of the EC. The Community is in fact anything but a simple 'enumeration' of, or an arena for, a wide variety of societal interests. Policy making in Brussels is strongly determined by the institutional relations between the two levels of governance involved. The access and influence of private actors can only be understood against the background of those relations.

The various forms of corporatism have in common their emphasis on formalised relations between a limited number of closed and

hierarchically structured interest groups and the State. In exchange
for influence on the content of policies, the groups commit
themselves to the decisions made and usually play an active role in
their implementation (Schmitter, 1974). Corporatism was developed
in the 1970s in response to the, at that time dominant, model of
pluralism. Pluralists reacted principally by contesting the distinctive-
ness of corporatism: it was depicted as just an institutionalised form
of pluralism (Williamson, 1989: 60–63). Later, after the emergence of
several versions of the theory, corporatism was also criticised for
becoming an increasingly broad and meaningless concept, describing
any kind of group–government relations (Smith, 1993: 36–37). The
major reason why a corporatist approach does not qualify for the
analysis of policy making in the EC, however, is the fact that the
paradigmatic exchange of representation and influence versus co-
operation and assistance in policy implementation (Frouws, 1993:
42ff.) does not occur, at least not between public and private actors.
If an exchange of this kind takes place at all, it is in the highly
formalised relation between the Member States' governments and the
EC institutions. It does not appear to be particularly illuminating to
regard such a system of 'joint decision making' (Scharpf, 1985, 1988)
as a case of corporatism.

It turns out that neither pluralism nor corporatism provides an
adequate basic view of the EC political system. Whereas both
pluralist and corporatist theories deal with the essentially dual
relationship between public and private actors at one level of
governance, the crucial feature of the Community is its two-level
character. This inevitably draws much of the attention to the
complex, institutionalised, hierarchical relationship between public
actors at both levels. In this interplay, the role and influence of
interest groups can be an important but by no means the only subject
of investigation. This observation once more underlines the need for
an encompassing political theory of the EC political system.
Considering the difficulties encountered in the preceding chapter in
finding or constructing such a theory, however, the conclusion to be
drawn at this point is that a middle-range analysis of EC policy
making requires a conceptual framework which is not too closely
bound up with either school of thought.

The notion of policy networks is particularly suited for this
purpose. It was developed in order to characterise and to analyse
different types of arrangements between State and society in the

context of policy making (Jordan and Schubert, 1992). Rather than being inspired by one of the macro-theories of the State, the meso-concept of policy networks is 'multi-theoretic'. This means that it can and in fact should be applied in combination with a wider theory of the distribution of power in the political system (Rhodes and Marsh, 1992; Jordan and Schubert, 1992; Van Waarden, 1992; Smith, 1993: 73). The concept of policy networks, in other words, mainly offers a description, characterisation and typology of relations and inter-actions between the State and societal interests, whereas a broader theory of, for instance, European integration and co-operation is needed for the explanation of the observed phenomena.

Although most elaboration of the concept of policy networks was directed to relations between public and private actors (Richardson and Jordan, 1979; Wilks and Wright, 1987; Grant *et al.*, 1988; Smith, 1990; for an overview, see Rhodes and Marsh, 1992), a second strand of research was devoted to relations between local and central government (Rhodes, 1981, 1986). Recently, a certain consensus has emerged about the meaning of the central notions of the policy network approach, based particularly on the work by Rhodes (Marsh and Rhodes, 1992; Smith, 1993).

The starting point of Rhodes's approach is power dependence or resource dependence, that is, the dependence of one actor upon others for resources. Rhodes (1986: 17), drawing partly upon Benson (1975), distinguishes five types of resources:

(i) authority (or legal resources);
(ii) money (or financial resources);
(iii) political legitimacy (or political resources);
(iv) information (possession and control of data);
(v) organisational resources ('possession of people, skills, land, buildings, material and equipment').

With some qualifications, Rhodes's categorisation can be applied to the relationships between both public and private actors in this study. Particularly the first two categories of resources betray their origins in the study of relationships between administrative agencies. Obviously, legal resources in the strict sense of laws, regulations or treaty provisions play an important role in EC decision making, but also, more than suggested by Rhodes, informal rules governing relations between actors should be taken into account. The category of money in Rhodes's and Benson's approach focuses on funds available to public agencies to perform their functions and raised usually by taxes. I will extend this category to resources located in the economic dimension in a broader sense, that is, money (raised by taxes or by the sales of products, for instance), but also other economic capacities of actors that may prove relevant in interaction, such as competitive positions of firms or groups of firms or the capacity to contribute to the national income or to the creation of jobs. Although it might be argued, furthermore, that in the end 'every resource could be seen as a species of political resource' (Rhodes, 1986: 20), I prefer to retain 'political legitimacy' as a separate category, since the EC and its Member States differ considerably in public support and democratic legitimacy. Those differences can be expected to play a role in the perceptions and behaviour of actors and therefore deserve some more visibility than if they, probably with some difficulty, were formulated in terms of the other categories. The importance of data, expert knowledge, and so on (informational resources) in all kind of relations is obvious. Organisational resources, finally, could arguably be reduced to the possession of money and authority (cf. Benson, 1975: 232), but as a way of directly denoting the 'physical' capacity of actors to carry out certain activities (policy preparation, lobbying, etc.), the category may be useful.[1]

Like every form of social interaction, policy making involves the recursively monitored reproduction of structures of resources and rules (Giddens, 1984: 25). This means, for the present purposes, that actors in bargaining processes draw upon sets of rules and resources which are at the same time gradually adapted and transformed in the course of those very processes. Bargaining, moreover, takes place *about* as well as *with the help of* resources: resources are to be considered as both 'prizes' and 'weapons' (Rhodes, 1986: 19–20). Strictly speaking, rules are distinct from resources, as the latter are controlled by certain actors whereas the former are part of actors' mutual knowledge (cf. Giddens, 1984: 17–18). Many rules, including for instance decision-making procedures, do however assign rights and obligations to specific actors and as such they can be (strategically) used as resources in bargaining.

Rhodes (1986: 22ff.), following Benson (1982), defines a policy network as a 'complex of organisations connected to each other by resource dependencies and distinguished from other clusters or complexes by breaks in the structure of resource dependencies'. He then identifies four dimensions along which the structure of power dependence in policy networks can vary:

(i) functional interests or policy focus – the interests or the policy issue around which the policy network is built;
(ii) membership – the actors participating in the network such as government agencies, possibly at different levels, and private interest groups;
(iii) vertical interdependence, that is, power dependence between the members of the network;
(iv) horizontal interdependence, that is, relationships with structures of power dependence around other functional interests.[2]

With the help of these dimensions it is possible to distinguish different levels of structure of policy networks on a sliding scale. At the 'stable', 'integrated' end are structures of power dependence that are characterised by a well identified policy focus, substantially closed membership, relatively stable vertical relations based on shared responsibility, and strong insulation from other structures. They are denoted as policy communities. Networks at the open, more unstructured extreme of the continuum are labelled issue networks (Rhodes, 1986: 22–23; Marsh and Rhodes, 1992: 249–251; also Smith, 1993).[3]

The concepts of power dependence and policy networks can also be applied at the international level, as demonstrated for instance by Peterson's analysis of EC technology policy (Peterson, 1992) and by the study on government and the chemical industry in Britain and Germany by Grant *et al.* (1988), which includes explorations of relevant international, particularly EC, aspects. This appears to be particularly true for situations of complex interdependence, where States and other international actors also try to deal with mutual dependence through negotiation and co-operation. As hinted at in chapter 2, the evolution of the Community's environmental policy could in principle even be viewed as the establishment of an environmental regime at the EC level. Policy networks and international regimes both seek to pin down the institutional forms in which interaction takes place. In both cases, moreover, the issues and issue areas to which they refer can range from the very broad to the highly specific. The two basic notions of complex interdependence and power dependence cannot easily be compared, however, because they refer to different levels of analysis. Complex interdependence defines conditions under which certain relations between actors and certain mechanisms of conflict resolution prevail in the specific context of international relations. *If* those conditions are met, however, the theory does not say much about *how* interactions actually take place. This is in fact one of the main reasons for the weak theoretical foundation of the regime concept. Rhodes's concept of power dependence can be used to close this gap. It offers tools for the analysis of multi-actor decision making at the sectoral level, and the characteristics of policy networks are directly derived from the basic dimensions of power dependence. It thus provides a framework for the study of day-to-day policy making in the EC.

With the theory of power dependence and policy networks, the principal concepts for the empirical study are available. If the supposed process of the Europeanisation of policy, in the sense of a growing intertwining of national and EC policy making, is interpreted as the gradual emergence of policy networks encompassing both the domestic and the EC level, then the nature of this process can be characterised along the four dimensions of power dependence introduced above. As such, the notions embodied in the power dependence approach cannot explain the dynamics of the Europeanisation of policy, but as sensitising concepts (Bulmer, 1984; Nooij, 1990: 57–58) they can draw attention to the relevant expression of the process.

Four dimensions of power dependence

The Europeanisation of policy can be described as the build-up of policy networks increasingly interlacing the domestic and the Community level. The emergence and development of the relations of power dependence that are the basis of those policy networks can in turn be made visible by analysing the interaction in concrete decision-making situations along the four dimensions of power dependence: functional interest or policy focus, membership, vertical interdependence, and horizontal interdependence. Changes in the interaction can then be related to the evolution of the underlying structure of power dependence.

This section will offer a more detailed discussion of the four dimensions of power dependence. In combination with the short history of EC environmental policy in chapter 1 and taking into account the theoretical observations made in chapter 2, this will lead to the formulation of a number of specific, substantial working hypotheses regarding the Europeanisation of environmental policy.[4]

Policy focus

The dimension of functional interests, substantive interests or policy focus refers to the perception and definition of the policy issue by the actors in the network (cf. also the section on membership, below). As the point addressed here is the perception of 'what the policy is about' and which types of arguments are 'valid' rather than the identification of a particular (common) interest pursued by the members of the network, the term 'policy focus' is most appropriate for the purpose of this study.

In the context of EC environmental policy, the question of policy focus particularly entails the balance between an economic and an ecological valuation of environmental problems and the level of governance at which those problems should be dealt with. The two aspects are interrelated. As shown in chapter 1, the deterioration of environmental quality may be considered as an ecological problem domestically, but mainly as an economic harmonisation problem at the international level. It is also possible, by contrast, that international negotiations focus on ecological objectives, while leaving the economic ramifications of measures to the national level. As demonstrated, the first decade of EC environmental policy was in fact characterised by the simultaneous occurrence of both situations, or, in other words, by a considerable gap between the handling of the economic and the ecological aspects of environmental problems.

In the 1980s, I further argued, this gap was gradually closed by the introduction of measures, such as Community-wide emission standards, that combined the setting of environmental goals and the control of the economic consequences of pursuing those goals. It was suggested that this development was stimulated by the emerging perception that problems of increasing international interdependence in the economic and in the ecological field could not be adequately dealt with separately. This view was formally laid down in the Single European Act.

If this shift in policy focus towards a more integrated perception of economic and ecological aspects of environmental issues at the EC level can indeed be traced back in the case study in the second part of this book, at least among the key actors in the policy networks involved, this would point to a process of maturation of EC environmental policy networks. In particular, it would mark the transition of the EC level from a framework considered suitable only for some specific elements of environmental policy to a fully fledged alternative to the domestic level.

Membership

The members of a policy network are those actors who actually take part in the exchange of resources. In other words: members distinguish themselves from non-members by interacting in relation to the policy issue in question. As Grant *et al.* (1988: 57–58) point out, this interaction is not necessarily direct: it can take place for instance through specialised magazines or newsletters. In addition, participation in the network may be 'delegated'. Particularly in the multi-level policy system addressed here, such delegation can even involve more than one step, for instance when national branch organisations, themselves representing a group of companies, are represented in Brussels by European umbrella organisations. Most policy networks, furthermore, consist of a core of key actors who interact frequently and determine the basic policy direction, and a number of peripheral actors with lower and often occasional influence and involvement (Laumann and Knoke, 1987; Smith, 1993). In the case study I will start with key actors and let them help identify the more peripheral ones (see also chapter 4).

Complex interdependence theory (chapter 2) at a very general level identifies three basic types of relations in international policy making: intergovernmental, transgovernmental and transnational relations. In the EC, with its emphasis on detailed technical regulation, the role of official intergovernmental relations is relatively limited. Although the Minister of Foreign Affairs in The Hague, with the help of a number of interdepartmental bodies,[5] is formally responsible for the co-ordination of Dutch EC policies, Van den Bos (1991, chapter 4 and *passim*) shows that, particularly in matters requiring a high level of specific expertise, the role of the directly involved minister and his or her departmental staff is often considerable, not only in the domestic preparation of EC policies but also in the negotiations in Brussels themselves. As a typical example he mentions the environmental field (Van den Bos, 1991: 145). Transgovernmental relations, with professional ministries on the national side and specialised agencies such as Commission Directorates-General on the Community side, will therefore probably dominate in the case study. Industry and environmental organisations are likely to be the most important non-governmental (transnational) actors in EC environmental policy. The choice of route into involvement in Community policy making of actors in the latter category particularly deserves some more attention.

Keeping in mind the basic hypothesis that the increasing intertwining of national and EC environmental policy will lead to the emergence of encompassing policy networks, the build-up of a more or less closed group of actors who participate in policy making at both levels can be expected, with an acceleration after the Single Act. With regard to transgovernmental actors this would mean that increasingly the same group of government agencies, or even the same persons, deal with domestic and parallel EC affairs. For private actors, there appear to be a direct and an indirect option for closer involvement in Community policy making. The direct option, sometimes referred to as the 'orthodox strategy' (Averyt, 1977), entails the articulation of private interests in Brussels, usually through umbrella organisations but increasingly also individually. The latter particularly applies to large firms, for instance in consumer electronics (Cawson, 1992) or car manufacturing (McLaughlin and Jordan, 1993). The indirect or 'national' strategy (Averyt, 1977) is aimed at the national government in its capacity of member of the EC Council of Ministers. The increase in the number of Euro-groups since the Single Act (Andersen and Eliassen, 1991; Mazey and Richardson, 1993b) suggests the growing importance of the direct option (Greenwood *et al.*, 1992: 22ff.). This does not, however, rule out the persistent relevance of the indirect route and the deployment of both strategies in combination (see for instance Grant, 1993; McLaughlin and Jordan, 1993). The direct route is in itself not more 'European' than the indirect one: in fact an active national campaign can be the expression of more intense interest in EC matters than routine participation in a European umbrella organisation. The choice in favour of one or the other channel does, however, have consequences for the position of the national government, as this is either passed over or assigned a pivotal function in the mediation of private interests.

Vertical interdependence

Vertical interdependence refers to relations of power dependence between actors within a policy network, that is, to the dependence of actors upon other network members for resources. Vertical interdependence, therefore, is characterised by a certain pattern of distribution and exchange of resources between the actors of a policy network. With increasing Europeanisation and the build-up of encompassing, more tightly knit networks, the development of more intensive interaction between actors may generally be expected. The question of particular interest here is how shifts in patterns of this interaction can be related to changes in the structure of resource dependence. In this section a number of expectations and questions will be developed that may help to identify relevant phenomena in the case study.

Probably the most conspicuously contested resource in EC policy making is the formal competence to act. The transfer of legal authority from the nation state to the EC is also the most tangible expression of the supposed 'erosion' of national sovereignty.[6] It should be realised, then, that the issue of legal authority in the EC can be regarded from two angles. On the one hand, the Community is ultimately dependent on the Member States for its power to act: the Community has competences only if they are based on the Treaty and/or specific legislation, to be enacted by the Member States gathered in the Council. On the other hand, as soon as legislation has been enacted, it is binding upon the Member States and it limits their right to develop or maintain national legislation. The fight that is *based on* as well as *about* legal competences is central to all systems of joint decision making, including the EC (Scharpf, 1985, 1988).

In chapter 1, the evolution of the EC's role in environmental policy, from the instigation of the harmonisation of a limited number of environment-related product standards and the co-ordination of some very basic environmental goals in the 1970s to the regulation of more substantive aspects of environmental issues in the 1980s, was sketched as a step-wise process. It may be expected that controversies arose particularly around the preparation for new steps, notably the introduction of new, more powerful policy instruments such as emission standards. The Single Act of 1987 formally established the Community's environmental competences and probably constituted a new balance in the distribution of legal resources between 'Brussels' and the Member States.

In addition, legal resources can be at stake in relations between policies in the EC and at the broader international level, for instance if some or all of the Member States (and in some cases also the Community as such) are bound to other international agreements, or if the Commission has been given the competence to negotiate on behalf of the Member States or to co-ordinate their positions. The substantive and/or normative connections following from this kind of embeddedness in a broader international framework may be expected to facilitate concrete linkage of policies at both levels (see chapter 2).

Relations between the Community and the Member States are not, however, governed by formal arrangements alone. As illustrated by the erratic development of EC environmental policy before as well as after the establishment of an explicit legal basis for it, more substantive aspects of policy issues were at stake as well. The gradual broadening of the range and impact of the Community's environmental policy logically brought about an increasing interference with national sovereignty in the economic and the ecological dimensions. With a view to bargaining processes, this in principle enabled – or forced – actors both at the Community and at the national level to bring more momentous resources into play, such as the economic and competitive power of States or industries, or damage to public health or crops, forests, and so on, caused by environmental pollution. In the context of EC harmonisation, in addition, the relative lack of economic or competitive power, particularly of 'less developed' Member States or regions, may also be used as a resource in bargaining. But also other types of resources can be involved in the process of Europeanisation. The demand for technical or statistical information at the EC level or the public and political interest in the issues discussed in Brussels may for example increase. This in turn could give certain actors new (informational, political) resources. Private actors – industry and environmental organisations – also play an important role here.

Industry's most powerful resource with regard to environmental policy making is no doubt the capacity to generate income, employment, and so on, which can be offset against public actors' formal authority to regulate. In addition, industry usually possesses specific technical knowledge, which can be an important resource, especially in the making of more far-reaching, detailed policies (Grant *et al.*, 1988: 60–61).

Information can also be relevant to environmental organisations, but it can be argued that their main trump is in the field of political resources. In this context, the continuously weak position of the EP and the virtual absence of 'European public opinion' should be kept in mind.[7] The direct means for articulating public opinion at the Community level is thus seriously underdeveloped; it may be expected that growing public involvement in EC environmental policy making will mainly take place through indirect channels, that is, through the national public debate and through (national and/or European) interest organisations, particularly environmental groups.

Among private actors, finally, the distribution and exchange of various resources play a role as well. On the one hand, in order to be able to lobby Brussels, Euro-groups are dependent upon their members at the national level for information and organisational resources (money, personnel). Individual firms, national branch organisations or environmental groups, on the other hand, will be prepared to provide such resources only if this is reciprocated in the form of influence and information about current EC developments (Mazey and Richardson, 1993b; Hull, 1993). Rules – for instance decision-making rules in Euro-groups or the room for taking unilateral action in Brussels – also affect this interaction. As pointed out in the previous section, however, the relationship between umbrella organisations and their members should not be mistaken as an expression of the interest of private actors in EC matters in general. It can serve only as an indicator for the route chosen by private actors to influence EC policy making.

With regard to vertical interdependence, the case study should give more insight into the ways in which resources are distributed among and used by actors in EC environmental policy networks. What types of resources are controlled by what types of actors and in what contexts can they be used effectively? Did the emergence of more encompassing EC policies indeed lead to shifts in the pattern of resource exchange? If the latter proves to be the case, it highlights changes in the underlying structure of power dependence between the domestic and the EC level.

Horizontal interdependence

A policy network is characterised by a certain degree of insulation from policy networks around other issues or issue areas (Rhodes, 1986: 23). On the one hand this means, among other things, that membership is more or less restricted and that resource dependencies inside the network (vertical interdependence) are considered more important than those outside the network (horizontal inter-dependence). On the other hand, it does not imply that no interaction with other policy networks takes place at all. Environmental issues in particular often touch upon many other policy fields. Establishing a balance between insulation and effective co-ordination with related issues and issue areas indeed is a crucial element of a developed policy network. It may therefore be generally expected that in the process of Europeanisation of environmental policy networks, horizontal resource dependencies are increasingly perceived and dealt with at the EC level. It should be noted that relations between the ecological aspect and the economic, internal market aspect of environmental issues are not discussed under the heading of horizontal interdependence, as those aspects are regarded as the very basis of the perception and definition of the networks' central policy problems (see the section on policy focus, above). The present section will deal with relations between issues within the environmental field, with relations between environmental issues and other sectoral fields, such as energy or agriculture, and with the embeddedness of EC environmental policy in the broader EC context.

In the previous chapter, the notion of linkage was introduced to characterise different types of relations with other policy issues and issue areas (Haas, 1980). In terms of power dependence, linkage is based on the perception of relevant resource dependencies and entails the use and exchange of resources between actors in different policy networks. The concept of linkage makes it possible to look at horizontal relations from an alternative angle. Whereas different categories of resources can be distinguished according to their own specific character (information, legitimacy), the different types of linkage focus on actors' motives to establish interaction. For instance, this can be for substantive or tactical reasons, but also on the basis of the perception of general, long-term reciprocity (fragmented linkage), that is, the anticipation of (profitable) resource exchange on future issues.

In two decades of EC environmental policy, the range of policy issues broadened and the gap between general ecological objectives and technical harmonisation measures designed primarily to take away barriers to trade was gradually closed. As a result, the Community got involved in a more and more comprehensive package of environmental problems. This in itself created more points of contact and overlap between policy measures and probably enhanced the need for co-ordination. Moreover, the establishment of links between different environmental policy issues was explicitly required, particularly in the Third and Fourth Environmental Action Programmes (EAP 1982–1986; EAP 1987–1992). In fact, in a national context too, the extent to which the problems have been solved of fragmentation of the environmental policy field into a large number of distinct, largely unrelated measures, can be taken as an indicator of the level of institutionalisation of the policy field (Van Tatenhove, 1993; Van Tatenhove and Liefferink, 1992). It can therefore be expected that the maturation of EC environmental policy networks went together with an increasing perception of the interconnectedness of environmental issues at the EC level and that this in turn led to increasing linkage of concrete policies. This probably involved primarily substantive linkage between environmental issues, for instance because the same substances, the same categories of sources or the same ecological effects were at stake, but the higher issue density may also have stimulated tactical linkage of issues.

Essentially the same applies to relations between environmental issues and other EC issue areas. The more far-reaching character of EC environmental policies probably led to increasing conflicts with other policy areas, for instance regarding claims on economic resources or the legal competence to act. The 'integration' of environmental considerations into other EC policies has been a priority ever since the early 1980s. It has to be seen in the case study to what extent resources related to other issue areas were in fact brought into play at the EC level. Here too it may be assumed that linkage predominantly had a substantive basis.

Fragmented linkage can affect willingness to accept compromises and short-term losses (see chapter 2). As the environmental policy area got better established in the EC policy system, culminating in its formal inclusion in the Single Act, it seems reasonable to assume that the Member States' attitude towards European integration in general became more relevant to environmental policy as well. At the same time, of course, the widespread 'Euro-sclerosis' of the early 1980s and the considerably greater confidence in the Community in the wake of the '1992' project must be taken into account. Both things together give rise to the expectation that the influence of the general EC climate on environmental policy making steadily increased and that the quality of this influence turned more positive in the mid-1980s. In addition, it was suggested that '1992' and the Single Act brought back the condition of basic programmatic agreement necessary for spill-over processes (see chapter 2). Although the penetration of environmental policy into other sectors turned out to be problematic, this does indeed not preclude the possibility that the (re)vitalisation of other policy areas, for instance transport or regional policy, led to stronger pressure to deal also with environmental aspects of those areas at the EC level.

Conclusion

This chapter was devoted to the search for a set of middle-range concepts for the empirical investigation of the dynamics of decision making between the Member States and the EC. As it had turned out that broader theories of international relations did not provide sufficient basis for analysing what actually happens when 'sovereign' States co-operate so intensively on so many and often so specific issues, the theory of power dependence and policy networks was proposed instead. It was originally developed as a 'multi-theoretic' approach at the meso-level, to be used within the context of one of the macro-theories of the State in capitalist societies – notably pluralism and corporatism. When applied to the political system of the EC and its Member States, the notions of power dependence and policy networks offer a useful analytical vantage point from which to describe and analyse the shifting structure of policy making between various types of governmental and non-governmental actors at both levels of governance.

The basis of the policy networks approach is the idea that actors in decision-making processes are dependent upon each other for different types of resources, namely authority (legal resources), money (financial resources), political legitimacy (political resources), informational or organisational resources. Bargaining takes place about as well as with the help of those resources. Around such relations of resource or power dependence, complexes of actors evolve that can be denoted as policy networks. Their structure can vary along four dimensions:

 (i) policy focus – the policy issue around which the policy network is built;
 (ii) membership – the actors participating in the network;
 (iii) vertical interdependence – relations of power dependence within the network;
 (iv) horizontal interdependence – relationships of power dependence with other policy networks.

Interactions and shifts between actors operating at the national and the Community level in concrete cases of EC environmental policy making can now be investigated along these four dimensions. Such shifts in turn reflect the changes in the structure of power dependence that lie at the heart of the Europeanisation of policy networks.

Notes

 1   'Ecological' resources are obviously lacking as a category in this list. As pointed out in the previous chapter in relation to the concept of sovereignty, the ecological dimension does not provide capacities that can be used to exert pressure on other actors directly. For that purpose, ecological problems have to be 'translated' into other resources, for instance economic ones.
 2   In later work, Rhodes includes 'resources' as an additional dimension (Rhodes, 1988; Rhodes and Marsh, 1992: 23). As the distribution and use of resources are the very bases of vertical and horizontal interdependence, however, I prefer the earlier categorisation.
 3   In a number of earlier publications, for instance by Richardson and Jordan (1979) and Grant *et al.* (1988), 'policy community', instead of 'policy network', was used as the generic term. Wilks and Wright (1987) proposed a distinction between 'policy communities' as groups of potential actors gathered around a common policy focus, and 'policy networks' as cases of concrete interaction between the members of a policy community, usually around a more specific issue (cf. also the critique in Rhodes and Marsh, 1992: 22–23). I will follow the terminology offered by Rhodes and Marsh.
 4   The 'hypotheses' developed below are not hypotheses that can be subjected to testing, leading to falsification or verification in a strictly positivist sense. They are rather expectations designed to guide the empirical

observations. As such they have a function complementary to that of the sensitising theoretical concepts. In the following, mainly the word 'expectation' will be used.

5   In the Netherlands, the two most important co-ordinating bodies with respect to EC environmental policy are the Co-ordination Commission for International Environmental Affairs (*Coördinatiecommissie Internationale Milieuvraagstukken*, CIM) and its working group on EC matters, and the Co-ordination Commission for European Integration and Association Problems (*Coördinatiecommissie voor Europese integratie- en associatievraagstukken*, CoCo), chaired by the State Secretary of Foreign Affairs. Dutch standpoints in the Community's Environment Council are discussed in joint sessions of CIM and CoCo.

6   Sub-national relations, that is, between national actors and actors at the local or provincial level, will not be taken into consideration in this study.

7   The practical non-existence of a 'European public opinion' able to exert pressure on policy making in Brussels is due to a vicious circle of lack of interest and lack of channels (European newspapers, broadcasting services, etc.). The persistence of this vicious circle cannot, of course, be attributed to one specific policy field alone: it is rather an expression of the embeddedness of EC environmental policy in the EC as a whole. In fact the situation with respect to public opinion in Brussels might be interpreted as an indicator that the Europeanisation of policy *in general* has not yet proceeded so far as to mobilise sufficient forces to break this vicious circle.

Part II
Case study: acidification policy

4

Acidification policy in the EC and in the Netherlands: an introduction to the case study

Introduction

In the first part of this study some theoretical concepts and questions were developed to approach the process of the Europeanisation of environmental policy. In chapter 2, the discussion remained at a relatively abstract and general level, but chapter 3, using the theory of policy networks, provided more concrete and operational tools. Elaboration of the four dimensions of power dependence resulted in a set of sensitising concepts for the characterisation of the build-up of policy networks between the national and the EC level. Together with a number of substantive expectations with regard to the development of EC environmental policy making, those concepts constitute the basis of the empirical part of this study.

The most suitable method to study the evolution of interactions and dependencies between a limited group of actors in the context of a policy-making process is qualitative field research, that is, a case study (Yin, 1984; Nooij, 1990: 22ff.). The detailed analysis of the behaviour and underlying perceptions and interests of actors in the struggle for policy outcomes with regard to a limited number of topics can give insight into the changing structures of power dependence in which interaction takes place. A more generalised approach, for instance in the form of a survey covering a more extensive range of policy issues, would presumably overlook the complex dynamics of the intertwining of policy-making processes at two levels and is therefore not employed here.

Crucial points in the design of a case study are the choice and delimitation of the field of study. It is an important factor in determining the representativeness of the empirical work. A narrowly defined case study area allows for in-depth investigations, but makes it more difficult to separate contingent factors from more general trends and limits the extent to which the results can be applied to a broader context. The reasons for selecting the issue area of acidification and the concentration on the interaction between one Member State – the Netherlands – and the Community level will be given in the first part of the next section. In the second part of that section, the methods used in the case study will be explained. As an introduction to the following chapters, the basic problem of acidification will then be sketched and a brief overview of the history of policies in the field of acidification in the EC (including the international background) and in the Netherlands will be given. The final section will explain the structure of the next chapters.

The case study: selection, delimitation and method

Selection and delimitation of the case study area

In the 1970s, EC environmental policy centred around single issues (see chapter 1). In the 1980s, the issue density increased and a broader range of policy instruments became available, but policy making continued to be concentrated around specific directives. Especially in comparison with the much more encompassing domestic environmental policy planning in some of the northern Member States – Germany, Denmark and the Netherlands – environmental policy at the Community level remained rather fragmented (Van Tatenhove and Liefferink, 1992). Apart from the Environmental Action Programmes with their ambiguous status and a few specific policy programmes, institutional mechanisms to ensure the coherence of environmental policy measures have been few. This makes it difficult and not particularly meaningful to approach the build-up of EC environmental policy at the aggregate level of general policy programmes and orientations.

The process of the making of an individual directive, therefore, is the predominant context in which actors meet and interact. This has to be taken into account in every study of EC environmental policy. One way to investigate empirically the long-term development of environmental policy making in the EC would be to select a number of directives from different periods and different sub-fields (water pollution, pesticide regulation, nature conservation, etc.) and to analyse and compare the decision-making processes. Although this approach has the advantage of offering a broad perspective, it would probably neglect the gradual build-up of connections between issues, which was in fact regarded as one of the expressions of the maturation of the policy field (chapter 3). If such connections are being established, this can reasonably be expected to have begun between the more related issues *within* sub-fields. For that reason, I decided to focus on one issue area within the environmental field.

In the selection of the issue area, the following had to be considered. First, to be able to follow long-term trends, the issue area should cover the two decades that have passed since what has come to be regarded as the start of EC environmental policy, the Paris summit of 1972. This requirement practically limits the choice to the 'classic', usually sectoral fields of environmental policy, for instance water or air pollution. Concerns such as nature conservation or industrial risks only started to play an appreciable role in Brussels around 1980. Secondly, for the assessment of shifts in the orientation of EC environmental policy during the period, the issue area should include the different basic types of measures applied in the Community. In particular, it should include the two types of measures prevalent in the 1970s, that is, both product norms and broader, more 'detached' environmental quality provisions, as well as examples of the instruments that started to play a more significant role in the 1980s, especially emissions standards. This rules out for instance noise policy, as this almost exclusively entails product standards. Thirdly, and perhaps most importantly, the case study area should give room for addressing the basic questions of this study. The issue area to be selected, in other words, should provide instances of substantial interaction between various public and private actors at both levels of governance. This can be expected to be the case particularly where major, politically salient issues and the possible transfer of notable powers from the national to the Community level were at stake.

The fields of water pollution, air pollution and waste appear to be potential case study areas, but the above criteria are probably most fully met by the field of air pollution and acidification. During the 1970s, the problem of 'acid rain' was discussed mainly in

Scandinavia. Sulphur dioxide, however, the chemical compound considered most important in early acidification policy, was subject to debate and regulation in the Community in the mid-1970s, in the form of both air quality standards and limitations to the sulphur content of fuels. The policy processes around those two issues, that may be regarded as 'precursors' of genuine acidification policy, will constitute the start of the present case study. Although the policies in this period strongly focused on local air pollution problems, the importance of internationally co-ordinated product standards was recognised at both national and EC level.

In the 1980s, rapidly increasing attention to the problem of acidification gave rise to two of the most protracted and con-troversial issues in the history of EC environmental policy: the introduction of catalytic converters in motor vehicles and the limiting of emissions of sulphur and nitrogen oxides from large combustion plants. Considering the high political salience of the problem of acidification in a number of Member States and the remarkably quick response at the Community level (see below), it can be argued that air pollution not only followed the general trend from relatively insubstantial air quality and product norms to more drastic measures (see chapter 1), but probably acted as one of the driving forces behind this trend. The case of acidification policy, therefore, is particularly suited to the study of this shift. The decision making behind the large combustion plants directive, eventually adopted in 1988, and the car emissions standards concluded (for the time being) in 1991, form the core of the case study and also in principle mark the end of its time span.[1]

In addition to the issues mentioned, policies regarding the third major acidifying agent, ammonia, will be taken into account. As will be shown, such policies are actually as good as non-existent at the EC level. This part of the case study will focus on the question why this is so. In the absence of distinct 'episodes' of non-policy, the chapter on the ammonia issue includes data up to the moment that the collection of empirical material was concluded, that is, summer 1993.

Apart from the selection of a case study area, the empirical work had to be focused on the relationship between the Community level and domestic policies and actors in one Member State. This practical necessity obviously narrows down the empirical basis of the work, but it should be remembered that it is not the purpose of this study to provide an overall picture of the historical development and present situation of State–EC relations in environmental policy. The study rather seeks to unveil mechanisms and trends underlying such relations. A detailed study rather than a bird's-eye view can provide insight into the complex forces behind the gradual intertwining of domestic and EC policies.

The Netherlands seemed to be particularly suited for this purpose. First, the country is one of the Community's founding members and has always maintained an open and positive attitude towards the goal of European integration. In contrast to many other Member States, ideological discussions have seldom thwarted the Dutch commitment to the EC. For that reason, the Netherlands offers an excellent opportunity for studying the dynamics of the process of Europeanisation under relatively 'pure' and constant conditions. Secondly, the Netherlands has always supported the development of environmental policies by the EC. Without actually taking the lead – this role was mostly left to Germany, as demonstrated below – the country was consistently in the forefront of the Community's air pollution policy. As the Netherlands was among the first countries to establish domestic policies in the field of acidification and actively participated in the European policy making, the policy field gives ample room for the study of the interrelation and interaction between both policy levels.

The specific features referred to above thus make the Netherlands a particularly good choice for the analytical purposes of the present study. At the same time, however, they may to some extent colour the outcomes. It would no doubt be interesting to conduct similar, detailed studies in other countries, notably those with a less outspoken or persistent pro-European attitude and those where environmental policies are less elaborated and institutionalised, for instance Denmark, the UK and the Mediterranean Member States. Findings in the Netherlands could then be checked and supplemented with the help of data from those countries. The final chapter of this book returns to the question of the representativeness of the case study.

Research method
The aim of the case study was to provide the empirical basis for the analysis of the interaction and possible shifts in this interaction between the domestic and the Community level in EC environmental

policy making. For this purpose, the build-up and functioning of policy networks around the different issues of acidification policy and encompassing the domestic and the Community level were investigated. The empirical study therefore had to provide a reconstruction of the policy processes in question, both in Brussels and in the Netherlands, with special emphasis on the different kinds of action taken by public and private actors at different policy levels. The empirical study was conducted to collect the data necessary for this reconstruction. The method applied for this was a combination of the study of written (primary and secondary) sources and interviewing of key actors.

Two types of written sources were used in the case study. Primary sources included legal texts (directives, laws, decrees, etc.), policy documents (policy programmes, memoranda, etc.) and internal documents, access to which was in most cases obtained in the context of interviews. Particularly with regard to the 'clean' car and the large combustion plants issues, notable secondary sources were available in the scientific literature in the form of case studies of (parts of) the decision-making processes in question. They usually focused on the Community level, particularly on the negotiations in the Council, and in some cases on the roles of big, influential Member States such as Germany or the UK.[2] In some cases newspaper articles and professional magazines were used as pointers to specific developments, but never as decisive evidence. As media coverage or the public perception of the issue or the policy making were not part of the research, no systematic study of newspapers or other periodicals was conducted. Written sources were initially used to gain an overview of the policy process, and later to check information obtained in interviews and to trace the context of statements.

The principal source of data with regard to the roles of Dutch policies and actors in EC decision making were interviews with twenty-three representatives of public and (collective) private actors involved in the policy making under consideration. The list of interviewees included officials working in the relevant policy fields at various government departments and in the EC Commission, as well as staff of environmental and business organisations and individual firms (see List of persons interviewed, pp. x–xi). The aim of the interviews was, first, to obtain factual information in order to fill the gaps that remained after the initial study of written sources. This kind of information, for instance about chronology, specific events, type and frequency of meetings, contacts with other actors, and so on, was needed for the reconstruction of the policy processes. Secondly, the interviews were used for 'testing' the specific expectations with regard to the build-up of encompassing policy networks developed in chapter 3. Questions – for instance regarding the policy focus, the mutual relations and the use of different kinds of resources in the network (vertical interdependence) and the co-ordination or conflict with other policy issues and issue areas (horizontal interdependence) – were reformulated and concretised for the context of the issues under consideration and raised during the interviews. On this basis it was possible to assess the dominant definitions of the policy issues (in terms of both substance and policy level), the processes of resource exchange and the underlying resource dependencies in and between the policy networks.

The criterion for selecting the interviewees was the extent to which they participated in the interaction in the network. It was attempted to cover the relevant government departments at the Dutch domestic level, the Commission officials directly dealing with the matter, the industrial sectors most directly involved (either directly or through their branch organisations) and the environmental organisations. This turned out to be possible in most cases, with the partial exception of the two issues from the 1970s: some key officials in the air quality issue had retired or passed away. The persons actually interviewed were selected using a cumulative method. In all cases the search began at the Dutch Ministry of Housing, Physical Planning and Environment (*Volkshuisvesting, Ruimtelijke Ordening en Milieubeheer*, VROM), because officials from this department played an important and active role in domestic policy making as well as in the co-ordination with EC standpoints with regard to all issues in the case study and could therefore be supposed to have a broad overview of the relevant policy networks. Through the VROM officials responsible for the issue in question, actors in other ministries and in the Community institutions, as well as private actors that they regarded as actively contributing to the policy process, were identified. In interviews with those persons the list was checked and in some cases new names were added. While all actors confirmed the central position of VROM in the issues in question, this procedure reduced the risk of overlooking a significant actor.

Interviews were held between December 1992 and June 1993 and usually took between one and two hours. Interviewees were informed in advance about the aim and character of the project and, in general terms, about the points of attention. The interviews themselves, however, were open ended, leaving much room for going more deeply into the matter or into 'sidelines' that appeared to throw additional light on the subject. As far as possible, interviewees were confronted with statements by and the opinions of other interviewees. This was usually done in an implicit way so as to avoid prejudices connected to particular persons or organisations. On the basis of written notes taken during the conversation, a detailed report was prepared and sent to the interviewee within two weeks. In an accompanying letter it was explained that the absence of a reaction would be interpreted as approval of the report. Most of the interviewees did not reply; in a few cases comments and additional information were received.

In view of the confidential character of much of the information and as agreed in advance with the interviewees, interview sources are generally not indicated in the text. As a rule, the absence of a reference to literature or documents implies that the information in question was drawn from interviews. Only in cases where the origin of the statement is crucial for its meaning or significance is the position of the interviewee mentioned.

It should be noted that no quantitative data were assembled in the case study. Although they could be helpful in assessing certain specific aspects of policy networks, for instance the size of membership or financial resources of umbrella organisations, the careful collection of qualitative data was considered more important for the purpose of this study, particularly in view of the limited time available.

Acidification: the problem and the sources

Acidification is, chemically speaking, the input of an excessive amount of hydrogen ions (H^+) into the environment, for instance into the soil or into surface water. This in turn has a range of negative effects on ecosystems. For instance, certain kinds of fish are directly affected if the acidity of lakes and streams increases. In soils, surplus acidity causes damage to micro-organisms, influences the supply of nutrients and can mobilise (toxic) metals such as aluminium. In the longer term, this can affect the quality of ground water and the health of plants and trees. The consequent reduction of agricultural and forestry yields may also lead to economic losses. Effects of this kind were first recognised in southern Scandinavia, but during the 1980s increasingly in other countries as well.

Acidification is caused by a number of airborne pollutants, notably sulphur dioxide (SO_2), nitrogen oxides (NO_x) and ammonia (NH_3). With the help of water contained in clouds or raindrops or present on the earth's surface, sulphur and nitrogen oxides are converted into sulphuric acid (H_2SO_4) and nitric acid (HNO_3). Ammonia can under certain circumstances be converted to nitric acid by micro-organisms in the soil. In the northern part of Europe, temperature is one of the limiting factors for the latter process (Nilsson, 1986). Sulphuric and nitric acid in turn provide the hydrogen ions that are directly responsible for acidification.

Acidifying substances can be transported over thousands of kilometres. Research since the 1970s (Eliassen, 1978) has for instance shown that a considerable share of acid deposition in Scandinavia originates from countries such as the UK, the Netherlands, Germany and Poland. Approximately eighty per cent of sulphur and nitrogen oxides emitted in the Netherlands are 'exported'. Similarly, some eighty per cent of the amount deposited comes from abroad. For ammonia, a particularly important pollutant in the Netherlands, 'exports' amount to about seventy per cent and 'imports' to thirty per cent (RIVM, 1988: 111).

The anthropogenic emission of sulphur and nitrogen oxides is strongly related to the burning of fossil fuels. Oil and coal contain variable amounts of sulphur that are converted into sulphur dioxide during combustion. The emission of sulphur can, at considerable cost, be reduced by the desulphurisation of fuels or flue gases. Natural gas contains hardly any sulphur. The most important sources of sulphur dioxide are therefore coal- and oil-fired power plants, oil refineries and other industrial combustion processes. In most countries they together account for eighty to ninety per cent of all sulphur emissions (RIVM, 1988; CEC, 1990).

Nitrogen oxides are emitted in every combustion process. They are formed by the reaction of nitrogen and oxygen in the air under the influence of the heat produced by the burning of any kind of fuel. Technological abatement of emissions of nitrogen oxides entails the adaptation of the combustion process itself or the (catalytic) cleaning of flue gases. The dominant source of nitrogen oxides is road traffic: it is responsible for more than fifty per cent of total emissions in most West European countries. Other major sources are electricity generation (fifteen to forty per cent) and various other industries (RIVM, 1988; CEC, 1990).

Apart from a limited amount from industrial processes, agriculture is solely responsible for the emission of ammonia (more than ninety per cent of total Dutch emissions; RIVM, 1988). Livestock (including pigs and chickens), stables, manure storage and spreading of manure on land release large amounts of ammonia into the air. The most serious effects occur in the vicinity of sources, for instance in some regions in the eastern and southern parts of the Netherlands, but long-range transport should not be underestimated, as noted above. Technological measures range from covering of storage tanks to advanced methods of injecting manure into the soil.

Air pollution and acidification policy in the EC

The international background

Although the Scandinavian countries, particularly Sweden and Norway, had attempted to bring broader attention to the issue at the UN Conference on the Human Environment in Stockholm in 1972, the OECD was the first to launch a programme of research into the international aspects of acidification. Its findings (Eliassen, 1978) pointed out the considerable transboundary transport of sulphur compounds. As the OECD itself had a tradition of issuing only non-binding resolutions and recommendations, the Soviet suggestion to turn to the ECE for more concrete steps was rapidly taken up by the Scandinavians. In spite of the primarily strategic motivation for the suggestion, negotiations led to the Convention on Long-Range Transboundary Air Pollution in Geneva in 1979. The Convention did not contain any concrete commitment to limit emissions of air pollutants, but as it was signed by most States in Eastern and Western Europe (as well as the USA and Canada) it was regarded as an important political signal and as the starting point for further negotiations (see Wetstone and Rosencranz, 1983; McCormick, 1985).

Little happened in the years immediately after the signing of the Convention. In 1982, however, serious damage to domestic forests, presumably caused by 'acid rain', gave rise to massive public and political concern in the Federal Republic of Germany (FRG). Although originally one of the more reluctant partners to the 1979 Convention, Germany now became an active promoter of effective international measures. It first expressed its new views at the Conference on the Acidification of the Environment in June 1982 in Stockholm. Soon after, it also started to press the EC.

Under the influence of the 'conversion' of the economically most powerful European State, things started to move again. In March 1984 in Ottawa, ten countries (Austria, Canada, Finland, Norway, Sweden and Switzerland, and the EC Member States Denmark, France, the FRG and the Netherlands) informally agreed to reduce sulphur dioxide emissions by thirty per cent by 1993 from 1980 levels. In June 1984, the '30% Club' was joined by eight others, including the Soviet Union, and in July 1985 a Protocol to the 1979 Convention of similar purport was signed.

In 1988 the SO_2 Protocol was followed by a second Protocol, requiring a standstill of emissions of nitrogen oxides in 1994 relative to 1987. Eleven of the twenty-five signatories (including EC Member States Denmark, France, Germany, Italy and the Netherlands) committed themselves to a thirty per cent reduction by 1998. In 1991, a Protocol on volatile organic compounds (VOCs), an important link in the formation of ozone in the lower atmosphere, was signed. In the meantime, the ECE had started preparations for a second step in the reduction of sulphur dioxide emissions. It was to be based on the concept of so-called critical loads, that is, deposition targets taking into account regional characteristics of the environment. The full protection of all ecosystems in Europe against acidification, however, would require very far-reaching measures, amounting to reductions of more than ninety per cent in many countries. The new SO_2 Protocol was signed in spring 1994 and aims to close the gap between actual (i.e. 1990) emissions and critical loads by sixty per cent by 2000, but for several countries exemptions and longer lead times are allowed (Ågren, 1994).

The start of EC air pollution policy in the 1970s
Community environmental policy started with the declaration of the Paris summit in October 1972 and the publication of the First Environmental Action Programme in 1973 (EAP 1973–1976; see chapter 1). With regard to air pollution, the Programme followed the

general trend in the Member States in those years and focused on health effects. It was proposed to develop 'criteria', that is, scientific dose–effect relationships, for a number of important substances, including some air pollutants. The OECD work on transboundary air pollution was only briefly referred to (EAP 1973–1976: 15). Considerable attention was paid to environmental problems connected with agriculture. In this field several research initiatives and policy intentions were announced, concerning among other things the environmental aspects of bio-industry (EAP 1973–1976: 40).

The measures with regard to air pollution taken in the years that followed did not live up to the ambitions of the First Action Programme. The establishment of scientific criteria soon appeared to be very difficult and had to be replaced by a more political approach, eventually leading to the first air quality directives in 1980 and 1982 (80/779/EEC and 82/884/EEC, see chapter 5). The control of local, particularly urban sources of air pollution remained limited to the regulation of the sulphur content of gas oil (75/716/EEC), used mainly for household heating and for diesel engines (chapter 5). Apart from that, the rather undemanding emission standards for motor vehicles decided in the framework of the ECE were translated into EC directives (70/220/EEC, 74/290/EEC, 77/102/EEC, 78/665/EEC, 83/351/EEC; chapter 6).

The rapid rise of the issue of acidification in the 1980s
Whereas the Second Environmental Action Programme (EAP 1977–1981) did not contain significant new elements in the field of air pollution, the Third Action Programme was prepared and published in the period of the German about-face with regard to *Waldsterben* (forest die-back) and acidification. The Programme contained a number of new ideas for EC environmental policy (see chapter 1), but progress in the field of air pollution was limited. More explicit reference was made to the possibility of setting emission standards, particularly for large stationary sources, and for the first time the problem of 'acid rain' was mentioned (EAP 1982–1986: 10–11).

This did not prevent the Commission from reacting relatively quickly to the new situation, however. Under German pressure, discussions about concrete measures to limit emissions from industrial sources had already started by the end of 1982. In the spring of 1983 an official proposal for a 'framework' directive on air pollution was issued, followed later that year by the draft of a 'daughter' directive setting limits for the emission of sulphur and nitrogen oxides from large combustion plants, that is, power plants, refineries and large industrial boilers (see chapter 7). In November 1983, furthermore, the Commission disclosed its view on the issue of acidification in a communication to the Council (COM(83)721). In addition to the drafts just mentioned, a considerable reduction of car emissions formed part of the approach. Proposals to this end, also strongly stimulated by Germany, were published in 1984 (see chapter 6).

Whereas agreement on the general provisions of the framework directive was reached in a relatively short time (84/360/EEC), controversies about the issues of the 'clean' car and the large combustion plants dominated the Community's air pollution policy until the end of the decade. This was reflected in the Fourth Environmental Action Programme, which gave highest priority to the issue of acidification (EAP 1987–1992: 22–24). On the basis of the strong impulse to integrate environmental policy into other policy areas contained in the Third and Fourth Action Programmes and the Single Act, the issue of agriculture and environment was seriously taken up for the first time since the 1970s in a communication from the Commission (COM(88)338). Later in 1988, it was followed by draft legislation regarding nitrate pollution from diffuse (i.e. mainly agricultural) sources. The directive was adopted in 1991 (91/676/EEC), but did not refer to the related problem of the emission of ammonia (see chapter 8).

Although not strictly relevant to the present case study, it is interesting to note that in the early 1990s the global problems of the depletion of the ozone layer and the 'greenhouse' effect acquired considerable weight in EC air pollution policy. The unresolved issue of a tax on the use of energy repeatedly topped the agenda of Council meetings and in the Fifth Environmental Action Programme (EAP 1993–2000), which attempted to bring about a more integrated approach to environmental policy by organising policies around environmental 'themes' and 'target groups',[3] 'climate change' was given a prominent place beside 'acidification and air quality'.

Air pollution and acidification policy in the Netherlands

The first broad environmental law in the Netherlands was the Nuisance Act (*Hinderwet*).[4] It was first enacted in 1875, thoroughly revised in 1952, and firmly rooted in public health policy of the nineteenth century (Van Zon, 1986). As in most industrialised countries, however, the systematic development of specific legislation aimed at the protection and improvement of environmental quality started in the 1960s. The first milestones were the enactment of the Surface Water Pollution Act (*Wet Verontreiniging Oppervlaktewater*) in 1969 and the Air Pollution Act (*Wet Inzake de Luchtverontreiniging*) in 1970. In 1971, the importance of the new policy field was acknowledged in the establishment of a new Ministry of Public Health and Environmental Hygiene (*Volksgezondheid en Milieuhygiëne*, VoMil). In 1972, it produced the so-called Emergency Memorandum on Environmental Hygiene (*Urgentienota Milieuhygiëne*, 1971–1972), the first of a long and ever more elaborate series of government memoranda on the environment. In the 1970s and early 1980s, policy plans were worked out in periodical Indicative Multi-year Programmes (*Indicatieve Meerjaren Programma's*, IMPs) for different sectors of the policy field (water, air, soil, etc.). In 1982, departmental organisation was changed and the environment brought under the new Ministry of Housing, Physical Planning and Environment (VROM). In response to problems connected with a lack of coherence in environmental policy, it developed a more integrated approach to planning and policy making. From 1984, the sectoral IMPs were gradually replaced by one comprehensive IMP that laid down specific, integrated policies for different 'target groups', for instance industrial sectors, transport and traffic or households. The 'target group' policies were to be based on a communicative approach. At the same time, environmental goals were formulated around 'themes', such as acidification, eutrophication and disturbance (see *IMP-Milieubeheer*, 1985–1989; Winsemius, 1986). At the end of the 1980s, finally, the IMPs were succeeded by a system of strategic National Environmental Policy Plans (*Nationaal Milieubeleidsplannen*, NMPs), to be published every fourth year, and annual progress reports (Environmental Programmes, *Milieuprogramma's*). In addition, numerous memoranda dealing with specific problems were issued throughout the period (for a general discussion of Dutch environmental policy, see Liefferink, forthcoming).

The gradual emergence of the issue of acidification in the 1970s
In the Netherlands as elsewhere, environmental policy in the 1970s focused on direct effects on public health, animals, plants and

materials. The acidification of lakes in Scandinavia and the desirability of internationally co-ordinated action were briefly mentioned in the first IMP-Air, but no relation was established with concrete effects or measures in the Netherlands. Apart from that, international regulation was mainly advocated for reasons of trade and competition (IMP-Lucht, 1976–1980: 52, 85–86).

As a major component of urban air pollution, sulphur dioxide attracted most attention in the 1970s. The 150-page Sulphur Dioxide Policy Framework Plan (*SO₂-Beleidskaderplan*, 1979–1980), pub-lished in 1979, aimed at improving air quality, that is, concentrations of sulphur dioxide in the air, but 'related' problems were discussed quite extensively as well and it was recognised that active policies to reduce emissions were needed, for a number of reasons. One such 'related' problem was acidification, the effects of which were reported to occur in several countries, including for the first time the Netherlands, although they were assumed to be restricted to lakes fully dependent on rain water. On the basis of Swedish estimates of tolerable deposition limits in Europe (Persson, 1976) on the one hand and the number of inhabitants on the other, an overall emission target for sulphur dioxide for the Netherlands was constructed, which happened to be approximately equal to the actual figure for 1980 (SO₂-Beleidskaderplan, 1979–1980: 37–46; Dovland and Saltbones, 1986). The approach of the Framework Plan was basically continued in the IMP-Air for the period 1981–195, published only in September 1982 (IMP-Lucht, 1981–1985).

The build-up of acidification policy in the 1980s

The next IMP-Air (IMP-Lucht, 1984–1988), issued only one year later, made clear that the German acidification fever had also touched the Netherlands (for a detailed discussion see Hajer, 1993). On the basis of the preliminary results of a pilot study, suggesting a considerable domestic impact of acidification, specific emission and deposition targets for sulphur dioxide as well as nitrogen oxides and (in more general terms) ammonia were formulated. They were further detailed in a special memorandum, 'The problem of acidification' (*Problematiek van de verzuring*, 1983–1984). In the meantime, negotiations had started about a Dutch equivalent to new German legislation to control emissions from large stationary sources (chapter 7). Furthermore, the Dutch Government increas-ingly supported the Germans in promoting the EC-wide introduction of catalytic converters in motor vehicles (chapter 6). In subsequent IMPs and the Interim Evaluation Acidification Policy (notably IMP-Lucht, 1985–1989 and IMP-Milieubeheer, 1985–1989; *Tussentijdse evaluatie verzuringsbeleid*, 1987–1988), emission and deposition targets were refined and tightened.

In 1988–1989, public and political attention to environmental policy in the Netherlands reached a temporary maximum, related among other things to the escalating controversies about the first NMP (NMP1), which even proved decisive in the abdication of the Cabinet in May 1989. In the EC context, Dutch unilateral action helped to provoke a breakthrough in the 'clean' car negotiations in early 1989. The NMP, in combination with the Acidification Abatement Plan (*Bestrijdingsplan verzuring*, 1988–1989) and a draft plan of approach for ammonia emissions (*Plan van aanpak beperking ammoniak-emissies van de landbouw*, 1990–1991) published almost simultaneously, once again revised the policy objectives with regard to acidification.

In the early 1990s, similar to what was observed in the EC, the issue of climate change increasingly competed with acidification for the attention of policy makers. Acidification policy in this period primarily aimed at the implementation of the objectives set out earlier. Some adjustment of targets, for instance with regard to nitrogen oxides and ammonia, were proposed but the basic approach of the first NMP was not changed (NMP-Plus; NMP2: 77–81).

Outline of the case study

In the following chapters the making of policy concerning acidification (including the 'pre-acidification' period) in the EC and its interrelations with Dutch domestic policies and decision making will be reconstructed. This reconstruction is, however, not an end in itself. Insight into the perceptions and roles of various actors with different interests and institutional positions forms the basis for the characterisation of the policy networks evolving around each of the issues in the case study. Considering the complexity and the documentary value of the empirical material, however, the two steps will be separated. Chapters 5–8 will describe the relevant policy processes and highlight the roles of different types of actors. In chapter 9, the findings will be analysed in terms of the four dimensions of power dependence, and conclusions about the build-up of encompassing policy networks will be drawn.

Chapter 5 draws together the two air pollution issues of the 1970s: air quality and the sulphur content of fuels. In chapters 6 and 7, the dominating issues of the 1980s will be considered in detail: the 'clean' car and the large combustion plants, respectively. Chapter 8, finally, deals with the 'non-issue' – at least at the EC level – of the role of ammonia in the acidification of the environment.

The discussion of each issue will be divided into five sections. A short historical account of the process in question will first be given. Secondly, the relations with Dutch domestic policy will be examined. The positions and roles of Dutch governmental actors in the decision making in Brussels, that is, mainly in and around the Council of Ministers, are assessed against the background of the relevant domestic policies. In addition, crucial connections with domestic policies in other Member States, notably Germany, and relevant bilateral contacts will be discussed here. The third section focuses on public actors at the Community level. This primarily involves the Commission – DG XI and its relations with DGs covering other policy fields – but also other Community institutions such as the EP or the Court of Justice as far as they proved relevant. Under the same heading attention is paid to connections between EC policies and the broader international context. The fourth section goes into the contribution of private actors to the process. It particularly describes the involvement of Dutch industry and Dutch environmental groups in EC policy making, either through contacts with the national government or through European umbrella organisations. The final section provides a short summary as a starting point for the analysis in the third part of the book.

Notes

1   At the end of 1992, a new round in the 'clean' car negotiations started, but it was not considered useful to include only the early beginnings of a new phase of the process in the case study. New steps with regard to large combustion plants had not yet been initiated when data for this case study were collected (1992–1993).

2   An exception is the study by Hajer (1993) on acidification policy in the UK and in the Netherlands. It focuses on the perception and conceptualisation of the problem of acidification in the domestic policy debates, using the

method of discourse analysis. However, its direct value in the context of the present study is limited, because the international and EC aspects are hardly taken into account.

3   This approach was strongly inspired by the Dutch philosophy of environmental policy planning, developed since the mid-1980s (see below).

4   The official Dutch names of legislative texts and policy documents are introduced in italics. They are used for reference and listed separately at the end of the book. For names frequently used in this study, the usual Dutch abbreviations are given and used thereafter. Abbreviations are listed on pp. xii–xiv.

Air pollution policy in the 1970s: air quality and sulphur content of fuels

Introduction

This chapter will review policy making over the establishment of air quality standards, particularly those for sulphur dioxide and suspended particulates, and the regulation of the sulphur content of fuel. Both issues can be connected with the focus on local, particularly urban air pollution prevalent in the 1970s, both at the Community level and in individual Member States. The air quality issue represents the strand of general EC environmental legislation initiated in this period, whereas the measures regarding the sulphur content of fuels belong to the category of product norms, directly related to trade and the functioning of the internal market (see chapter 1). Both issues emerged in the mid-1970s. Three air quality directives were eventually adopted between 1980 and 1985. A directive limiting the sulphur content of gas oil was decided in 1975 and updated in 1987. The establishment of similar limits for other types of fuels failed after repeated attempts.

The 'clean' car will not be discussed here. Although the setting of emission requirements for motor vehicles has its origins in the 1970s as well, the more exciting part of the process took place in the 1980s, when concern about acidification brought the introduction of the catalytic converter on the agenda (see chapter 6).

Air quality

Introduction and overview
The first air quality directive decided in the Council was Directive 80/779/EEC regarding sulphur dioxide and suspended particulates. It

had been proposed in February 1976 (COM(76)48). Almost one year earlier, on 16 April 1975, a directive concerning the concentrations of lead in the air had been submitted to the Council (COM(75)166). Member States were, however, very reluctant to take up the latter proposal and in 1977 agreed first to carry out an investigation into the exposure of the population to lead (Directive 77/312/EEC; see Johnson and Corcelle, 1989: 116–117). Negotiations about the air quality standards for lead were not seriously resumed until 1981, when the first results of the screening project became available and after the sulphur dioxide directive had been adopted. For that reason the main political controversies around the setting of EC air quality standards focused on the directive concerning sulphur dioxide and suspended particulates. These circumstances happen to coincide with the greater relevance of the sulphur dioxide directive for acidification policy, the subject of the case study, and explains the emphasis on this directive in the following discussion.

The problem of high concentrations of sulphur dioxide in the air was one of the first air pollution issues to be recognised. In the mid-1970s awareness of the health effects of smog in urban areas was widespread in Western Europe. The most dramatic smog episode, causing an immediate sharp increase in mortality, took place in London in 1952 (Wetstone and Rosencranz, 1983: 67), but many other big cities and industrial areas in Western Europe had suffered from comparable episodes.

At the time the directive concerning air quality standards for sulphur dioxide and suspended particulates was proposed, the FRG was the only Member State having binding, although quite lenient, national ambient standards for these substances. They had been set already in 1964 and tightened in 1974. Some other countries had guidelines for air quality, but they were either applicable only in certain situations (e.g. Italy) or not legally binding (e.g. the Netherlands, see below) (Weidner and Knoepfel, 1981: 47ff.).

There is no indication that a particular Member State stimulated the Commission to draft the proposal for sulphur dioxide. In fact, the idea of setting EC-wide ambient standards as such generally aroused neither strong opposition nor strong enthusiasm. Only the UK initially contested the principle of EC competence in air quality, but:

> when some of the more environmentally progressive Member States, most notably the Netherlands, began disparaging the proposed air quality

standards as inconsequential, and urging the adoption of more meaningful emission controls, the British receded in their opposition. Other countries also became more favorably disposed.

(Wetstone and Rosencranz, 1983: 150–151; for the role of the Dutch, see below)

Resistance from Ireland, France and Germany, for instance, had to do with the level of the proposed standards and focused on their scientific basis or on measurement methods.

As mentioned above, the lead directive (the later Directive 82/884/EEC) was negotiated mainly after the one for sulphur dioxide, but it had been proposed first. Here too, however, no indication could be found of objections in principle to the transfer of competences. It was rather doubts about costs and benefits that led to the postponement of the decision by launching a large-scale screening project. At the time the draft reappeared on the agenda of the Council, the question of the Commission's competence to initiate this kind of legislation was in any case no longer a topic. The discussions then focused on the level of the standards. The same was true for the directive regarding nitrogen dioxide (85/203/EEC, proposed in September 1983). In the latter case, some Member States, including the Netherlands, stimulated the draft of the proposal, but it was obviously considered to have low priority compared with the emission requirements for cars and large combustion plants that were under discussion in the same period.

Negotiations about the sulphur dioxide directive were long and difficult. As the strategy of developing scientific 'criteria' for a number of major pollutants, set out in the First Environmental Action Programme (EAP 1973–1976: 13), had soon proved to be impracticable, a more political basis was sought for the draft directive regarding air quality standards, making use among other things of the respected recommendations of the World Health Organisation (WHO) (WHO, 1972; revised in WHO, 1979; see below). This could not prevent the issue continuing to be heavily discussed, not only by Member States that feared the economic consequences of too strict standards, such as France, Ireland, the FRG and the UK, but also by some other countries that considered the proposed values too lax, notably the Netherlands and Denmark.

In the compromise finally reached (see SO_2-Beleidskaderplan, 1979–1980: 86) the standards proposed by the Commission were maintained as obligatory limits, but a set of stricter guide values was added. These guide values were identical to the 1979 WHO recommendations. They are meant to be applied in zones requiring special protection (80/779/EEC, Article 4) and serve as long-term objectives (Article 5). The system of limit values and guide values was used again in the air quality directives for lead and nitrogen dioxide without much discussion.

Additional complications in the negotiations were caused mainly by Germany, which brought up the issues of the method to be applied to measure concentrations of suspended particulates in the air and the date of compliance with the requirements of the directive. Other Member States suspected the FRG of using the issue as a smoke screen for the poor air quality in some regions of the country (Wetstone and Rosencranz, 1983: 151).

Relations with Dutch domestic policy
In the Netherlands, before the draft directive, only advisory standards had been set by the Health Council, an expert body advising the Dutch Government, in 1971 (Gezondheidsraad, 1971). In the negotiation process in Brussels, they functioned as the point of departure for the Dutch delegation.

The special role of the Netherlands in 'converting' the other Member States in the first stage of the negotiations about EC-wide ambient standards, suggested by Wetstone and Rosencranz (1983: 151, see above), could not be confirmed by the present research. A reconstruction of the debates in Brussels and the situation in the Netherlands at that time, however, may support their interpretation at least partially.

The formulation of air quality standards in the 1970s originated from the idea of developing 'criteria' for certain air pollutants (EAP 1973–1976). Such criteria were regarded by the Commission as a foundation for further policies. Indeed, the Commission was convinced that an effective air pollution policy would be possible only on the basis of a broader, more source-oriented approach, encompassing more than air quality standards and trade-related product norms. Notably, this approach would include emission standards. The Commission had started to express this view in the mid-1970s, that is, about the time when initiative was being taken towards the first air quality directives (for instance EAP 1977–1981: 13ff.). At that time, however, formulation at the EC level of emission standards for air pollution was unacceptable to most Member States.

A similar approach to ambient standards as a frame of reference for environmental policies could be observed in the first debates about environmental norms in the Netherlands, for instance in the Health Council document already referred to, and notably in the 1976 Memorandum on Environmental Health Standards (*Nota Milieuhygiënische Normen*, 1976–1977). In addition, the latter document first raised the possibility of establishing binding air quality standards. In the next few years, however, the situation gradually changed. Even though the 1979 Sulphur Dioxide Policy Framework Plan announced the preparation of an amendment to the Air Pollution Act necessary for introducing binding air quality standards in the Netherlands, the document generally showed an increasing emphasis on emission standards as a more direct and effective instrument for reducing pollution by sulphur dioxide (SO_2-Beleidskaderplan, 1979–1980: 74–81, 84). That the air quality approach was indeed given lower priority was clearly demonstrated by the fact that the draft amendment to the Air Pollution Act was presented to the Parliament only in 1983 and eventually adopted in 1986, almost four years after the formal date of compliance of the directive (see Bennett, 1991: 73–78).

This gradual shift in priority did not prevent the Dutch from playing a constructive role during the whole process of negotiating the sulphur dioxide directive. They generally supported the Commission in its efforts to pilot the directive through the Council. At the same time, however, it is not unlikely that the first signs of the Dutch shift to a more emission-oriented approach in this period coincided with the Commission's first efforts to broaden its range of policy instruments. Probably without being intended by the Netherlands, the emergence of this perspective may have inspired the other Member States to accept what might be called the smaller evil of quality standards, as suggested by Wetstone and Rosencranz.

During the negotiations, the Netherlands consistently argued for stricter standards than most other countries. For example, the Dutch Sulphur Dioxide Policy Framework Plan complained that, although the negotiations in 1979 were far advanced, 'still differences of principle exist[ed], particularly with regard to both short term and long term objectives' (SO_2-Beleidskaderplan, 1979–1980: 86; author's translation). The Dutch were in favour of 'as much as possible correspondence with the [stricter] values as formulated by the Health Council' (*ibid.*). The Plan supported this argument with reference to comparable standards applied in Japan and the USA and to the WHO recommendations. The Dutch wishes were – partially – accommodated in the directive's guide values. The Government Decree that finally implemented the directive in the Netherlands in fact strongly relied on the Health Council values and thus implied the designation of the entire territory of the country as a special protection zone under Article 4 of the directive, where the stricter guide values would apply (explanatory memorandum to *Besluit luchtkwaliteit zwaveldioxide en zwevende deeltjes (zwarte rook)*).

Community-level public actors

The Commission was the main initiator of the sulphur dioxide and lead proposals in the mid-1970s. The motive to produce both draft directives was almost exclusively the wish to protect public health, particularly in urban areas. The internal market aspect was negligible.[1] As a consequence, other parts of the Commission than DG XI (or rather its predecessor, the unit for Environment and Consumer Protection) were hardly involved in the preparation of the directives.

The Commission's proposals immediately followed from the strategy set out in the First Environmental Action Programme to develop 'criteria', that is, scientific dose–effect relationships, for important pollutants, including some major air pollutants such as lead and sulphur compounds (EAP 1973–1976: 13). On the basis of such criteria, environmental quality objectives had to be established and those, in turn, might lead 'if necessary' to common norms (EAP 1973–1976: 13–14). In doing so, the Commission followed an international trend of developing environmental quality standards. This trend could be observed not only in countries in other parts of the world, such as Japan and the USA, but also in other international organisations, most notably the WHO. The Commission was ready to claim the competence in this new field for the Community.

In the first years after the First Action Programme it was indeed attempted to establish criteria for major pollutants, such as sulphur dioxide and particulates, but it soon appeared that scientific opinions about environmental quality and protection diverged so much that in practice every interested party could select the 'scientific' basis that suited him or her best. The Commission then turned to formulating quality objectives and standards on a more political basis. The 1975 proposal for lead in the air and the first draft of the directive for sulphur dioxide and suspended particulates, both containing somewhat arbitrary limit values, may be regarded as a first attempt to do so. This approach was later explained in the Second Action Programme, which stated that standards might be set before the finalisation of criteria and quality objectives if there were urgent reasons relating to the protection of human health or the environment (EAP 1977–1981: 14). The approach was not readily accepted by the Member States, however. As set out above, the main reason for this was probably the Member States' unwillingness to bear the (economic) consequences of measures the necessity of which had not yet sufficiently been demonstrated. In the case of lead, therefore, the Council could agree only on a large-scale monitoring programme in order to provide scientific background for the later establishment of standards. In the case of sulphur dioxide and particulates, the basis and character of the standards together with some more or less technical aspects of the proposal long remained the central problem.

For the establishment of criteria, the Commission had suggested the use of as much as possible of the work already done in this field, notably by the WHO (EAP 1973–1976: 14; WHO, 1972, 1979). Also, after the original plan of formulating criteria for the Community had been abandoned, the Commission attempted to establish a link between the draft directive and the WHO work. This would have saved at least some of the scientific credibility of the directive's values and it would have explicitly linked the Community's activities to the broader international debate in this field. Even though the WHO criteria were not claimed to be scientifically unassailable, and their formal status was nothing more than recommendations, none of the Member State really dared to contest them directly. This had to do with both the reputation of the Organisation and the fact that renowned experts from most of the Member States had been involved in the relevant WHO committees. At the same time, however, most Member States agreed that the WHO criteria were too strict for the situation in the Community. For this reason, the WHO work was not even alluded to in the 1976 draft, but it lent additional force to later Dutch/Danish pressure to include both limit values and stricter guide values in the directive. Once the principle of two types of standards had been accepted, it was obvious to all parties, and strongly supported by the Commission, that the WHO recommendations should be used as a model for the guide values.

It should be mentioned in this context that the draft of a new directive on air quality standards was under discussion in the Community in 1993. It was intended to constitute the framework for Community limit values for more substances than those covered by the three directives adopted in the first half of the 1980s. The Commission again attempted to establish as close as possible links with the findings of the WHO and (together with the Dutch Government, among others) actively supported a recent updating of the WHO recommendations.

Private actors
There is no indication that either industry or environmental organisations played any significant role in the initial phase of the air quality directives.

As far as Dutch private actors are concerned, it was not possible to be sure, from the material in this study, whether, for instance, the Netherlands Society for Nature and Environment (*Stichting Natuur en Milieu*, SNM) or the Association of Dutch Employers (*Verbond van Nederlandse Ondernemingen*, VNO)[2] had any information about the preparation of the draft directives for lead and for sulphur dioxide and particulates before they were published in the EC's official journal. This would have made little difference, though, as it was clear from the beginning that the Community directives would hardly affect the Dutch situation. With regard to sulphur dioxide and suspended particulates, it was obvious, in the first place, that the limit values proposed by the Commission would barely be exceeded in the Netherlands. In the second place, and of course connected to the first point, the discussions between the Government and interested parties in the preparation of the Sulphur Dioxide Policy Framework Plan that were also taking place in the second half of the 1970s were heading towards designation of the advisory standards set by the Health Council (Gezondheidsraad, 1971) as guidelines for the future establishment of binding national standards. The recommendations of the Health Council were much stricter than the Commission's proposals. For those reasons, Dutch industry had no interest in influencing the EC process regarding the directive for sulphur dioxide and particulates.

Approximately the same applied to lead and nitrogen oxides: in those cases the negotiations between Government and industry had already taken place in the framework of the IMPs for air preceding the decrees setting legally binding standards (particularly IMP-Lucht 1984–1988 for nitrogen dioxide, and IMP-Lucht 1985–1989 for lead).

Dutch environmental organisations also concentrated on the Dutch policy process, but in addition SNM was active at the EC level. The directive for sulphur dioxide and particulates was not one of SNM's priorities, but the organisation saw the value of meaningful EC-wide air quality standards. Through the European Environmental Bureau (EEB)[3] it attempted to mobilise environmental organisations elsewhere. In the mid-1970s, however, the main interests of most of them did not include air pollution, and thus the EEB was not at all active on this issue. SNM's interest in air quality standards for nitrogen dioxide mainly concerned the national level. Around 1985, the Dutch limit values were exceeded in a considerable number of streets, as were, in some cases, the relatively lax limit values of the directive (Eerens *et al.*, 1989). SNM hoped that this would stimulate the Dutch Government to reduce air pollution from cars.

Sulphur content of fuels

Introduction and overview
The serious concern about urban air pollution in several European countries in the first half of the 1970s not only led to the air quality directives discussed above, but also to the directive on the approximation of the laws of the Member States relating to the sulphur content of certain liquid fuels (75/716/EEC).

Bungarten (1978: 186–187, 210–211) asserts that several countries in this period prepared and adopted legislation regarding the sulphur content of fuels, especially in urban areas. He reports that the Netherlands was the first to notify the Commission of its intentions in this field, on 2 May 1973. This happened on the basis of the notification agreement that had been made only two months earlier (EC, 1973; amended by EC, 1974). The Commission succeeded in announcing a draft within the time limit of two months, mainly because it had already been unofficially informed about the Dutch plans (Bungarten, 1978: 186–187).

The draft directive itself, however, was not published until February 1974 (COM(74)158). Moreover, it referred only to the lightest type of fuel oil, used for household heating and diesel engines, so-called gas oil. The Dutch Decree (*Besluit zwavelgehalte brandstoffen*), which was eventually accepted in September 1974, contained limit values for all types of liquid and solid fuels.

The directive on gas oil was adopted in November 1975. It restricted the sulphur content of gas oil to 0.5 per cent from 1 October 1976 and 0.3 per cent from 1 October 1980. In certain areas to be designated by individual Member States 0.8 per cent (0.5 per cent from 1 October 1980) was allowed. The Dutch Decree originally set the limit for gas oil at 0.7 per cent, but it already provided for a further limitation up to 0.5 per cent from 1 December 1975. Thus, the Netherlands, like Germany (Bungarten, 1978: 211), did not make use of the possibility of regional relaxation of the requirements in the directive.

Parallel to the preparations of the draft directive on gas oil, the Commission had set up a working group on heavy fuel oil (Bungarten, 1978: 187). This led to a draft (COM(75)681) published one month after the adoption of the gas oil directive. It proposed limit values for the sulphur content of heavy fuel oil of two per cent from 1978 and one per cent from 1983, to be applied only in areas (designated by the individual Member States) with high sulphur dioxide concentrations in the air. The philosophy was thus opposite to that of the gas oil directive, where special zones could be created for the application of laxer standards.

The heavy fuel oil draft was discussed without result until February 1978. Italy in particular was strongly opposed to it, in view of its high dependence on heavy fuel oil. This also explains why Italy, as well as France, would accept costly standards for heavy fuel oil only if the sulphur content of solid fuels was also regulated (Prittwitz, 1984: 140). This option was indeed considered for a short time in the late 1970s, but from the beginning this appeared to be highly controversial. Coal from many areas in Western Europe has a relatively high sulphur content, and as desulphurisation of coal is complicated and expensive, this would lead to a considerable competitive disadvantage vis-à-vis low-sulphur coal from outside the Community. Member States with big interests in coal mining strongly objected, and the Commission recognised the serious consequences in terms of social and regional policy. In 1981, eventually, the heavy fuel oil proposal was officially withdrawn by the Commission (Johnson and Corcelle, 1989: 109, 123).

In the 1983 communication from the Commission concerning environmental policy in the field of air pollution (COM(83)721), the idea of regulating the sulphur content of heavy and solid fuels was once again put forward, but at that time the proposal on large combustion plants (see chapter 7) was already being discussed. The approach of restricting sulphur *emissions* from plants with the help of end-of-pipe technology had already been chosen in Germany and would soon dominate the EC debate on industrial emissions as well.

Regulating sulphur *content* of fuels thus remained limited to small sources for which end-of-pipe technology was not available or practicable, such as household heating and diesel engines. In 1985 the Commission proposed a revision of the gas oil directive. It reversed the system of the original directive by setting a general limit of 0.3 per cent and allowing Member States to tighten this to 0.2 per cent in certain areas. The draft directive (COM(85)377) explicitly indicated that such zones could also comprise a Member State's entire territory (Article 5). This point became the bottleneck in the negotiations. Germany and the Netherlands, among others who would have preferred a limit of 0.15 per cent (cf. explanatory memorandum to Besluit zwavelgehalte brandstoffen, amendment 1988), supported the Commission's proposal, whereas for instance France and the UK advocated a single limit value to avoid (continued) splitting of the market. The latter group eventually conceded, perhaps because the refinery sector appeared to have little problem supplying two different grades (see below). Although the reference to the 'entire territory' was replaced by a more indirect formulation in the final directive (87/219/EEC), no fewer than five Member States decided to apply the stricter standard to the whole country, namely Belgium, Germany, Italy, Luxembourg and the Netherlands (explanatory memorandum to Besluit zwavelgehalte brandstoffen, amendment 1988).

The most recent amendment to the gas oil directive took place in early 1993 (93/12/EEC). Its main element was the tightening of the limit value for gas oil used as fuel in diesel engines to 0.2 per cent in 1994 and 0.05 per cent in 1996. This amendment is not part of the present case study, however.

Relations with Dutch domestic policy

The initiating role of the Netherlands claimed by Bungarten (1978: 186–187, see above) could not be discerned in the case study. In interviews it was put forward that the German *Heizölverordnung*

(Fuel Oil Decree) rather than the Dutch Decree had been the main inspiration for the Commission. The German *Verordnung* was decided in January 1975 and notified to the Commission on 18 October 1973, about five months after the Dutch notification (Bungarten, 1978: 211 and 187). Formally speaking, therefore, there are no arguments against Bungarten's version, but the findings of this case study suggest a less significant role for the notification procedure than for more informal contacts. Bungarten himself reports that the Commission had already been informed about the Dutch plans before the notification in May 1973. It is quite likely that the Commission also knew about similar intentions in Germany and maybe in other Member States as well. In that case the Commission would have perceived its initiative of setting up a working group and preparing a draft as a reaction to a more general tendency in the Community rather than to the plans of (or pressure from) one particular Member State. This interpretation is supported by the reference to the possible regulation of the sulphur content of fuels in a preliminary draft of the First Environmental Action Programme that was published in May 1972 (SEC(72)666). The Dutch notification as described by Bungarten would then have had the effect mainly of speeding up the process (in the light of the tight time schedule prescribed in the notification agreement) rather than initiating it.

The Commission's proposal regarding heavy fuel oil of 1975 was a logical counterpart to the gas oil directive. Preparations for the two drafts started simultaneously and there is no indication that an individual Member State exerted specific pressure on this point, apart from the national regulations notified by the Netherlands and other Member States in 1973, some of which also covered heavy fuel oil. The attitude of the Netherlands to the proposal was more or less neutral: an EC directive on heavy fuel oil could be accepted if it did not interfere with the Dutch Decree, but the Dutch Government did not actively promote the initiative. As the limits laid down in the Decree and envisaged for the near future and those proposed in the draft for special protection zones were of the same magnitude, such interference would not occur if the entire territory of the Netherlands was designated as a special protection zone. The draft did not set limits for areas outside such zones. In view of distortions of the conditions of competition potentially following from such an arrangement, the Dutch Government – if there was to be a directive – would have preferred standards throughout the Community, as noted above.

Similar to the case of the original gas oil directive of 1975, the impetus for reviewing it was a combination of Dutch/German pressure and Commission initiative. The updating of Directive 75/716 had already been announced (for 1984) in the Commission's communication about air pollution of 1983 (COM(83)721), but around 1985 the Netherlands and Germany stimulated the Commission to carry out its intention. During the negotiations, the two countries were the principal advocates of a limit considerably lower than 0.3 per cent, preferably 0.15 per cent. They argued that setting the standard at 0.3 per cent would constitute no improvement at all for them and some other Member States that had already applied the stricter standard of the 1975 directive to their entire territory. Controversy over this point persisted, but never reached a level of politicisation comparable to that over the 'clean' car or the large combustion plants. In the Netherlands, the option of unilateral action was considered irrelevant in this case. This may be partly due to the strongly export-oriented position of Dutch refineries, but also to an estimation of this option as too 'hard' for this relatively minor issue. In the end the parties agreed on the compromise of 0.3 per cent generally and 0.2 per cent in designated zones, which in fact had already been proposed by the Commission in its draft of 1985.

Community-level public actors

Leaving aside the question of whether the first impulses to regulate the sulphur content of fuels came from within the Commission or from one or two of the Member States (see above), it is interesting to consider why the Commission took up the challenge and decided to start preparing a draft directive.

In the early 1970s, as pointed out, the Netherlands and a number of other Member States were formulating legislation on the sulphur content of fuels (cf. Bungarten, 1978: 210–211). There can be no doubt that the avoidance of trade barriers that could arise from diverging national standards was an important motivation for the Commission to take up the issue. This is obvious for instance in the preliminary draft of the First Environmental Action Programme, where the need to regulate the use and/or quality of fuels at the Community level was primarily connected to the preservation of conditions of free trade (SEC(72)666). At the same time, genuinely environmental considerations played a role. This point was stressed by the Commission. The emerging national regulations in this field were mainly a reaction to increasing levels of air pollution and the more frequent occurrence of smog in urban areas. Household heating, causing emissions from numerous low stacks, was seen as one of the most effective targets for policies to reduce the sulphur emissions in the urban environment. At the level of the Commission, just having started the build-up of its environmental policy and naturally following the general concern about human health and urban pollution (see EAP 1973–1976), this was of course also realised. The oil crisis of 1973 was seen as an additional, clearly environmental reason for measures, because it stimulated the use of cheaper types of oil richer in sulphur.

This dual motivation at the Community level was reflected in the involvement of different Directorates-General. The fuel issue first came under the responsibility of DG III (Internal Market and Industrial Affairs) and the Council working group dealing with technical barriers to trade. The unit for Environment and Consumer Protection (the predecessor of DG XI) had a hard job convincing the others of the importance of the environmental aspect of the issue and only in the course of 1973 was responsibility shared between the two DGs. Later in the 1970s, probably in the context of the preparation of the directive on lead in petrol (78/611/EEC), a more permanent division of tasks in this field was reached, leaving the entire package of vehicle requirements (including emission limits) to DG III and assigning the environmental requirements for the quality of fuels to DG XI. Nevertheless, in the run-up to the 1987 amendment of the gas oil directive, disagreement between the two DGs again surfaced. This probably added to the Commission's inability to mediate effectively over the question of the establishment of a stricter standard beside the general limit value of 0.3 per cent.

Direct reference to the Community's energy policy was seldom made in the context of the fuel issue. Even the preamble to the heavy fuel oil proposal did not say a word about the possible connection with the objectives of the common energy policy agreed only one year earlier in the wake of the oil crisis, such as less dependency on imported oil, increased use of nuclear energy and gas, and energy saving (Hawdon, 1988: 106ff.). The Member States, however, did realise the consequences of the proposed legislation for national energy supply and energy prices: it was the principal reason for Italy and some other countries objecting to it. As discussed above, the suggestion of regulating the sulphur content of solid fuel as well was then put forward as an attempt to break the deadlock. This idea quickly disappeared from the stage, however, because of its expected social effect on European mining areas and because the (second) oil crisis made policies restricting the use of oil alternatives unacceptable. The oil crisis was also the main argument for withdrawing the heavy fuel oil proposal in 1981: energy saving and the shift to nuclear energy and coal was supposed to have reduced emissions from burning heavy fuel oil so considerably that the directive was no longer needed (Johnson and Corcelle, 1989: 123; Prittwitz, 1984: 140, quoting the responsible DG XI official).

The renewed suggestion of regulating the sulphur content of all fuels in the Commission's communication of 1983 (COM(83)721) can hardly be taken seriously. None of the persons interviewed actually remembered it. As the choice for end-of-pipe measures on cars and combustion plants had in fact already been made by then (see chapters 6 and 7), the suggestion in COM(83)721 must have been intended by the Commission as a tactical statement to increase the pressure on parties unwilling to support stricter acidification policies.

The Commission's role in initiating the 1987 amendment to the gas oil directive, finally, was discussed above. It is most likely, in short, that signs of the Dutch/German wish to start the process of reviewing the directive reinforced the intention of the Commission to do so.

Private actors
The refinery industry was involved in the fuel issue in the Netherlands through the Oil Contact Commission (*Olie Contact Commissie,* OCC) and at the European level through its unofficial umbrella organisation, CONCAWE.[4]

With regard to gas oil, the main priority of the sector was to avoid fragmentation of the market. As desulphurisation up to about 0.15 per cent is technically feasible at modest cost, the exact level of the limit values discussed in the EC in the 1970s and 1980s were not of much concern to the refineries. From the point of view of storage and transport, however, marketing of more than two different grades in the Community was considered undesirable. In addition, the use of a single grade was preferred in smaller areas with highly integrated markets, such as the Netherlands and Belgium. As the introduction of more than two limit values was never a serious option in the Community, CONCAWE was not very active on the issue. This was in line with the (formally) independent, research-oriented character of the organisation. Active lobbying was undertaken by CONCAWE only if the sector's interests were substantially challenged. Between the OCC and the Dutch Government too, there was little disagreement on this matter.

The refineries' interests were more seriously at stake in relation to the heavy fuel oil proposal. Here CONCAWE produced a number of reports, stressing the high costs of the desulphurisation of this type of oil and the political obstacles and potential consequences for the security of supply if such requirements were made of oil imports from the Middle East. The CONCAWE reports supported arguments put forward by other actors, including the Commission, and thus assisted in the rejection of the proposal.

For the environmental organisations, the sulphur content of fuels was not a priority. In the years around 1975, the EEB had frequent contacts with DG XVII (Energy) about energy issues, but this mainly involved nuclear energy (EEB, 1984). In the 1980s, the gas oil issue was overshadowed by the negotiations on the 'clean' car and the large combustion plants. In 1985–1987, and probably also in 1973–1978, EEB's activities were limited to issuing position papers shortly before relevant Council meetings. SNM assisted in preparing those papers on the basis of its experiences in the national context. Particularly in the 1970s, when the Decree on the sulphur content of fuels was one of the few means to control (urban) air pollution, SNM had been heavily involved in the Dutch policy making.

Summary

In its efforts to establish EC-wide standards for air quality, the Commission followed a general international trend rather than initiatives or pressure from one or more Member States. Particularly the respected work of the WHO served as a source of inspiration. Formulation of scientific 'criteria' for air quality soon appeared to be infeasible, as the levels to which this would lead were considered too strict by most Member States and thus became subject to (political) interpretation. For the same reason, the WHO recommendations, prepared by a group of scientific experts, could not be used as a basis. After several years of negotiations they were included in the directive as guide values, together with considerably laxer (but obligatory) limit values. The Netherlands was among the countries supporting relatively strict standards, based on the fact that its own, so far advisory standards were of the same magnitude of those recommended by the WHO. Particularly towards the end of the 1970s, however, the involvement of the Dutch Government in the issue was small because domestic priorities at that moment gradually started to shift to more direct measures to control air pollution. Both the existence of stricter domestic air quality standards and the prospect of a more demanding approach can explain the lack of interest of Dutch private actors in the EC process, as it implied very little difference for them.

In contrast to the air quality issue, the initiative to regulate the sulphur content of fuels in the Community was primarily motivated by the wish to avoid fragmentation of the internal market by diverging national legislation in this field. The Netherlands was among the first to develop such legislation and helped to draw the Commission's attention to the issue. Setting standards for gas oil did not lead to serious conflicts, as illustrated by the small amount of involvement of private actors and the relatively quick adoption of a directive. Slightly more controversy arose around the updating of the directive in the mid-1980s, but the two camps could both be satisfied by retaining the system of two different grades of gas oil, which in practice posed few problems to the refinery sector. The sulphur content issue also showed the limits of market-oriented environmental measures in the EC, however. The attitudes of the Member States as well as the refineries with regard to comparable standards for heavy fuel oil and possibly solid fuel (coal) ranged from neutral to a strong aversion. The direct effects on the cost of energy production and, more importantly, the indirect effects on security of supply and employment, particularly in countries dependent upon high-sulphur fuel, clearly did not outweigh the economic advantages related to Community-wide standards. Environmental arguments were barely at stake here.

Notes

1   The drafts for sulphur dioxide/particulates and for lead (COM(76)48 and COM(75)166) were both based exclusively on Article 235 of the EEC

Treaty. This was retained in the final version of the lead directive (82/884/ EEC). In the final version of the directive for sulphur dioxide/particulates (80/779/EEC), however, more explicit reference was made to the internal market aspect by adding Article 100 to the formal Treaty basis of the directive and by including a formula about the risk of unequal conditions of competition as a result of diverging standards in the Member States in the preamble.

2   Among Dutch environmental organisations, SNM is the most actively involved in influencing government policy. Its work, including participation on several advisory bodies to the Government and lobbying, is based on scientific expertise rather than action strategies. VNO is the largest and most influential Dutch employers' organisation. It works closely with the Association of Dutch Christian Employers (*Nederlands Christelijk Werkgeversverbond*, NCW).

3   The EEB was for a long time the principal EC-level umbrella organisation of the environmental movement. It was founded in 1974 and now represents more than 100 national environmental groups. With only a few staff, its activities are almost exclusively aimed at influencing EC environmental policies. During the 1980s, other environmental organisations established offices in Brussels as well, such as Friends of the Earth, Greenpeace and the Worldwide Fund for Nature (WWF) as well as some single-issue groups (Lowe and Goyder, 1983; Rucht, 1993; Hontelez, 1993; Hey and Brendle, 1994).

4   The Dutch refinery sector is among the largest in Europe. For a long time, contacts with the Government in the environmental field were co-ordinated informally among the refineries. In 1985, environmental affairs were formally brought under the OCC. This body had been instigated by the Ministry of Economic Affairs (*Economische Zaken*, EZ) as an intermediary for discussing questions of supply and marketing of oil products. The Oil Companies' European Organisation for Environmental and Health Protection, CONCAWE, based in Brussels and previously in The Hague, was set up by the oil industry in Western Europe (including a number of non-EC States) mainly for technical research purposes. Although formally independent, it used to function as the oil industry's mouthpiece in the EC as well as in other relevant international organisations. In 1989, a separate European lobby organisation, called Europia, was set up by the refineries.

6

Acidification policy in the 1980s: the 'clean' car

Introduction and overview

Of the issues included in this case study of EC acidification policy, the 'clean' car is the most well known. Indispensable, particularly for the period until 1989, is the excellent and highly detailed study by Holzinger (1994). Many other publications give additional information regarding certain aspects or about developments after 1989 (Corcelle, 1985, 1986, 1989; Roqueplo, 1988; Becker, 1988; Boehmer-Christiansen, 1990; Dietz *et al.*, 1991; Arp, 1991, 1993; Boehmer-Christiansen and Weidner, 1992; Bennett and Liefferink, 1989, 1993). The complicated negotiations in Brussels are particularly well covered by this literature and will be only briefly reviewed in the present section. The other sections will concentrate on the interaction between the Community process and Dutch policies and policy actors.

A slow start

Until the early 1980s, EC regulation of motor vehicle emissions ran parallel to the ECE regulations on this matter. Discussions in the Community framework were often used to reach a common position before the ECE negotiations. Details were then worked out by the ECE's technical working group and included in identical ECE and EC legislation (Directives 70/220/EEC, 74/290/EEC, 77/102/EEC, 78/665/EEC and 83/351/EEC). The ECE/EC standards of the 1970s were not very stringent. With the exception of carbon monoxide, they broadly followed technical developments and did not stimulate innovation. As early as 1977, the FRG, together with Switzerland and supported by the Netherlands, made its first attempts to accelerate the pace of regulation at the ECE. The initiative had no success and was repeated in 1981, this time both in the ECE and in the EC Environment Council. Even at that time, before the broad public concern about forest die-back, Germany threatened unilateral measures (Boehmer-Christiansen and Weidner, 1992: 38). Obviously, the EC, devoted to the objective of the common market, was more sensitive to this threat than the ECE and this may have been one of the reasons for the relatively quick response of the Commission. At the beginning of 1982 it established the ad hoc group 'Evolution of Regulations, Global Approach (ERGA) – Air Pollution' in order to study future European car emission standards. With hindsight, this may be considered the moment when the Community started to take the lead from the ECE.

From 1982, public concern in Germany about *Waldsterben* (forest die-back) rapidly increased. The problem became one of the major issues of the 1983 elections. Under this pressure, politicians and car producers, the latter united in the Association of the German Automobile Industry (*Verband der deutschen Automobilindustrie*, VDA), agreed that catalytic conversion was the best way to achieve the major reductions of emissions from cars that were required. The introduction of unleaded petrol was a prerequisite for the application of this technology. From the beginning, the VDA insisted on a European or at least EC-wide approach, partly for fear of a splitting of the market (which would cause efficiency losses and possibly barriers to trade), and partly in view of the fact that most German car producers, because of their exports to the USA, had already gained considerably more experience with catalyst technology than most of their European competitors.

In May 1983 the FRG first brought its wishes to the attention of the EC Council of Ministers. Referring particularly to the effects of lead on human health, however, only the lead issue was seriously taken up by the Council. The group of countries supporting the idea of further reducing the lead content of petrol included the UK (Haigh, 1988: 25). In this way, ironically, one of the greatest opponents to stricter emission standards in later years helped to pave the way for the introduction of the catalytic converter.

Dissatisfied with this outcome, Germany then threatened to 'go it alone'. This eventually provoked a proposal from the Commission dealing with all aspects of motor vehicle emissions, published in June 1984 (COM(84)226). It was, however, strongly coloured by the sceptical attitude of DG III, primarily responsible for the draft, and the resistance from the European car industry, represented mainly by the *Comité des Constructeurs d'Automobiles du Marché Commun* (CCMC).[1] Standards equivalent to those introduced in the USA in 1983, requiring catalyst technology for all cars, were scheduled only for after 1995. From 1989 for new models and from 1991 for all new cars, considerably lower limits would apply that could be achieved without a catalyst in most types of cars, except for the largest models. This arrangement would give the European car manufacturers sufficient time either to develop the alternative (predominantly British) lean-burn engine or to adapt to the application of catalysts.

The fruit of German pressure: a problematic compromise

None of the Member States was satisfied with the proposals: Germany, supported by Denmark, Luxembourg and the Netherlands, considered them too lax, whereas the others, including the UK, France and Italy (as well as CCMC), rejected them as too ambitious. The German Government once again increased the pressure by officially deciding upon the obligatory introduction of US standards and unleaded petrol in 1989 and a programme of fiscal incentives in order to promote the sales of 'clean' cars and unleaded petrol beforehand. A directive ensuring the EC-wide availability of unleaded petrol from 1989 was nevertheless adopted relatively easily in March 1985 (85/210/EEC). A compromise over emission limits was finally reached in Luxembourg in June 1985 on the basis of a revised Commission proposal (COM(85)228). The most important element was the differentiation of standards for different sizes of cars. Standards for cars with an engine capacity above 2.0 litres, applicable from 1 October 1988 for new models and 1 October 1989 for all new cars, were so stringent that they could be achieved only with a three-way catalyst. Limits for cars with an engine capacity between 2.0 and 1.4 litres would enter into force only in 1991/93 and were attainable for a lean-burn engine combined with a simple oxidation catalyst. Small cars, with an engine capacity below 1.4 litres, would be affected only in a second, as yet unspecified phase from 1992/93. The Luxembourg compromise was supported by all Member States except two. Greece, having no car industry but experiencing severe damage from car-emitted pollutants in Athens, desired quicker progress, particularly in the category of small cars.

Denmark categorically insisted on US standards for all cars. Thus, as unanimity was still required at that time under Article 100 of the Treaty, the formal adoption of the compromise was blocked.

The long-expected result: catalytic converters in all cars

The situation changed in July 1987 with the entering into force of the Single European Act. Under the qualified majority requirement of the new Article 100A, the compromise could now be adopted against the will of Denmark and Greece. Denmark, being in the chair of the Council of Ministers in the second half of 1987, forced a (positive) common position, speculating on rejection of this position by the EP. In its final reading, the Council could then have adopted the proposal only unanimously and in that case it would again have been confronted with a Danish veto. However, the Parliament did not reject the Council's position, and in December 1987 the Luxembourg compromise was finally enacted by qualified majority (88/76/EEC).

A draft for the second phase, for small cars (COM(87)706), requiring only lean-burn technology and a simple oxidation catalyst, was blocked by Denmark, Greece, the Netherlands and Germany. Germany, however, at that time holding the presidency of the Council, was eager to find solutions both for the 'clean' car issue and for the continuous problems around the emission standards for large combustion plants. After more than five years of negotiation, the German Government needed some kind of Community 'result' in the field of acidification to show to its home front. In the last phase, France succeeded in wresting some extra concessions by linking the two issues (see also the next chapter) and basic agreement was finally reached in the Council in June 1988. With regard to small cars, the package included acceptance of relatively flexible 'medium-size' standards together with the commitment to start discussions about a third phase by the end of 1991.

The Netherlands, together with Denmark and Greece, had voted against this deal, and now chose a confrontational strategy. Against protest, especially from France, it provoked a test case before the Court of Justice by announcing its intention to introduce a scheme of tax incentives stimulating the sales of small cars equipped with three-way catalysts, which was in obvious conflict with the agreement just reached.[2] The June 1988 agreement was nevertheless adopted as the Council's common position in November 1988 and sent to the EP, which succeeded in making optimal use of its new powers under the Single Act. The Parliament showed itself in favour of three-way catalysts in all small cars from 1992. The Commission had indicated in advance that it would support the EP's amendments and actually did so in its revised proposal of May 1989 (COM(89)257). According to the co-operation procedure, the Council could now either reject this proposal unanimously or adopt it by qualified majority. It did the latter during its session in July 1989 (Directive 89/458/EEC). The still pending procedure against the Netherlands was then withdrawn, as the directive allowed Member States to anticipate future standards with the help of fiscal incentives.

The 1989 directive had now set the tightest standards for the smallest categories of cars. This somewhat paradoxical situation was resolved by the so-called Consolidated Directive of 1991 (91/441/EEC), which aligned the standards for large and medium-size cars to those for small cars. The Consolidated Directive thus put a (temporary) end to a process of negotiation unprecedented in EC environmental policy in terms of length, complexity and political controversy.

Relations with Dutch domestic policy

The Dutch position in the early 1980s

The ECE regulations regarding motor vehicle emissions in the 1970s and early 1980s can hardly be characterised as 'environmental' policy. They were part of a much broader programme of uniform technical standards for cars, aiming to facilitate international trade and to create conditions for large-scale, efficient manufacturing of cars. Emission limits were not very demanding.

The first attempt to introduce environmental objectives to the ECE regulatory process was made in 1977. Both the FRG and Switzerland submitted proposals for considerably tighter emission limits. They were, however, supported only by the Netherlands. Though unsuccessful, this early attempt to some extent corrects the established picture of Germany as a country that was originally 'largely unconcerned about international air pollution' (Wetstone and Rosencranz, 1983: 79), but suddenly converted after the discovery of serious forest damage in the early 1980s.

The Community's first environmental policy initiative related to car emissions was, as discussed, taken in 1981, again by Germany. At that time the role of the Dutch Government was limited. One highly qualified civil servant had been in charge of the ECE regulations since the early 1970s but the issue had not been given high priority. The German proposals were not rejected, but they were not actively supported either (IMP-Lucht 1981–1985: 28–30).

One year later, a remarkable change had taken place as a result of rapidly increasing concern about the effects of acidification, not only in Scandinavia and Germany, but also in the Netherlands. In spring 1983, the Netherlands, together with the UK, was among the countries supporting the German initiative to head for unleaded petrol in the EC, but for the Dutch Government this step was not only motivated by health effects of lead but also by the wish to create the conditions for the introduction of catalytic converters (IMP-Lucht 1984–1988: 43). The question of catalysts itself was approached somewhat more carefully at that time: the position of the Dutch Government in Brussels was based on requiring catalysts only for large cars (IMP-Lucht 1984–1988: 88; IMP-Lucht 1985–1989: 81). By then, the German Government had already committed itself to US standards and catalysts for all sizes of car. The UK, France and Italy, on the other hand, were considerably more reluctant than the Netherlands.

The Dutch Government retained this intermediate position between the Member States strongly advocating strict standards (Germany, Denmark) and those opposed to catalyst technology. In fact, the general philosophy of the Luxembourg compromise, with its differentiation between three categories of cars and catalytic converters required only for the largest category, was not too far away from the Dutch position of 1983 (this was also concluded by the Government itself, in IMP-Milieubeheer 1986–1990: 105). The Dutch never seriously questioned the basic approach to this agreement as it gradually emerged during the negotiations in 1984 and 1985. Instead, they urged for the strictest possible standards *within* the margins of the emerging compromise (for instance regarding the requirements for medium-sized cars – see Corcelle, 1986: 126; Holzinger, 1994: 245). This policy was also motivated by the mediating role that the Netherlands had taken upon itself, allegedly at the request of Germany, France and the UK. The

Netherlands was supposed to be particularly suited to this role for a number of reasons, including the availability of high-level and 'impartial' technical expertise within the Ministry of VROM and the Dutch interest both in effective environmental policies and in the further development of the lean-burn engine (because of the activities of Volvo Car in this field – see below), without at the same time being too deeply involved in the controversies between the big car-producing Member States. The self-perception as a broker made it practically impossible not to agree with the Luxembourg compromise, even though some aspects were not entirely satisfactory for the Dutch Government.

It should be mentioned, however, that Commission officials involved in the process merely remembered the 'constructive approach' of the Dutch delegation in EC environmental negotiations in general, but no particularly active role as a mediator in the compromise. There is no clear indication for this in the literature either.

A Dutch hobbyhorse: the test cycle

One favourite topic of the Dutch Government was the revision of the ECE test cycle, on which approval of new models was based. The theme had appeared on the Dutch agenda as early as 1983 (IMP-Lucht 1984–1988: 51). The original ECE test, dating from 1970, only covered urban traffic (low speed, many short stops, etc.). This can be explained by the focus at that time on carbon monoxide, which causes problems only in local (urban) settings. The effects of nitrogen oxides, however, are not restricted to the direct surroundings of the source and, moreover, emissions of nitrogen oxides increase with speed. The US test was slightly better in this regard, but for genuine representativeness, the ECE test cycle would have to be extended by an 'extra-urban' part.

The Dutch Government first put forward its ideas about the test cycle in a meeting of a Council working group in July 1984, as part of an attempt to overcome the differences between Germany on the one hand and France, Italy and the UK on the other (Holzinger, 1994: 229–230). According to the Dutch proposal, US standards would form the basis of the new EC legislation, but they would be adapted to European conditions, to become a new European test cycle.[3] The other Member States reacted positively, particularly France and Italy, but during the further negotiations the proposal was considerably transformed and probably no longer met the original Dutch expectations. The idea of 'US equivalence' was gradually developed into a 'somewhat adventurous' concept (Becker, 1988: 10), requiring 'equivalent effects on the environment' of US and EC standards and eventually 'equivalent total emissions' from the car fleets in the US and the Community. Obviously, this formula gave enormous room for interpretation and that is why it could still be maintained that the Luxembourg compromise (including the second phase for small cars) was 'US equivalent'.[4] One of the more important reasons for the Netherlands accepting the compromise at all was in fact the agreement on the development of a new test cycle. The limit values included in the agreement were, however, still based on the old, urban test cycle. The old cycle was replaced only in the Consolidated Directive of 1991.

Unilateralism
Between 1983 and 1985, the German Government repeatedly threatened with *Alleingang*, that is, unilateral (or at least earlier) introduction of unleaded petrol and mandatory use of catalysts. There can be no doubt that this provocative behaviour had an effect: it showed the Commission and the other Member States that Germany was serious about the matter and it certainly helped to speed up the process. In addition, and perhaps even more importantly, the German threat had an important domestic aspect: it showed the voters that the Government (the CDU/CSU/FDP coalition) was prepared to do the utmost for the German forests. At the same time, however, it was clear to most people directly involved that the execution of the German plans was very unlikely. The powerful German car industry was fiercely against it, for obvious commercial reasons. Economic interests, including the common European interest to stand firm against Japanese car producers, were far too big to risk an intra-European trade war (Arp, 1993: 5–6; Holzinger, 1994: 199–201, 213). The German threat of unilateralism was indeed a balancing act between industrial interests on the one hand and the display of environmental activism for the German voter and intensification of pressure on European political partners on the other hand. This was illustrated by the skilful German handling of Cabinet decisions between July 1983 and September 1984: they evolved from statements of intention to impressively detailed schemes for the fiscal stimulation and eventual mandatory introduction of

'clean' cars (Holzinger, 1994: 201–202, 224–225). With the official notification of the plan to the Commission in late 1984 and debates in the Council about possible complaints against Germany before the European Court of Justice (Holzinger, 1994: 237–238) the pressure was raised to a maximum, but from that moment the German Government showed increasing willingness to come to terms with the other Member States. In the last months before the Luxembourg compromise the threat of unilateralism rapidly disappeared.

The careful handling of the option of *Alleingang* by the German Government can be contrasted with the Dutch strategy after the small car compromise of June 1988. At that time, the Netherlands had unambiguously committed itself to the US standards for motor vehicles (Milieuprogramma 1988–1991: 60, published September 1987). The lenient standards of the 1988 compromise, therefore, were highly unsatisfactory to the Dutch Government, and it decided unilaterally to introduce tax reductions for small cars complying with US standards. Germany in fact would have liked to do the same, but left the role of guinea pig in a possible Court procedure to the Netherlands (Holzinger, 1994: 313–314). Boehmer-Christiansen and Weidner (1992: 51) suggest that, after Luxembourg, Germany had 'learnt from its mistakes, a diplomacy which had tended to generate resistance rather than co-operation' and, consequently, became 'more conciliatory'. Here, however, it may have been more important that the German Government felt committed to the agreement of June 1988, which had been reached under its own Council presidency. The fact that this agreement had been reached at all may be explained better by the strong German wish to bring home at least some kind of result rather than by a move to a more conciliatory style motivated by experiences in the earlier negotiations.

Considering the events in Brussels, the Dutch unilateral action was a clear success: contrary to the 1988 compromise, the small car directive of 1989 (89/458/EEC) allowed for tax arrangements stimulating the sales of cars complying with future EC standards, including the proposed Dutch scheme. This was no doubt partly due to the Dutch initiative, in addition to the activism of the EP in early 1989 (see below). The impact at the EC level, however, does not seem to have been the prime motivation for the Dutch Government to go ahead with its tax proposals. Of course, the Government was aware of the risk of a Court complaint. In fact this was the principal reason for the Ministry of EZ to be strongly against the project. Only at the highest Cabinet level was Nijpels, the Minister of VROM, able to overcome this resistance. Under such conditions, the argument that Dutch unilateralism would benefit the EC negotiations could not be used openly, but it did not play an important role within the Ministry of VROM either. The measure was motivated almost entirely by *domestic* policy goals related to acidification. Only later, when the controversy with the Commission and France, among others, started to develop, was the effect on negotiations in Brussels fully realised and was eventually presented as a Dutch victory over unwilling EC partners.

Coalitions with other Member States

Thus, after a hesitant start in the early 1980s, the Netherlands became one of the Member States most strongly advocating stringent car emission standards in the Community, together with Germany, Denmark and sometimes Greece. Considering the negotiations from the German initiative in 1981 to the Consolidated Directive in 1991, it is remarkable that those countries did not manage to join forces. In practice, they sometimes supported each other in the Council, but in many other cases they obstructed each other's strategies. These cases included such important moments as the Luxembourg compromise (supported by Germany and the Netherlands, but blocked by Denmark and Greece) and the 1988 compromise on small cars (constructed by Germany, with considerable concessions, but rejected by Denmark, Greece and the Netherlands).

The recurrent fragmentation of the 'pro-catalyst' group was often due to genuine differences of priorities and strategies. This certainly refers to Greece, which was mainly motivated by the serious situation in Athens, but also to Denmark. Whereas Germany and the Netherlands were generally prepared eventually to accept a compromise, Denmark mostly rejected anything other than US standards for all categories of cars. In Brussels, it was generally felt that the country thereby placed itself 'off side'. This situation was worsened by the fact that the technical basis of the radical Danish positions did not always meet the standards of the other members of the Commission's and the Council's working groups. As Arp (1993: 162) points out, particularly in the Commission's influential Motor Vehicle Emissions Group (MVEG), 'expertise is what counts'.

The reasons for the lack of co-ordination between Germany and the Netherlands are not so obvious. Correspondence of domestic policies and attitudes towards the EC process was considerably greater here, and some Dutch attempts to bring about closer bilateral co-operation were made, but did not materialise. One explanation may be that the German Government, in view of the complicated domestic political struggles around *Waldsterben* and the option of *Alleingang*, preferred to keep its hands free for tactical manoeuvring in Brussels. This may also explain why one of the few instances where Germany sought foreign support for its car emission policy involved a group of countries largely not members of the EC: the so-called 'Stockholm Group', an informal working group consisting of Norway, Sweden, Finland, Switzerland, Liechtenstein, Austria and Canada as well as the EC Member States Denmark, Germany and the Netherlands. In July 1985 the Group produced a declaration urging for US standards and the US test cycle. Germany and the Netherlands, however, had committed themselves to the Luxembourg compromise only one month earlier and were therefore not free to embrace the declaration. Denmark had rejected the Luxembourg compromise and was the only EC country that actually signed (Donkers, 1988: 221). The Stockholm Group may have had an indirect impact on the EC process by once more showing the high priority given by Denmark, Germany and the Netherlands to stricter standards.

Community-level public actors

The Commission's reactions to the first German initiatives concerning the 'clean' car were almost exclusively motivated by its responsibility for the functioning of the internal market. The rapid establishment of the first ERGA working group in January 1982 showed that the Commission took the German plans seriously, and probably the threat of *Alleingang* in particular (Boehmer-Christiansen and Weidner, 1992: 38). In addition, it illustrated the economic importance of the car sector: no risk could be taken here, especially in view of the keen competition from Japanese producers.

Relationships within the Commission

The Commission's focus on the internal market was reflected in the consistent leading role of DG III on the issue of car emissions. This was partly the heritage of the preceding decade, when the regulation of car emissions standards was regarded as just one element of the harmonisation of numerous technical requirements of motor vehicles in the ECE, logically dealt with by the DG for the internal market. The market aspect of course still existed in the 1980s, but now environmental considerations were the underlying motivation for adaptation (viz. tightening) of the common standards. This, in turn, was acknowledged in the assignment of the issue to the Council of Environment Ministers rather than to the Internal Market Council. Correspondingly, it was Environment Commissioner Narjes who had the first responsibility within the Commission. Nevertheless, the influence of DG XI on the process remained limited for a long period. This is significant, because the views of DG XI often differed markedly from those of DG III.

Holzinger (1994: 202–210) reports that during the preparations of the draft directive of June 1984 (COM(84)226), DG XI dedicated itself to catalyst technology as the best available option, but without success. This position can also be found in the Third Environmental Action Programme, published as early as February 1983, which stated that the Commission would examine the possibilities for the mandatory introduction of 'anti pollution provisions or fuels' that 'considerably' diminished the level of pollution from exhaust gases (EAP 1982–1986: 10). This formulation clearly referred to the catalytic converter and to unleaded petrol, but in no way corresponded with the line pursued by DG III.[5] Fundamental differences of opinion persisted between the two DGs. The Dutch tax reduction scheme of 1988, for example, was disapproved of by DG III, whereas DG XI, supported by the Commission's Juridical Service, defended the Dutch opinion that the scheme did not constitute either State support or discrimination against certain producers. It hoped that the Dutch initiative would give a new momentum to the negotiations after the compromise of June 1988. Again, assisted by French protests against the Dutch plans, DG III could assert its will, which led to the start of two Court proceedings against the Netherlands.[6]

The 'clean' car case is thus a good example of an asymmetrical compromise *within* the Commission. It cannot be maintained that the 'pro-catalyst' camp met wholly without sympathy, but at the same time the strong influence of DG III was reflected in the ample consideration of the interests of the car manufacturers (see the illuminating analysis by Holzinger, 1994: 206–207). This may help to explain why Dutch officials characterised the Commission's input in the process, especially in the early years, as not particularly constructive. It should be added, though, that the situation gradually changed after the general acceptance of catalyst technology in the 1989 small car directive and the 1991 Consolidated Directive. Conflicts between DG III and DG XI have diminished considerably since that time, more or less in parallel with the fading away of the most serious controversies in the Council on this issue.

The role of the European Parliament vis-à-vis the Dutch tax incentives regarding the small car directive

In the events around the small car directive, the EP played a remarkable role, which had been made possible by the procedural changes resulting from the Single Act. There can be no doubt that the 'environmentalist' amendments from the EP were in line with its earlier critical comments on the 'clean' car negotiations (Holzinger, 1994: 194, 215–221), but there were also broader political motivations. With European elections coming up in June 1989, the Parliament was eager to present itself as a factor that could no longer be neglected. The 'clean' car, one of the most visible 'green' topics of the moment, was an excellent opportunity to do so.

It is interesting to compare the different views on the causes of the Community's about-face regarding the catalytic converter in the first half of 1989. The Dutch Milieuprogramma 1990–1993 proudly claimed that 'it is uplifting to note that *inter alia* this Dutch position [concerning fiscal incentives] and the recommendations of the European Parliament on the matter have persuaded the Commission to propose eventually making US standards compulsory' (Milieuprogramma 1990–1993: 107). Dutch civil servants who had been involved in the matter, however, toned down this interpretation. They stressed the importance of the EP amendments and also the role of the then new Commissioner for the Environment, Carlo Ripa di Meana, who wanted to make a forceful start and helped to convince the Commission to accept the Parliament's amendments. Moreover, they pointed out that, if the Netherlands had not re-opened the debate about fiscal incentives, this undoubtedly would have been done by Denmark or Germany, who were preparing comparable arrangements at the time. Commission officials also focused on the role of the EP and the Commissioner. According to them, the role of the Dutch initiative had been limited to triggering the directive's provisions on the specific point of tax incentives.

In the same period, in addition, Renault and Fiat were gradually moving to the 'pro-catalyst' camp. Fiat, for instance, in reaction to the Dutch tax reductions, started to sell catalyst-fitted cars in the Netherlands. Peugeot advertised catalyst-fitted cars in Switzerland, one of the countries of the European Free Trade Association (EFTA) most strongly advocating strict limits (Arp, 1991: 28). This development weakened and finally removed French and Italian opposition to catalyst technology. Thus, the gradual splitting of the European market, due among other things to the Dutch tax incentives, at least indirectly helped tighten Community standards.

Connections with other issue areas
A final word should be said about the connection between the 'clean' car and EC transport policy: this connection was virtually non-existent. From the beginning, the DG for Transport (DG VII) was represented in Commission working groups on the issue of car emissions (for instance in the ERGA working groups in 1982/83; see Holzinger, 1994: 194), but its contribution was considered insignificant by all officials interviewed. Throughout the process, the 'transport' aspect of the issue was overshadowed by its ramifications for the functioning of the internal market.

Private actors

The Netherlands has only one producer of passenger cars: Volvo Car (which changed its name to NedCar in 1992, when Mitsubishi participated in the company). At the time of the negotiations considered here, two-thirds of Volvo Car was owned by the Dutch State and one-third by Swedish Volvo. The Dutch Association of the Bicycle and Automobile Industry (*Rijwiel- en Automobielindustrie Vereniging*, RAI) represents the interests of the importers of all makes of car in the Netherlands. Volvo Car was also represented in RAI.

RAI
There are close ties between RAI and the Dutch Government. Regular meetings take place between RAI and the Ministries of VROM, Transport and Public Works (*Verkeer en Waterstaat*, V&W), and Finance. RAI has repeatedly shown it has access, when

necessary, to the highest political levels, but compared with other EC Member States the 'clean' car did not engender serious conflict between the car sector and policy makers in the Netherlands. Contacts between RAI and the Dutch Government on this issue remained at the administrative level, primarily at the Ministry of VROM, and mainly entailed the exchange of information. This situation can be explained by the history of the public debate about cars in the Netherlands and the position of RAI as an organisation mainly of car importers among the European car lobby.

In the Netherlands, the negative effects of motor vehicles on the environment were recognised relatively early (e.g. *Urgentienota Milieuhygiëne*, 1971–1972: *passim*). As a reaction, RAI stressed the advantages of cars, for example in the prolonged campaign *Blij dat ik rij* ('Happy to be driving'), but at the same time attempted to advance the use of technical means to reduce noise, air pollution, and so on.

Against this background, it is not surprising that RAI in principle supported the Dutch Government's strategy with regard to the catalytic converter, under one crucial condition: it should lead to policy at least at the Community level. RAI realised that on the Dutch market consumers would generally be prepared to pay a higher price for a cleaner car, but to avoid discrimination among the members (i.e. the importers of cars) cost increases should be equal for all. This attitude was most clear in the period around the Luxembourg compromise: the fact that a European agreement had finally been reached was considered more important than its exact content. Fiscal measures were seen as a useful temporary instrument to stimulate the introduction of 'clean' cars, as long as they did not discriminate. For this reason, RAI had no objections to the Dutch fiscal incentive scheme of 1988/89.

Within the European organisation of car traders, *Comité de Liaison de la Construction Automobile* (CLCA), RAI attempted to propagate a similar view, but for a long time it was joined only by the Danish sister organisation and later also by the Germans. Consequently, RAI was largely unable to use the European umbrella organisation to influence policy in Brussels. It should be noted, however, that CCMC was in fact the more important forum for the car industry. In CCMC the interests of German versus French, Italian and British car manufacturers directly met, but RAI was not a member of CCMC.

Thus, RAI was in a relatively weak position at the European level. For the work in Brussels it had to depend largely on the Dutch Government and the 'pro-catalyst' German car producers and Volvo (see below). As there were no fundamental differences with the Dutch Government on this issue, RAI could dedicate most of its time to the smooth introduction at the national level of the successive changes of technical and financial arrangements connected with the 'clean' car.

Volvo Car
For Volvo Car, the situation was to some extent similar. Swedish Volvo was one of the first European car producers to offer cars equipped with a catalytic converter. This had to do, among other things, with Volvo's considerable exports of catalyst-fitted cars to the USA and with the interest in less polluting cars in the Swedish home market. At the same time, Volvo was working on the lean-burn engine, like most other car producers in Europe. This was part of the company's long-term strategy of improving the fuel efficiency of cars. Reduction of the emission of nitrogen oxides was regarded as a secondary goal, which could be achieved to a large extent along the same route. As soon as the problem of exhaust gases started to dominate the issue of fuel efficiency in the EC, however, Volvo had no problem in shifting to catalyst technology for the European market as well. Moreover, like some German producers of large cars, Volvo saw the commercial advantage of a *quick* introduction of the US standards in the Community.

However, Volvo's position among car producers in the Community was not strong. Volvo was (and is) one of the smaller producers in Europe. Moreover, it should be remembered that Volvo Sweden was itself not a member of CCMC because Sweden was not part of the *Marché Commun*, but Volvo Car in the Netherlands functioned as the 'backdoor' through which it had entrance to the organisation.[7] From 1982, Volvo consistently belonged to the 'pro-catalyst' group in CCMC, but never acted in the forefront. It behaved pragmatically, following events and trying to adapt to the situation.

Similar terms may characterise the relationship between Volvo and the Dutch Government with regard to the 'clean' car. Essentially, both parties (as well as RAI) had the same goal: tightening emission standards in the Community. As a consequence, serious conflicts between Volvo and the Government did not arise, but at the same time concrete plans and strategies were not sufficiently alike to form a basis for close co-operation. An important difference between Volvo and the Ministry of VROM involved the test cycle. Volvo was unsure of the value of a 'representative' test cycle: emissions in practice were too dependent on contingent factors, such as actual driving conditions, driving style, maintenance of the vehicle, and so on. The crucial thing was to have a standard method of comparing different types of car. In the second place, Volvo would have preferred a worldwide test cycle, for reasons of efficiency. Interaction between Volvo and the Government thus seems to have been limited to certain specific points where Volvo's interests were directly at stake.

One such instance was the precise delimitation of the three categories for the Luxembourg compromise (i.e. the definition of 'small', 'medium-size' and 'large' cars). Even though Volvo was in principle strongly in favour of the catalytic converter, one of its models at that time had an engine that could be adapted only at high cost. This engine was, ironically, obtained from Renault and had a capacity of 1397 cc. It is obvious that Volvo had an interest in this engine being categorised as 'small', so that it would not have to be adapted. As France and Italy, among others, also happened to be strong supporters of the limit of 1.4 litres for 'small' cars, the point passed the Council without trouble, but the Dutch Government was well aware of the interests of its national car industry and would have defended them if necessary.

Environmental organisations

The environmental organisations quickly took up the issue of car emissions. In October 1982 the EEB, together with the *Bureau Européen des Unions de Consommateurs* (BEUC), launched a campaign against the use of lead in petrol. It was BEUC that was represented in the Commission's second ERGA working group, initiated in July 1983 to assist in preparing the draft directive. The focus of the BEUC–EEB coalition on lead in this period, which of course should be regarded partly as a consequence of the terms of the debate at the Community level in general, may have been reinforced by the leading role of BEUC, health effects of lead being more directly relevant to consumers than acidification. When the policy debate turned from reduction of the lead content of petrol as a goal in itself to unleaded petrol as a prerequisite for the use of catalysts, the co-operation between EEB and BEUC gradually became less intensive. In 1987, EEB organised an international seminar on the issue, now in collaboration with Friends of the Earth.

Parallel to this, the involvement of some of the EEB's member organisations increased, including notably Dutch SNM. SNM often had a significant share in the preparation of the EEB's positions and press releases on the issue of car emissions. Collaboration with German environmental groups was remarkably limited. German organisations, for instance the *Schutzgemeinschaft Deutscher Wald*, did play a role in the EEB, but their input was not as big as could be expected on the basis of the salience of the issue in Germany. This was probably due to the considerable differences in goals and character between environmental groups in Germany, which prevented the kind of concerted efforts SNM in the Netherlands was able to make.

In the case of the 'clean' car, moreover, the EEB was not quite totally dependent upon the contributions from its national member organisations. From the mid-1980s, the EEB and Friends of the Earth were assisted by an experienced former official of the US Environmental Protection Agency. He played a crucial role in providing the environmental lobby with a solid technical base. This greatly facilitated their being taken seriously in the Commission's technical working groups.

Activities of environmental groups regarding the 'clean' car at the Dutch national level, finally, were limited. There were regular contacts between the Ministry of VROM and SNM, but there were no serious conflicts over this issue. Both parties were convinced of the need for a European approach to the problem and both strove for application of the US standards. SNM did not doubt the Ministry's dedication to this goal and made no great effort to convince the Dutch Government to take a harder stand in Brussels. No public campaigns on the issue were organised. SNM strongly supported the unilateral introduction of tax incentives in 1988/89. Similar to the Dutch Government, SNM regarded the fiscal scheme primarily as a domestic measure, and any possible effect at the EC level only as a positive 'side-effect'.

Summary

In the 1970s moderate car emission standards were set jointly by the ECE and the EC, but from 1982 German pressure forced the Community to accelerate its pace. In response to rapidly increasing public and political concern about the effects of acidification on German forests, the Government in Bonn soon brought into action the powerful weapon of *Alleingang*. The prospect of the unilateral introduction of catalytic converters in Germany and the possible splitting of the European car market convinced the other Member States as well as reluctant parts of the Commission (DG III in particular) to take the German pressure seriously. In 1985, this led to a compromise amounting to the introduction of catalysts only for large cars. Its unanimous adoption by the Council of Ministers was however blocked by Denmark and Greece. The Dutch Government took an intermediate position in this period. It had not yet initiated domestic policies in this field and supported the 1985 compromise in view both of its reluctance to make catalysts compulsory for all sizes of car and of its attempts to act as a broker in the Council negotiations.

The events in the second half of the 1980s illustrated the sometimes crucial influence of institutional factors in EC decision making. In 1987, the shift from unanimity to qualified majority voting made it possible to enact, finally, the compromise reached two years earlier. In 1989, the EP used its extended powers under the Single Act in a strategic game with the Commission and the Council, resulting in a considerable tightening of the standards for small cars. This breakthrough was also stimulated by the Dutch, who had meanwhile fully moved to the 'pro-catalyst' camp. They now used the threat of unilateralism to underline their dissatisfaction with the half-hearted progress made in Brussels. In 1991, finally, standards for all cars were brought to the same level as those for the smallest category.

All through the 1980s, both the only Dutch car producer, Volvo Car, and the Dutch car trade association, RAI, in principle supported technological measures to reduce emissions and thus belonged to a minority among their European colleagues. This made it difficult for them to make use of their respective European umbrella organisations to influence decision making and as it were condemned them to rely on the Dutch Government to defend their interests. The environmental lobby in Brussels, in contrast, was quite effective with regard to the 'clean' car. The Dutch environmental movement, particularly SNM, significantly contributed to this.

Notes

1   Until 1990, CCMC was the organisation representing all car manufacturers that had their headquarters in an EC Member State. Note that also

Volvo Car in the Netherlands, owned jointly by the Dutch State and Swedish Volvo, was a member of CCMC. At the end of 1990, CCMC collapsed owing to profound disagreement about the strategy regarding Japanese car imports. It was succeeded by the *Association des Constructeurs Européens d'Automobiles* (ACEA). The French Peugeot/Citroen Group did not participate, but the new organisation included Swedish and American firms (Volvo, Saab, General Motors, Ford). Apart from CCMC/ACEA, the European peak association of national car trade groups (the *Comité de Liaison de la Construction Automobile*, CLCA) was active on the issue of the 'clean' car (see the detailed account of the European car lobby by McLaughlin and Jordan, 1993; see also below).

2   Plans for a similar scheme had in fact already been under discussion in Denmark in early 1988, but the conflict in Brussels centred around the Dutch tax scheme (Arp, 1993: 156). This was probably due mainly to the small size of the Danish car market and the absence of either a formal Danish decision or an official notification to the Commission (Holzinger, 1994: 317–318). Dutch notification in September 1988 constituted a basis for the Commission to act.

3   This had been the only substantial Dutch compromise proposal in the run-up to the Luxembourg agreement (see above). However, its ambitions and impact represent little more than the usual 'constructive approach' of the Netherlands.

4   I am indebted to Henning Arp for drawing my attention to the Dutch role in starting the juggling with the concept of 'US equivalence'.

5   This example also illustrates the status of the Action Programmes (see chapter 1): they often contain merely the views of DG XI and can be easily neglected by more powerful parts of the Commission.

6   The Commission had also been divided on the issue of the German tax reduction scheme in 1985. DG III had strong objections, whereas DG IV (Competition) and the Juridical Service argued that the German scheme did not discriminate among producers (Holzinger, 1994: 238).

7   Contrary to the parent company in Sweden, Volvo Car in the Netherlands was a member of CCMC. In 1992, the roles were changed: Volvo Sweden became a member of ACEA, whereas NedCar after the purchase of a one-third share by Mitsubishi was not allowed membership of the new organisation.

7

Acidification policy in the 1980s: industrial emissions

Introduction and overview

The Community's efforts to reduce the emissions of acidifying substances from industrial sources involves two directives that are closely connected both formally and historically. The more well known is the directive on large combustion plants, discussed from late 1982 and agreed almost exactly six years later (Directive 88/609/ EEC). It was preceded by the so-called framework directive on the combating of air pollution from industrial plants of June 1984 (84/ 360/EEC). In this chapter I will discuss the two directives together.[1]

The beginnings of the EC policy process regarding industrial emissions once again lie in Germany (see the previous chapter on the 'clean' car). At the Stockholm Conference on the Acidification of the Environment in June 1982, the Germans first made known to the international community their radical change in attitude to the problem of acidification under the influence of growing domestic concern about *Waldsterben* (forest die-back). In the same period Germany submitted a memorandum to the EC's Environment Council, advocating in general terms rapid and effective policies against air pollution in the Community. At the national level, priority was given to industrial emissions: in September 1982 the *Gross-feuerungsanlagenverordnung* (GFAV) was proposed. It aimed at considerable reductions of emissions from large combustion plants (electricity generating plants and large industrial installations such as refineries and steel works), achievable only through costly de-sulphurisation processes. The proposal was almost immediately followed by strong German pressure on the Commission to initiate similar legislation at the Community level.

The framework directive

When the Germans began to press for Community measures, the Commission had already started preparing a general directive on air pollution (see below). The proposal originally included emission standards for certain industrial sectors, but this soon proved to be unacceptable for several Member States, including the UK and France. In order to be able to accommodate German wishes, the Commission then decided to present two draft directives at the next Council meeting, in December 1982: a 'framework' directive containing more general provisions and a 'daughter' directive setting emission limits for large combustion plants.

Instead of setting emission standards, the draft of the framework directive officially submitted to the Council in April 1983 (COM(83)173) assigned to the Council the authority to establish such limits by qualified majority. In response to strong opposition, notably from the UK, this was changed to unanimous agreement and the directive was adopted in June 1984 (84/360/EEC). It should be noted that the latter concession made the article in question practically meaningless: Articles 100 and 235 of the Treaty gave the Council sufficient basis for establishing emission standards unanimously anyway. Thus, the two most important remaining elements of the directive were the obligations to establish a system of licensing for several industrial activities and to apply the 'best available technology not entailing excessive costs' ('batneec') to reduce pollution. The rather vague formulation 'not entailing excessive costs' was added under pressure from the British (see Boehmer-Christiansen and Skea, 191: 233).

The large combustion plants directive:
continued attempts to compromise

The very first draft of the large combustion plants directive contained emission limits for both new and existing plants. This element had been borrowed directly from the German GFAV and would require costly 'retrofitting' of most existing installations. In the draft officially submitted to Council in December 1983 (COM(83)704) it had been replaced by emission limits for each new plant and overall reduction targets for all plants together. The targets amounted to a sixty per cent reduction for sulphur dioxide and forty per cent for nitrogen oxides and particulate matter, relative to 1980 levels, to be achieved by 1995. This arrangement clearly took away some of the initial objections, but the percentage reductions were to become the most persistent source of controversy until the last phase of the negotiations, in 1988.

During the first discussions in the Environment Group of the Council[2] in April and May 1984, several Member States claimed that specific circumstances would make it difficult for them to comply with the proposed targets. The Commission, however, strongly opposed the Italian suggestion of differentiation of reduction targets and was willing to consider only exemptions for certain countries. However, no trace of this was to be found in the revised Commission draft of February 1985 (COM(85)47). It had adopted only the more cosmetic amendments proposed by the EP a few months earlier (EP, 1984; see Bennett, 1992: 109–112; Arp, 1992: 29–30).

In the first half of 1986 agreement seemed to be within reach. The prolonged negotiations and the risk of further complications due to the accession of Spain and Portugal finally made the Commission accept the idea of differentiation. A compromise proposal from the Dutch Council presidency aimed at an overall reduction of sulphur dioxide emissions by forty-five per cent in 1995, to which Member States would contribute in proportion to, among other things, total emissions in their country, gross national product (GNP), and expected economic development. A second phase, leading to a sixty per cent reduction by 2005, would be worked out later. A similar two-step approach was to be developed for nitrogen oxides, resulting in a forty per cent reduction by 2005. During a dramatic Council session in June, however, the compromise was blocked by Germany and the Commission, who considered both the system of differentiation and the time schedule inadequate (Bennett, 1992: 116–117).

From that moment on, all successive Council presidencies produced their own compromise proposals. The UK attempted to extend the proposal to *all* sources of sulphur dioxide. The Belgian presidency introduced a third phase and corrections for reductions achieved before 1980, as well as (in view of the second and third phases) for new capacity installed after 1980. Denmark, finally, further relaxed the requirements for the southern Member States and the UK and Ireland, but this proved unacceptable to the others.

Decision under German presidency
In the first half of 1988, the issue of the large combustion plants was back into the hands of its initiator: Germany. As pointed in the previous chapter, the German Government was particularly eager to close the two important files on European acidification policy – the large combustion plants and the 'clean' car – during its presidency, in order both to boost its environmental image at home and to put an end to a long period of uncertainty for German industry. In a German compromise proposal of February 1988, notable concessions were granted to Spain, among others, but not to the UK. During the Council session of March this led to a vigorous confrontation between the UK and the German presidency. From this moment, a number of sub-issues which had been discussed before mainly at a technical level received more and more attention. The British protest at the March meeting, for instance, was primarily aimed at the threshold size of plants at which the emissions standards for new installations would apply. Later the point of measurement of emissions and the conditions for incidental breaking of the limits were added to the negotiations by the UK. In addition to that, a solution had to be found for a forceful Spanish memorandum requiring more flexible emission limits for new plants and for the French problem of plants used only to cover peak demands. These sub-issues were increasingly seen in the context of the negotiation package as a whole, parts of which could be played off against other parts. In this period, bilateral contacts particularly between the German and British Governments parallel to intensive negotiations in the Environment Group played a major role. During two long Council meetings on 16 and 28 June, Germany again had to make considerable concessions to the UK and Spain. At the last moment, moreover, France suddenly stated that it could accept the large combustion plants directive only if Germany was prepared to make an important concession in the parallel negotiations about the 'clean' car (see the previous chapter). Under pressure of time and after the Commission had made clear that it would also accept the package, Germany had to give in to these demands (for a detailed account of the final phase, see Bennett, 1992: 123–130). This agreement was by no means the end of the story for the 'clean' car, but the large combustion plants directive could be formally adopted without change at the next Council meeting, in November 1988 (88/609/ EEC).

Relations with Dutch domestic policy

There can be no doubt that Germany was the decisive factor behind the initiation of Community legislation concerning air pollution from industrial installations. In the summer of 1982, the German offensive started with a memorandum pressing for Community measures against acidification in general terms. This memorandum stimulated the Commission's work on legislation regarding air pollution and also functioned as a 'warming up' for the communication of the draft GFAV to the Commission, accompanied again by strong political pressure, some months later. The motives for this unusually forceful diplomatic action were twofold. On the one hand, it was obvious that substantial reductions of acid deposition on German forests could be achieved only by international efforts. On the other hand, the competitiveness of German industry required that the considerable costs of abatement measures be shared as widely as possible (see Boehmer-Christiansen and Skea, 1991, chapter 10).

The German initiative was received with mixed feelings by almost all EC partners. More or less positive reactions came only from the Netherlands and Denmark, though the latter had some doubts about the feasibility of the proposals. The Dutch generally acclaimed the early drafts of the directive, including the initial idea of setting emission limits for all plants (implying 'retrofitting' of existing installations) but with the exception of the arrangement for refineries (see below). However, the Netherlands restricted itself to expressing its consent to the line set out by the Germans but did not actively support it. This seems to have been mainly because the preparations of the Dutch equivalent of the GFAV were still under way in this period. Finishing the Dutch legislation had priority.

The Dutch Decree

The foundations for Dutch policy with regard to large combustion plants were laid in the Sulphur Dioxide Policy Framework Plan (SO_2-Beleidskaderplan 1979–1980) and in an encompassing government memorandum on energy policy, published in 1980 (*Nota Energiebeleid*, 1979–1980, particularly part II, on coal). Concrete emission requirements for new coal-fired plants and existing plants adapted to the use of coal were set in two circulars, issued in 1981 and 1982 and addressed to the licensing authorities (*Circulaire over de luchtverontreiniging door kolengestookte installaties; Circulaire inzake de eisen met betrekking tot de uitworp van luchtverontreinigende stoffen door kolengestookte installaties).* In the same period, the idea of a more general approach, including all types of fuels, started to take form in the Dutch Government. The final result was laid down in the Decree Emission Requirements Combustion Installations (*Besluit emissie-eisen stookinstallaties,* BEES). The concepts behind the German GFAV were the main source of inspiration for this plan. In 1982 (or early 1983), a Dutch delegation visited Germany to study the design and effect of the GFAV. In this phase, communication about the preparation of the BEES was mainly between the ministries involved: the Ministry of EZ for energy policy, including electricity generation, and the Ministry of VROM for the environmental aspects. Differences between them were considerable and sometimes led to heated discussions. This situation continued throughout 1983 and this may explain the wait-and-see attitude of the Dutch in the first phase of the negotiations in Brussels. It may also have been one of the reasons for keeping the matter 'indoors' for some time: as will be shown below, important partners such as the Dutch electricity producers and the employers' organisation, VNO, got involved in the project only late 1983 or early 1984. Talks with the refineries may have started slightly earlier, as both ministries relatively quickly agreed that the GFAV model was not satisfactory for that particular sector. Not surprisingly, the question of the refineries was the point put forward most prominently by the Dutch in January 1984, that is, immediately after the submission of the official draft to the Council. For most other elements, they could simply join the Germans in pressing for a directive as close as possible to the GFAV.

In the course of 1984, the details of the BEES gradually took shape in negotiations with the target groups. The parallel talks about the EC draft only played a role in the background to the domestic policy process. Although it was already clear that the EC directive was to become generally more lenient than the BEES, this was hardly used by industry as an argument for laxer national standards. A number of factors may account for this. First, the latitude for this kind of argument probably was rather limited, as at that time also the Ministry of EZ had committed itself to standards comparable to those in the GFAV. Secondly, Dutch industry in the early 1980s mainly referred to its neighbours in questions of competitiveness, rather than to the EC as a whole. The fact that Germany, the Netherlands' dominant trading partner, was about to apply the same or even stricter standards made the acceptance of the BEES much easier. Thirdly, and more or less related to the second point, representatives of Dutch industry who were involved in the BEES negotiations appeared to have been surprisingly poorly informed about the state of affairs in Brussels. In most cases, their information was not sufficiently detailed to be able to use it strategically against the Government.

In September 1984, the principal elements of the future Decree were published in the IMP-Air for 1985–1989 (IMP-Lucht, 1985–1989). They included emission limits for different types of large combustion plant, retrofitting of a number of coal-fired power plants with a remaining lifetime beyond 2000, and the outline of a refinery regime. From that moment, the objectives of the Dutch Government in the negotiations in Brussels was clear: on the one hand to stimulate rapid decisions about standards as close as possible to those in the GFAV and the future BEES, and on the other hand to 'protect' particular elements of the BEES. The latter referred to more stringent standards, but also to the refinery arrangement, the maintenance of which was wanted even if no other Member States could be convinced of its advantages. From that moment, also, the Netherlands more actively supported German efforts in the Council, up to the Dutch presidency in the first half of 1986.

The Dutch presidency

The motives behind placing the large combustion plants high on the agenda of the Dutch Council presidency were comparable to those of Germany: first, the reduction of emissions in other countries would help to achieve the Dutch deposition targets; and secondly, a satisfactory EC-wide agreement would improve the credibility and acceptability of domestic acidification policy for the general public and for the industrial target groups. The publicity generated by an agreement under Dutch direction would further heighten the latter effect. Considering the meagre results of two years of official negotiations and the new Spanish and Portuguese membership, the Dutch Government believed that progress could be made only by accepting the pragmatic option of differentiation of reduction targets. With the help of an external consultant, who had started work a few months earlier, the Dutch Government developed a set of criteria to differentiate emission reduction among the Member States, taking into account the contribution to the problem of acidification and the present and expected future situation of the national economy. During an informal Council meeting in March 1986, the approach was in principle accepted and it was decided that the Dutch presidency and the Commission would jointly work on a more detailed proposal for the formal Council session in June. There, however, the Dutch attempt failed, mainly because of resistance from Germany and the Commission. There are four possible explanations for this failure, which do not exclude each other.

First, it is likely that Germany simply considered the Dutch proposal insufficient, especially after additional concessions had been granted to Spain and some other countries, and presumed that a better result was still within reach. The Commission shared this view. In the opinion of Bennett (1992: 117), this was a 'tactical error, for the agreement which was eventually reached after further protracted negotiations was to require less stringent measures'. It should be noted, however, that Bennett's qualification refers mainly to the reduction percentages for the 1990s. For the longer term, the final directive gives reduction targets of fifty-eight per cent in 2003, whereas the Dutch compromise contained only a general commitment to a sixty per cent reduction in 2005, to be worked out later. Weizsäcker and Schreiber (1988: 167) give a second explanation for the Commission's behaviour, by citing 'British critics' who claimed that the responsible Commissioner, Stanley Clinton Davis, blocked the agreement primarily because he did not want the British Conservative Government to boast a political success in the environmental field. It was indeed confirmed in the present case study that the relationship between Clinton Davis and the British delegation became increasingly tense during the negotiations. Thirdly, the personal relationship between the Commissioner and the Dutch delegation, which was not unproblematic either, may have affected the outcome of the Dutch presidency. The fourth factor relates to the fact that the Dutch, in April 1986, when they combined the roles of delegation and Council President, put forward a detailed proposal for a refinery regime. This proposal was badly received by all other parties and may have reduced the authority and credibility of the presidency. The last two factors can hardly have been decisive, but they may have thwarted effective informal communication between the presidency, the Commission and the major negotiating partners (including Germany), especially before and during the crucial Council session in June.

The Dutch refinery regime and the directive

Oil refinery is a major sector in the Netherlands, both in economic terms and in terms of its contribution to acidification.[3] It is not surprising, therefore, that special provisions for refineries were included in the BEES. The wish to maintain those provisions under the EC directive was one of the central themes of the Dutch delegation in the Council negotiations.

During the fact-finding mission to Germany in 1982/83, representatives of the Ministries of EZ and VROM concluded that the GFAV was predominantly aimed at big single sources, such as power plants. The specific situation of refineries, consisting of several smaller installations and burning mixes of fuels, was scarcely taken into account. The idea of a special refinery regime probably originated within the Ministry of EZ, but it was easy to convince the responsible divisions of the Ministry of VROM as well. The oil companies were strongly in favour, but in fact little pressure was needed from their side. The refineries, still co-ordinating their interests in relation to environmental issues in an informal group, were more directly involved in deciding *how* the special needs of the refineries were best met. After some months of discussion the oil companies succeeded in having their preferred option accepted: the establishment of a single emission limit for sulphur dioxide for all (existing and new) installations of a refinery. Together with the other building stones of the BEES, the exact values for the refinery 'bubbles' were published in September 1984: 2,500 mg/m^3 from 1 January 1986 (1 June 1987 in the final text of the Decree), 2,000 mg/m^3 from 1991, and 1,500 mg/m^3 from 1996, unless application of these values would lead to intolerable impacts on the competitiveness of Dutch refineries vis-à-vis Germany, Belgium, France and the UK (IMP-Lucht 1985–1989: 63; Besluit emissie-eisen stookinstallaties, Article 18).

As mentioned before, the Dutch first raised the issue of the refineries with the Council in January 1984. They argued that differentiation between new and existing installations, as proposed by the Commission (COM(83)704, Article 12), would be highly impractical and difficult to enforce in view of the complexity of refinery plants and the use of fuel blends of variable quality. In the course of 1984 and 1985, however, the question of the reduction targets dominated the agenda. As far as the refinery issue was discussed at all, the other Member States showed little interest. This became particularly clear during the Dutch Council presidency. Although the Netherlands preferred its own system, making no distinction between existing and new installations in the refinery, it proposed in April 1986 to extend the application of the emission limit of 1,700 mg/m^3 (reserved in the draft directive for installations smaller than 300 MW burning liquid fuel) to all *new* refinery installations. By remaining closer to the Commission draft, the Dutch Government probably hoped to meet with more approval than before. The proposal was seriously debated this time, but rejected by all Member States and the Commission.

In September 1986, the matter was discussed bilaterally with the Commission. The Dutch argued that, from 1991, there would be practically no difference between the BEES regime, which limited *total* refinery emissions to 2,000 mg/m^3 from that date, and the amendment proposed by the Dutch. The option of a single emission limit for all new and existing installations at the EC level had now entirely disappeared. As it was too far away from the basic philosophy of the directive, the Dutch delegation had given up trying to convince the other Member States of its merits. Instead, the Dutch now pursued a standard for new refinery emissions as close as possible to the domestic overall standard, so that it would be relatively easy for Dutch refineries to comply with both systems simultaneously; in other words, it would be possible to retain the BEES regime while at the same time correctly implementing the directive. The Commission showed somewhat more understanding for the Dutch position, but still rejected the idea of an exemption for one particular sector. In the British compromise proposal discussed in December, there was no trace of a refinery arrangement. The Belgian and Danish presidencies tried to meet the Dutch wishes to some extent, but the value of 1,700 mg/m^3 was generally considered too lax. In 1988, the Netherlands finally had to accept a value of 1,000 mg/m^3 for all new installations of a refinery taken together. Only the German presidency still had some doubts, but did not want to press this relatively minor issue. The agreement was included in the directive as a second option, in practice applied only by the Netherlands.

As touched upon before, the refinery issue did no good to the Dutch reputation in the negotiations and probably weakened its position as Council President in 1986. The Commission objected to the refinery arrangement primarily because it feared that the *principle* of an exemption for one specific sector would open the door for other exemptions. It may indeed be assumed that this demand by one of the most 'environmentalist' Member States facilitated similar demands from other countries. Most Member States, notably Germany, Denmark and France, rather objected to the *level* of the emission limit proposed by the Netherlands. They considered it too lenient and suspected the Netherlands of trying to favour the Dutch refinery sector. In this context it should be remembered that the Dutch refinery sector, apart from being relatively big as a whole, contained some of the largest single refinery plants in Europe. For this reason, the Dutch were interested particularly in flexible arrangements for new installations above the limit of 300 MW. Single installations forming part of the generally smaller plants in, for instance, France and Germany seldom exceeded the capacity of 300 MW. For this category of source, the limit value was to be 1,700 mg/m^3 anyway, whereas installations below 50 MW would not come under the directive at all (Article 9 and Annex IV of the directive; see also Roqueplo, 1988: 218).

The Dutch defence that the 1,700 mg/m^3 standard for new installations was an essential element of a domestic system that eventually aimed at higher *and* more efficient reductions by allowing the oil companies more flexibility did not make much impression on the EC partners. This may be partly because of the decision made by the Netherlands in 1986 to desist from further efforts to include a single limit value for both new and existing installations in the directive. On the one hand, this was a logical and realistic reaction to the negative response encountered before, but on the other hand it had the effect of leaving the Dutch delegation in Brussels with the difficult task of advancing a relatively lax standard for new refinery installations without the broader framework that actually made sense of this standard. From that point of view, it is not difficult to imagine that the other Member States primarily saw the Dutch strategy as an attempt to make life easier for the big refineries in the Rotterdam–Rijnmond area. In any case, it is clear that it was Dutch obstinacy and the circumstance that other sub-issues were considerably more important in the final stage of the process, rather than persuasion by arguments, that led to the eventual outcome.

Community-level public actors

Strong German pressure was crucial in the initial phase of setting emission standards for industrial installations. The German proposals were received by the Commission with mixed feelings, but this had to do with timing rather than with their basic content. In fact, the Commission – in any case DG XI – had long wished to have a broader range of policy instruments at its disposal for dealing with problems of air pollution than only quality standards and some product standards of limited scope. After it transpired in the late 1970s that the more encompassing option of limiting the sulphur content of heavy fuel oil was doomed to failure, the Commission carefully started to prepare the Member States for the introduction of emission standards at the EC level. This was reflected in the Second Environmental Action Programme (EAP 1977–1981: 14) and in a more explicit text in the Third Programme suggesting the possibility of setting emission limits for specific types of source, particularly large stationary ones with high stacks that contributed substantially to transboundary pollution (EAP 1982–1986: 10). It should be noted that this text had been included in the draft of the Programme, published in November 1981,[4] before the Germans first raised the issue of *Waldsterben* internationally. Considering this, there is no reason to doubt that the Commission welcomed the German about-face regarding acidification and the first German memorandum to the Council, in the summer of 1982, urging in general terms effective Community policies. It encouraged the Commission to continue the preparation of a general directive on air pollution. As mentioned above, the very first drafts of this directive contained emission limits, but these rapidly broke down on resistance from several Member States, including the UK and France. From that moment, it was clear to the Commission that the general directive should have a framework character, with emission limits being set in 'daughter' directives. Apart from its procedural elements and the general 'batneec' requirement, the framework directive thus mainly served as an intermediate step in the introduction of emission standards.

From this perspective, the communication of the German GFAV to the Commission in the autumn of 1982 was also in principle a support to the Commission's efforts. This may explain in part why Environment Commissioner Narjes quickly picked up the German call for an equivalent to the GFAV at the EC level, the other factor of course being the intensity of the German pressure. At the same time, however, the Commission and particularly the division responsible for the technical preparation of the draft directive, DG XI, felt somewhat surprised by the tight schedule pursued by the Germans. As it had hardly started the collection of the necessary information, the only way to cope with this schedule was to remain close to existing models, above all the GFAV itself. Despite warnings from the specialists in DG XI, the first draft was sent to the Environment Council in December 1982, without preliminary talks at the expert level. As could be expected, it proved to be not acceptable for most Member States and it was returned to the Commission (see also Donkers, 1989: 55, on the 'regrettable' tendency to send premature drafts to the Council under political pressure).

The connection with the ECE negotiations

From the beginning, the Commission perceived a connection between its activities in the field of industrial emissions and the work on acidification in the ECE (see chapter 4). In the Third Action Programme, it was pointed out that the reduction of emissions from industrial sources could be seen as part of the fulfilment of the Community's participation in the 1979 Convention on Long-Range Transboundary Air Pollution (EAP 1982–1986: 10). After the founding of a group of countries aiming at a thirty per cent reduction of sulphur emissions in March 1984 and the signing of the SO_2 Protocol in Helsinki in 1985, the Commission was eager to embark upon this more concrete obligation as well, but it was stopped from doing so by the opposition from the UK, Ireland, Greece and from 1986 also Spain and Portugal. The Commission then set its mind on joining the so-called 30% Club 'through the backdoor' of the large combustion plants directive. With the percentages envisaged in the Commission draft of December 1983, reductions in the EC as a whole would indeed have been sufficiently high to comply with the 1985 Protocol. The Commission's ambition, however, failed to impress the Member States. For the Member States who did not intend to sign the Protocol anyway, the possibility of the Community signing it was no reason to increase their efforts to reduce emissions. But Germany and the Netherlands were also averse to Community participation in the Helsinki Protocol because they did not want the others – and the UK in particular – to make good cheer even with an indirect membership of the 30% Club without fulfilling all the obligations. After the Dutch presidency, the entire matter became irrelevant because the gap between the Protocol and the reduction targets and deadlines then discussed in Brussels had grown too big.

The Commission and differentiation of reduction targets

The idea of differentiation of reduction targets was put forward at an early stage, but it was accepted by the Commission, unwillingly, only in 1986. The reasons for the Commission's opposition are not difficult to reconstruct. In the first place, differentiation among the Member States principally runs counter to the idea of harmonisation in a common market. From this point of view, serious problems of adaptation to the common rules should be dealt with in the form of temporary exemptions for individual countries rather than by differentiation as a basic principle of a directive. This was indeed the position taken by the Commission until 1986. Secondly, in this specific context, the Commission probably feared that if it accepted the principle of differentiation, the demands of Member States for relaxation of reduction targets would be even harder to contain than before. Among other things, it would imply the end of the Commission's strategy of isolating the UK by granting specific exemptions to its allies in the opposition to the directive, such as Ireland and Greece (Boehmer-Christiansen and Skea, 1991: 239).

The Dutch Government was also conscious of those drawbacks, but nevertheless regarded differentiation as the only way to break the deadlock in the negotiations. In order to give its proposal an objective appearance, it developed an elaborate set of criteria on which national reduction targets could be based. It was clear to all parties, however, that one unequivocal, 'objective' set of criteria for this kind of complex problem simply did not exist. The Commission simply used the argument of 'objectivity' in its eventual rejection of the Dutch compromise to express its discontent with the Dutch willingness to grant considerable concessions to a number of countries for the sake of reaching an essentially political agreement.

Relationships between the Community institutions

In the last two years of the negotiations, technical aspects of the directive increasingly moved to the background. The political task of formulating and informally discussing compromise proposals was carried out primarily by the Council presidencies. Consequently, the role of the technical experts in DG XI became less important. Within the Commission, the emphasis shifted to the higher ranks of DG XI and the Cabinet of the responsible Commissioner, Stanley Clinton Davis. Simultaneously, the involvement of the Secretariat-General of the Council increased. Formally, its role is that of an impartial liaison between the Commission, the Council presidency and the Council members. Regarding its very limited staff and the absence of technical expertise, the Secretariat-General may be assumed to restrict itself to this role. Probably its most important function in the case of the large combustion plants was to maintain at least some consistency between the successive compromise proposals and to 'preserve' those elements that had proved to be politically acceptable.

The increasing dominance of the Council also added to the almost total impotency of the EP in the last stage of the process. After the fulfilment of its only formal task under the unanimity rule, the advice of November 1984 (EP, 1984), the EP adopted two further resolutions to express its dissatisfaction with the slowness of the process and the lax targets and deadlines discussed so far (EP, 1985, 1986), but they were practically neglected by the Council and the Commission (see also Arp, 1992: 30).

Connections with other issue areas
The existence of substantive connections between emissions from industrial plants and particularly large combustion plants and energy policy is obvious: any intervention in the production or use of energy, be it for environmental or other reasons, has potential impacts on structure and prices in the energy sector. In the context of the large combustion plants directive, the question of indigenous energy sources was important. Some of those energy sources, particularly lignite and some types of coal, had a relatively high sulphur content, but their increased use had been consciously stimulated after the two oil crises in order to reduce the Community's dependence on oil supply from countries belonging to the Organisation of Petrol Exporting Countries (OPEC). Besides, the use of domestic fuels had positive effects on balance of payments and on employment. For those reasons, continued use of lignite in Greece, high-sulphur coal in Spain and peat in Ireland, for instance, were preconditions in the large combustion plants negotiations. In this sense, the large combustion plants issue was also indirectly related to regional and social policies. Apart from that, most Member States were worried more generally about the effects of

costly anti-pollution measures on energy pricing, industrial competitiveness, and so on.

It is beyond any doubt that these kinds of connections were in the minds of all negotiators in the large combustion plants process and, particularly at the lower (expert) levels, they were quite openly discussed. Nevertheless, this situation did not lead to intensive contacts with the relevant Community institutions. Good working relations between DG XI and DG XVII (Energy) existed but they were restricted largely to exchange of technical expertise. No attempts were made, for instance, to co-ordinate the environmental efforts with the policy of diversification of fuel supply pursued by DG XVII. The Energy Council issued some comments on the large combustion plants draft on the initiative of the Council presidency of that moment, but was in no way involved in actual decision making. This can be related to the tendency of all Councils to screen off their perceived field of competence. This tendency may be particularly strong in the relatively new field of environmental policy. At the same time, however, the laboriousness of the large combustion plants process, and its close connections with energy, social and regional policy, was one of the reasons for the Commission to stress once again the point of integration of environmental policy into other policy fields in the Fourth Action Programme, published in 1987 (EAP 1987–1992; see also chapter 1).

Private actors

Dutch industry got actively involved in the policy process regarding acidifying emissions relatively late. The two circulars on the emissions from coal-fired combustion plants, issued in 1981 and 1982 (see above), were the subject of consultations between the Ministry of VoMil (in 1982 succeeded by the Ministry of VROM) and the most affected sector – electricity generation – but not for instance the Association of Dutch Employers, VNO, which was later to play an important role in the process around the BEES. The so-called target group approach in Dutch environmental policy had not yet been developed at that time and the relationship between the Ministry and industry was still rather polarised. The Ministry of VoMil/VROM obviously did not regard the circulars as the start of a considerably broader policy, the implementation of which might be easier with the support of the relevant industries.

Dutch industry did not pay much attention to the EC initiative for the framework directive and the following negotiations. This may be to some extent due to the low level of contacts between the Ministry of VROM and industry at that time. VNO was informed about the project of the framework directive through the European Union of Industrial and Employers' Associations (UNICE), and the same probably applied to interested sectors such as electricity producers (through UNIPEDE) and the oil and (petro)chemical sectors (through CONCAWE and CEFIC).[5] They correctly realised at an early stage that the emerging framework directive was harmless, as all the major obligations that remained after the original idea of including emission standards had been dropped were already fulfilled in Dutch legislation (Bennett, 1991: 191–193). There was simply no reason for Dutch industry to act on the issue.

The making of the BEES marked the start of much closer involvement of industrial actors in Dutch policy on acidification. In the first stage, as mentioned above, the discussions between the Ministries of VROM and EZ were closed to outsiders. From 1984, however, after the most serious internal controversies had been overcome, contacts with the relevant sectors gradually intensified. Consultations with VNO, refineries and electricity producers, among others, were stimulated by the new approach to environmental management, introduced by Minister Winsemius in the IMPs 1985–1989 (particularly IMP-Milieubeheer 1985–1989; see chapter 4). It included the articulation of specific 'target group policies', to be developed in collaboration with the relevant sector. At the same time, however, the Government continued to take unilateral steps, which increasingly irritated the 'target groups'. A battle with the electricity generating sector was, for instance, begun by the Cabinet decision of August 1984 that three coal-fired power plants with an expected lifetime beyond 2000 were to be equipped with 100 per cent flue gas desulphurisation instead of fifty per cent as previously agreed. The conflict could only be hushed up with a Government contribution of DFl 110 million.

Oil refinery

As discussed above, oil refinery was probably the first sector to get actively involved in the preparation of the BEES. The Ministries of VROM and EZ quickly agreed that the special situation of the refineries justified a specific arrangement in the Decree. Although the refineries were represented on the VNO committees dealing with the BEES, the refinery regime remained a matter entirely for the Government and the oil companies.

Agreement about the main elements of the Dutch refinery regime was reached in 1984 and published in September of that year (IMP-Lucht, 1985–1989: 63). After that, attention shifted to Brussels. There was consensus among the parties that, ideally, the directive should contain a similar regime, or give sufficient room for the implementation of the national regime. All through the process, the refineries remained in the background. They did not attempt to use the Council's negative response to the Dutch proposals as an argument to relax the domestic requirements, but they did not contribute much to the Dutch efforts at the European level either. In the umbrella organisation CONCAWE, the idea of a single emission standard for the entire refinery did not meet with much enthusiasm. As explained above, the relatively smaller refineries in other countries would in fact be affected less by the source-by-source approach of the draft directive than by the regime advocated by the Dutch (for an illuminating analysis of the situation in France, see Roqueplo, 1988: 218–230). The German refinery sector, moreover, had already adapted to the GFAV regime and was not interested in a change. Consequently, the Dutch refineries, though keen to maintain the flexible Dutch legislation, were simply not able to assist in exerting pressure on the other EC Governments through their colleagues in CONCAWE. Instead, they had to rely on the activities of the Dutch delegation in the Council. As has become clear, they had no reason to complain about the Government's dedication.

Electricity generation
Like the refineries, the electricity sector had mainly direct contacts with the Ministries of VROM and EZ. The sector traditionally has strong roots in the Ministry of EZ, particularly in the Electricity Directorate, a part of the Directorate-General for Energy. This did not prevent the sector, however, from being unpleasantly surprised by the Cabinet decision of August 1984 regarding the installation of 100 per cent flue gas desulphurisation in some existing plants. In addition, talks with the Government about the BEES mainly took place between the sector's Committee for Environmental Affairs[6] and the Ministry of VROM. The impression therefore seems to be justified that the Electricity Directorate was less involved in the BEES

process than the Oil and Gas Directorate in the same ministry, which was one of the major partners in the making of the refinery regime. This is an indication that anti-pollution measures in the electricity sector were mainly seen as a matter of (costly) 'add-on' technology, not affecting the long-term planning of generating capacity, choice of fuels, and so on, which is the principal concern of the Electricity Directorate. For the refinery sector, in contrast, the reduction of emissions was more directly related to basic questions regarding processes and installations.

After the 'surprise attack' of August 1984, negotiations about the precise requirements to be included in the BEES were conducted in a co-operative atmosphere. The draft directive was already under discussion in Brussels, but it was hardly used by either party to influence the outcome of the domestic process,[7] nor was it attempted to introduce elements of the Dutch agreement into the EC negotiations. In fact, the process in Brussels was practically neglected in the talks between the sector and the Government; the electricity companies were informed about it almost exclusively through UNIPEDE.

There was good contact between UNIPEDE and DG XI. The divergent positions of the Member States in the Council were to some extent repeated in UNIPEDE. As the organisation had to accommodate individual wishes and priorities, UNIPEDE was not able to make particularly powerful statements. For the Dutch electricity sector, UNIPEDE's activities were not momentous. The sector was in principle interested in regulation at the European level, particularly in view of the increasingly international character of the electricity market, but in this case there was no direct interest, as it was clear from the beginning that the directive would be less stringent than the BEES. For the electricity companies from Member States more severely affected by the directive, such as Spain and Ireland, UNIPEDE's efforts were not crucial either. Electricity generation is of enormous economic importance and in all Member States the government and the electricity sector had very close institutional links – the privatisation of the British power plants had not yet started at the time. The national electricity companies could therefore be sure of their respective ministers in the Council.

Other industries
The interests of other industries affected by the BEES were taken care of by the 'Steering Committee on Air' (*Stuurgroep Lucht*) of

VNO. This standing committee dealt with all air pollution issues and had a broad composition. For the more specific field of the BEES, a sub-committee on industrial furnaces was appointed. The refineries and the electricity companies were represented, as were several others, such as branches of the chemicals and metals industries. The sub-committee was chaired by an association of industries with interests in the field of energy and environment (*Vereniging Krachtwerktuigen,* KW).[8] Most practical work was done in a core group, consisting of the major members of the sub-committee, again led by KW. As the reduction of sulphur emissions was most problematic for refineries and power plants, and since they maintained their own contacts with the Government, the VNO committees concentrated on requirements regarding nitrogen oxides. Like the electricity sector and unlike the refineries, the VNO committees mainly interacted with the Ministry of VROM. In doing so, their activities centred around the domestic regulatory process. Germany, being the Netherlands' major trading partner, was the point of reference for the acceptability of the BEES requirements, rather than the EC directive.

In the meetings of UNICE about the directive, VNO was represented. In contrast with, for instance, the British employers, VNO welcomed the idea of European legislation in this field for reasons of competition, but it did not actively support this position. This had to do firstly with the fact that priority was given to the satisfactory completion of the BEES process, and secondly with a perception of the relative ineffectiveness of UNICE, which was strongly divided on the issue. This perception was shared by VNO's members, who did not do much to support VNO's input in UNICE. Together with some individual large energy consumers such as the electricity generators, KW was represented on the European Federation of Industrial Energy Consumers (EFIEC). As with VNO in UNICE, however, KW did not play an active role in EFIEC on this issue. In general, KW acknowledged the value of EC-wide legislation for industry, but it actively dealt with EC matters only if they threatened to affect the domestic regulatory situation. This was not the case here.

Environmental organisations
Acidification was among the priorities of both EEB and SNM. As in the case of the 'clean' car, this led to close collaboration between the

two organisations and a leading role of SNM in the EEB's efforts to influence EC policy making.

Already around 1980 SNM worked together with Scandinavian organisations in actions aimed at the negotiations in the context of the ECE Convention on Long-Range Transboundary Air Pollution. This illustrates SNM's early awareness of the international character of the problem of acidification. Consistent with this approach, the BEES was seen as an important step at the domestic level, but at the same time SNM attached considerable value to the establishment of comparable standards across the Community. SNM prepared most of the EEB's comments and press releases regarding the large combustion plants directive and participated in direct contacts with DG XI and the EP. The contribution of German environmental organisations to those activities was, not unlike the 'clean' car case (see chapter 6), relatively limited.

The line followed by the Dutch delegation in Brussels was generally agreed with by SNM. It may be assumed that SNM's image of the 'ideal' directive differed from that of the Ministry of VROM, but in the given situation their goals were similar: finishing the negotiations with a directive as close as possible to the stringent requirements of the GFAV and the BEES. It should be noted, however, that SNM also supported the refinery regime. This may seem odd, as some other Member States looked upon the Dutch proposals in this field as unacceptable concessions to the Dutch oil companies. This apparent paradox is probably due to the confusion already explained above about the exact purport of the Dutch proposals in the Council and their relationship with the BEES regime. In its support of the refinery regime, SNM explicitly referred to the *domestic* version, applying to both new and existing installations. After adoption of the directive, SNM expressed its disappointment about the final text of the refinery arrangement, because it covered only new installations. It is doubtful, therefore, whether SNM was aware that the Dutch delegation had already in 1986 proposed a version applying only to new installations in order to be able at least to maintain the domestic BEES regime.

Summary

German pressure in the early 1980s not only initiated the 'clean' car process but also the regulation of acidifying emissions from stationary sources. The first result was a framework directive setting general provisions regarding air pollution from industrial sources but no emission limits. They were to be included in 'daughter' directives, the first of which was aimed at large combustion plants, that is, power plants, refineries and other large industrial burners. The most controversial element of the issue was the reduction of emissions of sulphur and nitrogen oxides from existing plants. Several Member States feared that rigorous cutbacks would be too costly and hamper their economic development.

For the Netherlands, the situation was different. Domestic measures regarding combustion plants had already taken shape in the course of 1984. They were modelled largely on the German regulation and contained limits of comparable magnitude, considerably stricter than those discussed in Brussels at the time. The domestic approach formed the basis for the position of the Netherlands at the Community level. Together with Germany it advocated significant emission reductions in the EC. For the Dutch environmental organisations, this meant that they could concentrate on targets other than the Government in The Hague in their attempts to influence EC decision making. SNM notably contributed through its work in the EEB. For Dutch industry, having already accepted the domestic measures, there was little need to engage actively in the EC process at all. There was, however, one exception. The Dutch domestic measures contained a special regime for the refinery sector that took into account the variable characteristics of fuel mixes and production conditions peculiar to the large Dutch refineries. The arrangement was different both from the German legislation and the EC proposals. As it was generally regarded as a concession to industry, Dutch attempts to include a similar arrangement in the EC directive met with serious objections. It was argued, however, that this was to a considerable extent because only parts of the original arrangement were presented in proposals to the EC partners. Refineries in other countries, moreover, did not support the Dutch regime either. As most of them were smaller than the Dutch ones, the directive confronted them with other types of problem.

Basic agreement about the directive was finally reached in 1988 under German Council presidency, at the price of considerable concessions, particularly to the southern countries. As had already been discussed for some years, the problem of emissions from existing plants was solved by the differentiation of reduction targets among Member States. The Dutch refinery regime was eventually included as a second option.

Notes

1   This chapter is based partly on a study of documents and interviews conducted in collaboration with Hélène Grijseels.

2   The Environment Group is one of the many standing working groups of the Council. It is composed of civil servants from the Member States and meets regularly to prepare for decision making at the ministerial level.

3   Partly because of a favourable geographical situation at the mouth of the Rhine, the Netherlands, particularly Rotterdam, has a large, strongly export-oriented refinery sector. Total capacities in France, Italy, Germany and the UK are only slightly higher. In addition, refineries in those countries generally serve more stable (largely interior) markets. Owing partly to the considerable size of the Dutch refinery sector and partly to the curbing of emissions in other sectors such as electricity generation, oil refinery had the highest percentage share of the emission of sulphur dioxide in the Netherlands in the 1980s (thirty-five per cent in 1985 compared with some ten per cent in the other countries mentioned; see RIVM, 1988: 106; VROM, 1988; CEC, 1987, 1988, 1990).

4   *Official Journal of the European Communities*, C305, 25 November 1981.

5   The Union of Industrial and Employers' Associations (UNICE) brings together the employers' organisations of the EC Member States and a number of other European countries (Collie, 1993). The International Union of Producers and Distributors of Electrical Energy (UNIPEDE) also covers more countries than the EC Member States. Since 1990, UNIPEDE has focused entirely on technical matters, whereas a separate organisation (Eurelectric) was set up for lobbying activities. Also, the *Conseil Européen des Fédérations de l'Industrie Chimique* (CEFIC) is broader than the EC. Apart from national associations for the chemical industry, some forty multinationals with their headquarters in Europe are direct members. For VNO and CONCAWE, see chapter 5, notes 2 and 4.

6   The Dutch electricity companies work closely together in a number of organisations. Until 1989, the Association of Directors of Electricity Companies in the Netherlands (*Vereniging van Directeuren van Elektriciteitsbedrijven in Nederland*, VDEN) was the most important channel for contacts with the Government. The Committee for Environmental Affairs was linked to the VDEN, which provided for instance the chairperson, but it also included representatives from other, more technically oriented bodies. After a restructuring of the sector in the late 1980s and the enactment of the new Electricity Law in 1989, the Dutch Electricity Generating Board (*Samenwerkende Elektriciteits-Produktiebedrijven*, SEP), previously mainly responsible for the management of the national transmission network, formally took over the function of VDEN.

7   There was one minor exception: the electricity sector was not content with the conditions for short-term, extreme transgression of the emission limits in the case of technical problems. Through UNIPEDE it successfully attempted to introduce a more flexible arrangement in the directive (based on mean values over forty-eight hours instead of thirty minutes; see BEES, Articles 30–34; 88/609/EEC, Article 15). The BEES was later adapted to the directive in this respect (1991 amendment, Article Z).

8   The main activity of KW is the rendering of technical assistance to its 2,500 members (including almost all large industries in the Netherlands) through its own consultancy group. In addition, the association occasionally represents the interests of its members in contacts with the Government. One such occasion was the preparation of the BEES.

8

A case of non-policy at the EC level: ammonia from agriculture

Introduction and overview

Whereas the main sources of sulphur dioxide and nitrogen oxides – industry, transport and households – gradually became subject to various forms of Community policy, the principal source of ammonia, the third major acidifying agent, did not. Contrary to the previous chapters, therefore, this chapter will not deal with a policy process that eventually led to one or more directives, but rather with the question why such a process did not occur. Also in this case of 'non-policy' at the Community level, the discussion will focus on the positions and roles of Dutch actors.

The First Environmental Action Programme, issued in 1973, already pointed to problems connected with the intensive use of 'certain' fertilisers and 'waste from bio-industry' (EAP 1973–1976: 34, 39). The Second Action Programme even expressed the Commission's intention to formulate draft legislation concerning collection, storage and spreading of manure from bio-industry (EAP 1977–1981: 21–22). No draft was published, however, and in the next Action Programme (EAP 1982–1986), the issue was not mentioned. It did re-appear in the Fourth Action Programme: the intended draft directive was narrowed down to limiting water pollution caused by liquid waste from the livestock industry and excessive use of artificial fertiliser (EAP 1987–1992: 24).

The draft was submitted to the Council in early 1989 (COM(88)-708). It aimed at protecting both surface and ground water against nitrates from 'diffuse' (i.e. mainly agricultural) sources. The main instrument was the obligatory designation of 'vulnerable' zones by the Member States, according to a number of criteria set out in an annex to the proposal. Within those zones, special protection measures should apply, including restriction of the amount of manure applied to the land. The final directive, which was adopted in December 1991 (91/676/EEC), also included a code of conduct to be (voluntarily) followed by farmers in both 'vulnerable' and other areas.

In the early 1980s, the first policies following upon the recognition of acidification as a serious environmental problem focused on sulphur and nitrogen oxides. In Dutch policy documents, the contribution of ammonia to acidification was mentioned for the first time in 1983 (IMP-Lucht 1984–1988). The Commission first paid attention to it in its Communication on Environment and Agriculture of 1988, expressing its concern about the environmental impact of ammonia, but not proposing concrete measures in this field (COM(88)338). The nitrate directive, the draft of which was published some months after the Communication on Environment and Agriculture, exclusively aimed at reducing pollution of surface and ground water. No reference was made to the consequences of the directive's requirements regarding the methods of manure application and manure storage for the emission of ammonia into the air. The EP did not pay attention to this point either (EP, 1989). The Fifth Environmental Action Programme once again pointed out the need to regulate the emissions of ammonia from the livestock industry, but it remained unclear which policy level would be most appropriate (EAP 1993–2000).

Relations with Dutch domestic policy

A bird's-eye view of Dutch manure policy
Manure from the livestock industry is a major environmental problem in the Netherlands. Excessive application of manure to the land has several adverse effects, including soil degradation, contamination of ground water, impairment of plant growth, and acidification. Although the problems had been recognised or at least anticipated earlier, substantial policies in this field were not developed before the mid-1980s. Based on two laws, the Soil Protection Act (*Wet Bodembescherming*) and the Fertilisers Act (*Meststoffenwet*), a large and rather complicated system of legislation

now attempts to regulate the amount of manure applied to the land, the time and methods of application and the handling of manure surpluses. The standards in the system are based on the amount of phosphate contained in manure. This compound rather than nitrate was selected because of its better traceability in the environment. The central element of the system is a maximum amount of phosphate to be applied per hectare, differentiated for three types of land (arable land, grassland, maize land) and gradually tightened in three phases between 1987 and 2000. All manure production exceeding the (legally allowed) capacity of the land that belongs to a farm is to be considered 'surplus'. This surplus is subject to a levy, used among other things to finance the so-called Manure Bank which co-ordinates the flows of surplus manure to other farms or to manure reprocessing plants. The principal instrument to control the implementation of the system is the registration of all manure produced, applied to the land, transported and reprocessed in the country. The system of manure registration (also referred to as manure accounting or manure 'book-keeping', '*mestboekhouding*') was initially based on the phosphate content of the manure, but in 1995 it was extended to a broader system of mineral registration, including nitrogen (see Baldock and Bennett, 1991: 96–124; Brussaard, 1993: 148–154; Frouws, 1993).

This general scheme to deal with the manure problem in the Netherlands, although based on phosphate and primarily aimed at protecting soil and ground water, also helps to reduce the emission of ammonia into the air. In addition, there is a growing amount of regulation specifically relating to ammonia, regarding for instance stall systems, storage facilities and the method of applying manure on the land (see generally: *Plan van aanpak beperking ammoniak-emissies van de landbouw*, 1990–1991; *Notitie mest- en ammoniakbeleid derde fase*, 1992–1993).

The international component of Dutch manure policy
Dutch policy documents are not specific about the relation between domestic policies and international initiatives in the field of ammonia pollution from the livestock industry. The foreign component of the document most specifically dealing with ammonia, the 'Plan of approach: limiting agricultural ammonia emissions', was restricted to the assumption of a twenty-five per cent reduction of ammonia emissions in neighbouring countries (Plan van aanpak beperking

ammoniak-emissies van de landbouw, 1990–1991: 4). Considering how little attention was given to the problem outside the Netherlands (see also below), this assumption seems optimistic. In 1989, consultation on the subject with neighbouring countries had already been announced in order to develop joint positions in EC and ECE negotiations. In the framework of the EC, notification of the Commission about relevant Dutch legislation was planned, as well as 'dissemination of information' about the role of ammonia in acidification and possible abatement strategies (with the option of initiating a proposal for regulating the nitrogen content of animal feed). In the ECE framework, the Netherlands agreed to act as 'lead country' for ammonia (Bestrijdingsplan verzuring, 1988–1989: 101–107, in particular).

By mid-1993, notable progress had been made only with regard to the ECE framework, where discussions about abatement strategies for ammonia had just started in the Working Group on Technology. Bilaterally, the issue had been discussed only with Belgium. In the EC, as pointed out, ammonia had not yet appeared on the agenda, except for some short references in general policy documents. Moreover, the Dutch Government had not made efforts to raise the issue in Brussels.

On the one hand, the fact that the international activities up to mid-1993 fell short of the unambitious proposals put forward four years earlier reflected the low popularity of the issue outside the Netherlands. Belgium – or more precisely Flanders – reacted to the Dutch consultations by announcing research efforts with regard to ammonia. In addition, the Ministry of VROM received indications that Germany had started developing its own ammonia policy. Nitrogen loads are nowhere as high as in the Netherlands, but environmental problems related to the livestock industry do occur elsewhere. In Denmark, environmental regulation of the livestock industry is strict but focused on (ground) water pollution. In France (Brittany) and Italy (Po Valley), particularly the problem of water pollution is recognised, but only limited measures have been taken, at the local level (Rijksplanologische Dienst, 1993: 11–69).

On the other hand, the low level of international activity on the part of the Dutch Government in the field of ammonia can be related to the domestic policy context. Dutch policies regarding nitrate and ammonia pollution from agricultural sources are relatively young and important parts had not yet been implemented or were even still under discussion in the early 1990s. Full development of domestic policies had much higher priority than international initiatives, basically for two reasons. First, it was argued that, even though emission reductions abroad were desirable in order to be able to reach Dutch deposition targets, the credibility of Dutch efforts to stimulate such reductions would be considerably higher if reference could be made to effective domestic policies. Secondly, there was a widespread fear that EC involvement in the issue would unfavourably interfere with the emerging domestic arrangements. The manure issue in the Netherlands was (and still is) a very complicated one. A combination of economic and social interests, increasingly serious environmental effects and intricate institutional relations between the agricultural and the public sector led first to a long period of inertia and then to a process of delicate negotiations, conflicts and compromises about possible solutions to the problem. This finally resulted in the present, highly complex package of legislation, parts of which still have to be finalised (for a detailed analysis of the process, see Frouws, 1993). Community legislation would unavoidably have a broader and more general character and would not be able to take into account all the special circumstances in the same way the Dutch legislation has done. In the worst case, Community obligations could totally upset the compromise that had been reached with so much difficulty.

The complexity of the national political and legislative context, in short, made Dutch policy makers prefer to keep the ammonia issue at the domestic level for a time. If EC policy measures become unavoidable, the Dutch position will be to try to keep them as flexible as possible.

One might ask, however, if this position was shared by all parties in the Dutch policy process. From the point of view of agricultural interests, represented in the Government by the Ministry of Agriculture, Nature Conservation and Fisheries (*Landbouw, Natuurbeheer en Visserij*, LNV), the fear seemed to be justified that relatively strict and undifferentiated EC measures could only work out negatively for Dutch farmers. For the Ministry of VROM, in contrast, this would in principle offer the possibility of using the EC as a crowbar with which to speed up the domestic policy process. With respect to ammonia, however, the Ministry of VROM appeared not to be prepared to risk destroying the emerging domestic compromise. This may have been related to a generally more co-operative relationship between the Ministries of VROM and LNV since the early 1990s (Van Tatenhove, 1993).

Community-level public actors

As described above, the Commission's references to the ammonia problem were rare, short and unspecific. The EP, while sometimes active in promoting otherwise neglected issues, did not seriously address the issue either. This situation can be generally explained by a lack of interest in practically all Member States, in combination with a number of other perceptions among policy makers in Brussels.

The limited interest of, for instance, France, Italy, Germany and Denmark in EC involvement in the ammonia issue was sketched above. In those countries, environmental problems related to the livestock industry existed, but policies were largely focused on water pollution, often at the local level. In most other Member States, the issue did not exist at all, simply because animals were kept at much lower densities (Rijksplanologische Dienst, 1993: 18).

Under such circumstances, the Commission had to have very good arguments to initiate policies by itself. One such argument could have been the direct chemical linkage between nitrate and ammonia. Both substances are part of the nitrogen cycle and lower emissions of one substance can result in higher emissions of the other. In Dutch manure policy, this fact is gradually being acknowledged, for instance in the intended system of mineral registration. In the EC, however, nitrate has so far been dealt with as a separate issue, without paying attention to ammonia. Another argument could have been the long-range transport of ammonia. There are strong indications that transboundary transport and effects are not negligible (RIVM, 1988: 111). This was picked up by the ECE's monitoring programme in 1987, but by mid-1993 these efforts were still in a preparatory stage and reliable data were not yet available. In view of that, the Commission had little basis for launching initiatives of its own and preferred to give priority to other issues.[1] A third and final argument could have been the effects of diverging levels of regulation on competition. Although the possibility of such effects cannot be denied, low priority was given to this aspect as well, particularly because no Member State had shown its dissatisfaction with the existing situation. The Netherlands, having relatively strict domestic policies in this field, would theoretically have been a candidate to do so. As argued, however, the Dutch preferred to deal with the problem domestically.

In sum, no serious efforts with regard to ammonia were to be expected from the Commission, nor may they be expected in the near future. The basic perception of the ammonia issue by the Commission is that of a regional problem that should and can be handled at a policy level below the Community. The wish not to increase further the burdens on the Common Agricultural Policy and on European farmers as well as the subsidiarity debate related to 'Maastricht' can be mentioned as additional, more general arguments for this position.

Private actors

The consensus among Dutch governmental actors not to stimulate the Europeanisation of the ammonia issue was shared by the agricultural sector. In this context, the Agricultural Board (*Landbouwschap*), a semi-public organisation representing the sector's interests vis-à-vis the Government (Frouws, 1988, 1993), emphasised the diversity of European agriculture and the specific features of Dutch intensive, technology-based farming. According to the Board, the large scale and high intensity of Dutch livestock farming on the one hand caused considerable environmental problems, but on the other hand gave room for technological solutions, such as low-emission stall systems, which require investments that would not be possible in most other countries. It was anticipated that EC measures, rather than taking into account these specific circumstances, would relate (the reduction of) environmental impacts to the amount of land available. This was done for instance in the nitrate directive and in the extensification programmes in the MacSharry proposals for reforming the Common Agricultural Policy, with obvious consequences for Dutch intensive farming. Therefore, the Agricultural Board preferred to deal with ammonia, as well as with manure in general, at the national level, at least as far as emission limits and specific requirements on farming methods were involved.

This position reflected the Board's general approach to international environmental policies, as laid down in a memorandum of 1988 (Landbouwschap, 1988). For the Board, the advantages of developing solutions specifically fitting the Dutch situation usually outweighed the disadvantages of unequal conditions of competition because of diverging environmental regulations. At the Community level, only broad environmental targets would be acceptable, for instance in the form of deposition targets for ammonia.

As pointed out, ammonia was hardly a policy issue in other Member States. The same was true for the European umbrella organisation COPA (*Comité des Organisations Professionelles Agricoles*), and the Dutch Agricultural Board did not attempt to get it on COPA's agenda. This was also motivated by the general climate in COPA in the early 1990s, which was particularly unfavourable to discussing any additional regulatory burden on agriculture in view of the many problems already threatening the sector, such as over-production, EC budget cuts and the negotiations on the General Agreement on Tariffs and Trade (GATT).

Environmental organisations also had little interest in the Europeanisation of the ammonia issue. Although the possibility was occasionally raised within SNM, no serious action was taken, because the chance of success was considered very low. Not only Member State governments outside the Netherlands but also other environmental organisations showed very little interest in the issue. Nevertheless, the EEB comment on the draft of the nitrate directive pointed out the direct relationship between the different forms of nitrogen pollution produced by the livestock industry – nitrate and ammonia. The background to this explicit (and at the Community level unique) reference was probably that it was SNM which was in charge of the technical preparation of the EEB opinion. It did not lead to any further efforts by the EEB in this field, however.

Summary

Although environmental problems related to the intensive livestock industry were recognised both in the Netherlands and in the EC in the early 1970s, concrete measures were initiated considerably later. In 1991, the EC adopted a directive limiting the emission of nitrates into surface and ground water by diffuse (i.e. mainly agricultural) sources that had been proposed some years earlier. It did not contain any provision regarding the related problem of the emission of ammonia into the air. In policy documents, the ammonia issue was only briefly touched upon. Although emissions in some European regions and transboundary transport of ammonia were not negligible, the problem received very low priority in most Member States and, consequently, in the EC.

In the Netherlands, in contrast, ammonia was recognised as a major environmental problem and formed part of domestic manure policy set up the mid-1980s. It was characterised by a succession of delicate compromises and a large number of highly specific arrangements. Apart from the lack of interest from other Member States, the wish not to let generic (and possibly even more costly) EC measures interfere with this fragile structure was the main reason for both public and private actors in the Netherlands not pressing for EC involvement.

Note

1   In addition, one could imagine that 'victim countries' would call for international action in order to reduce the deposition on their territory. Similar to Sweden and Norway with regard to sulphur dioxide in the 1970s, for instance, Germany could claim that it receives the lion's share of the Dutch 'export' of ammonia. So far, however, Germany (or any other country) has not followed the Scandinavian example.

Part III
Analysis and conclusions

9

Environmental policy between the Member States and the EC: an assessment of the findings

Introduction

In the preceding five chapters I have given an extensive account of the policy processes around the EC directives in the field of air pollution and acidification and their relations with domestic, particularly Dutch policies. In view of the complexity of the material and in order to retain the documentary value of the empirical work, I opted for a historical approach, with special attention to the roles of different types of actor in the political process. On the basis of this, it is now possible to study and interpret the findings of the case study in the theoretical terms of the first part of this book.

In doing so, it is useful to keep in mind the two principal limitations of the approach chosen in this book (see also chapter 4). The most obvious limitation as well as the strength of every case study is the restricted subject matter. The field of air pollution and acidification is one of the major themes of EC environmental policy and largely covers the two decades of its development from the 1970s up to the early 1990s. The question to what extent it is representative of the entire environmental issue area will be addressed in the next chapter, whereas the present discussion will confine itself to the empirical evidence collected in this case study.

Secondly, the case study was limited essentially to the relationship between the EC policy level and a single Member State, the Netherlands. This study attempts to identify mechanisms and trends prevailing in this type of relationship rather than giving an overview for a range of a countries. In view of its generally pro-European attitude and its long-standing interest in environmental policy, the Netherlands was thought to provide a particularly clear example of developing national–EC relations. Nevertheless, it soon appeared that Dutch positions on EC acidification policy, and even Dutch domestic policy in this field, cannot properly be understood without taking into account developments in Germany. German 'clean' car and combustion plants policies in particular preceded and inspired their Dutch counterparts. Where necessary, attention was paid to this in the case study. In this chapter, the findings derived from the Dutch case will be compared with evidence from other Member States, as available in the scientific literature. In the final section as well as in the next chapter the bias and specific features of the Dutch case will be discussed in more detail.

In the next section the findings of the case study will be examined in the terms of the four dimensions of power dependence introduced in chapter 3. Following the substantive expectations regarding the Europeanisation of environmental policy developed in the first part of this book, the next section attempts to identify shifts in the interaction between actors in the making of EC environmental policy and to relate them to changes in the underlying structure of resource dependence between the domestic and the Community level. This will provide the basis for a more general discussion of the transfer of sovereignty in environmental policy between the State and Brussels, followed by a short conclusion.

The build-up of policy networks in EC acidification policy

Policy focus
The first dimension of power dependence along which policy networks can be characterised is policy focus. In chapter 3 it was argued that the maturation of EC environmental policy would be marked, among other things, by a trend towards a more integrated perception of the economic and the ecological aspects of environmental issues at the EC level. This trend was expected to become visible in the early 1980s under the influence of the emergence of the pre-eminently transboundary issue of acidification, among other things (see chapters 1 and 3).

As far as the 1970s are concerned, the case study largely confirmed this view. The issues of the sulphur content of gas oil and air quality standards embodied the two types of environmental legislation developed in the EC at that time. The former was a typical example of an immediately trade-related harmonisation measure, whereas the latter belonged to the category of broad, general provisions with only indirect economic consequences.

In the gas oil issue, the ecological aspect was no doubt decisive for public actors at the national level. The threat to public health posed by high sulphur concentrations in urban areas must have been the sole motivation for the regulation of the sulphur content of fuels in the Netherlands, Germany and some other Member States in the first half of the 1970s, a motivation that was not outweighed by economic considerations. The Commission also stressed the environmental character of the issue: it regarded its gas oil proposal as one of the first instances where the interest of the internal market, that is, the avoidance of trade barriers by divergent national standards, and genuinely environmental goals could be combined. For the Member State governments, however, environmental considerations hardly played a role at this level. Their main focus in Brussels was an economic one: they primarily wanted to mitigate the economic effects of their *domestic* environmental measures by limiting the number of grades of gas oil to be marketed in the Community to two, which in fact corresponded with the wish of the oil companies. The prevalence of the economic aspects of the issue at the EC level became even more obvious in relation to heavy fuel oil. Here the Netherlands, being one of the countries that had set its own standards for heavy fuel oil and had thus shown its domestic environmental interest in the matter, supported the Commission proposal only as long as it did not interfere with the domestic legislation. For economic reasons it had a preference for one single standard throughout the Community, but it did not actively promote this view. For most other Member States, the environmental aspects of the proposal were not at stake at all. They saw only the negative economic effects of a European directive concerning heavy fuel oil (and possibly even solid fuel) and therefore blocked the initiative.

In the case of air quality too, a number of Member States, including Germany and the Netherlands, had already set their own, mostly advisory standards. They as well as the Commission were clearly tackling the environmental problem of urban air pollution. In contrast to the fuel oil issue, however, air quality standards had no direct impact on the conditions of trade or even competition. For the Netherlands the values discussed in Brussels had hardly any economic impact at all, as they were already being complied with. This explains why Dutch private actors were uninterested in the matter. The Dutch Government delegation could thus easily transfer its basically ecological definition of the issue to the EC level and advocate the stricter WHO and (Dutch) Health Council standards in the Council of Ministers. At the same time, though, the issue had low priority in other Member States, as illustrated by the very slow implementation of the directive. For some, including Ireland, the UK, France and Germany, the economic consequences of the proposal were more relevant. They generally saw neither ecological nor economic reasons for treating the problem at the European level, however, and only grudgingly agreed with the directive after five years of negotiation. As far as they perceived the (ecologically motivated) need to set air quality standards at all, they believed it should be at the local or national level. Particularly interesting in this sense was the case of Germany. The FRG was the only Member State having binding air quality standards in the early 1970s, albeit rather lenient ones. As it feared the consequences of the (stricter) directive in some heavily polluted areas, Germany most persistently obstructed adoption of the EC directive (Wetstone and Rosencranz, 1983: 150–151).

The two central issues of EC policy in the field of acidification in the 1980s – the emissions from large combustion plants and from motor vehicles – were indeed of a different kind and character. The large combustion plants directive aimed at formulating a full emission reduction programme for a number of major industrial sectors, taking into account both ecological goals and economic requirements. The introduction of car catalysts and unleaded petrol was in the end nothing other than product harmonisation together with some supporting measures, which had their roots in the 1970s, but the scale and the impact on both industry and consumers distinguished them from measures in earlier directives. At first sight, the fact that this large and direct impact was no reason to refrain from the project totally, as happened for instance in the case of heavy and solid fuel, illustrates the increased importance of environmental motives at the EC level.

It should be realised, however, that both issues were put on the agenda by Germany and that in both cases German efforts in

Brussels were preceded by substantial measures at the national level. Public concern about the consequences of acidification for German forests first led to domestic political debate and to the formulation of national environmental policy goals. Both the decision to introduce catalytic converters in passenger cars and the preparations for the GFAV were already far advanced when the German Government started to press the Commission and the Council. Community action was considered necessary by the Germans in order to reduce 'imports' of acidifying substances, but also to remove any competitive disadvantages for German industry. For a number of other Member States, such as the UK, France and most southern Member States, the environmental aspect of the issues was hardly at stake at all, neither at the domestic nor at the EC level (see, for instance for the UK, Boehmer-Christiansen and Skea, 1991: chapter 11; for France, Roqueplo, 1988: chapter 3; Héritier *et al.*, 1994: chapter IIC; for southern Europe, Brinkhorst, 1989: 65; Pridham, 1994: 93; Aguilar Fernández, forthcoming). They mainly perceived the political and economic need for harmonisation, after the matter had been put on the European agenda primarily by Germany.

Some northern Member States, including the Netherlands, were in a situation more comparable to that of Germany, although public feeling and political debate about acidification were neither as early nor as heated as in Germany. As far as the large combustion plants were concerned, however, in the Netherlands, as in Germany, decisions were taken domestically first. Only after the principal elements of the BEES had been established did the Dutch Government start to develop an active policy at the EC level. This policy aimed at creating favourable economic conditions for implementation of the BEES, including the refinery arrangement, rather than at (re)formulating environmental policy goals at the EC level. In fact only the environmental organisations (SNM and EEB) emphasised the latter aspect. The 'clean' car, in contrast, was regarded much more as a truly 'European' issue in the Netherlands, all aspects of which should be dealt with within the Community framework.[1] This can easily be related to the relatively small size of the Dutch car market and the absence of big domestic car manufacturers, which made it difficult to develop effective and credible independent national policies. The short period of Dutch *Alleingang* with regard to the small car in 1988/89 was clearly a second choice when agreement at the European level seemed unlikely in the near future. It was of high symbolic value, aimed mainly at the domestic level (see chapter 6).

In conclusion, it cannot be denied that environmental motivations were the basis of both the 'clean' car and the large combustion plants directives in countries like the Netherlands and Germany, but they played a role predominantly at the national level. The unacceptability for all Member States of a splitting of the European car market, in combination with the German unwillingness to depart from the policy measures that had been decided domestically, brought about the harmonisation of EC car emission standards.[2] In the case of the large combustion plants, trade was not directly threatened. Strong German political pressure, again based on a domestic policy line, was probably more decisive here. In Germany as well as in the Netherlands, the national level was regarded as most appropriate for taking the basic decisions on acidification policy. Those decisions then functioned as a virtually unassailable starting point for negotiations in Brussels. The Community level was mainly regarded as an opportunity to improve the conditions for the implementation of domestic regulation. The crucial difference between the 1970s and the 1980s was that in the latter period economic motives to urge for Community measures as near as possible to the domestic ones were reinforced by an environmental motive – the wish to reduce the foreign contribution to acidifying substances.

The ammonia issue is a special case in many senses, but it strongly underlines the point just made. Here it was particularly clear that all Dutch domestic actors defined the problem as a national one. Transboundary environmental aspects and the risk of competitive disadvantages were to some extent recognised but did not change the basic conviction that solutions should first be formulated at the national level. This view was shared by the Commission as well as by neighbouring Member States.

Membership

As an expression of the emergence of encompassing EC environmental policy networks, the build-up of relatively closed groups of actors taking part in policy making at both levels was expected (chapter 3).

Starting with governmental actors at the national level, the Ministry of VROM (and its predecessor, VoMil) in the Netherlands played a central role in all five issues in the case study. The input of other departments varied and tended to be stronger in issues with more economic impact, such as the large combustion plants (Ministry of EZ) and ammonia (Ministry of LNV). In all cases, however, VROM was the primarily responsible for national legislation and in practice co-ordinated the Dutch contribution to EC negotiations. This confirms the observation by Van den Bos (1991) that transgovernmental relations prevail in EC environmental policy.

In Germany a comparable formal and informal division of tasks prevailed. Although always subject to intensive consultation with other departments, the environmental section in the Interior Ministry (until 1986) and later the Federal Environmental Ministry was the central government agency that prepared both national and international policies in the field of air pollution and acidification (Boehmer-Christiansen and Skea, 1991: 106ff.; Boehmer-Christiansen and Weidner, 1992: 38; Héritier *et al.*, 1994; and more generally Pehle, forthcoming). In other Member States, however, the situation was different. For instance in France, the Environment Ministry played a pivotal role in the making of domestic policies, but was described as considerably weaker with regard to the preparation of positions to be taken in Brussels (Roqueplo, 1988: 137–138). Environmental concerns have traditionally had a subordinate administrative status in the UK. All through the negotiations described in the previous chapters, the hands of the Department of the Environment were tied by others, such as the Department of Trade and Industry and the Department of Energy, and by decisions from the highest political levels (Boehmer-Christiansen and Skea, 1991: 109–113 and chapter 11; Boehmer-Christiansen and Weidner, 1992: 61–63). The often younger environment ministries in the southern Member States generally had even more difficulties in asserting their positions against more established parts of government (Pridham, 1994; La Spina and Sciortino, 1993). These differences to a large extent coincide with (and as it were provide the institutional background to) the variations in appreciation of the environmental vis-à-vis the economic aspects of the issue of acidification, referred to above.

At the EC level, all five issues were discussed and decided by the Environment Council, that is, by the Member States' Ministers of the Environment. Within the Commission, however, the involvement of different Directorates-General was more ambiguous. With regard to air quality standards and surprisingly also the more substantial issue of industrial emissions, on the one hand, DG XI could act almost independently of other DGs. DG XVII (Energy) was consulted frequently for technical aspects of the large combustion plants directive, but does not appear to have had much political influence. The issues of sulphur content of fuels and car emissions, on the other hand, started their EC career under the competence of DG III (Internal Market and Industrial Affairs). At the end of the 1970s, the sulphur content issue moved to DG XI, but DG III retained a substantial interest in the subject. The primacy of DG III in the 'clean' car issue was not diminished and recurrently triggered controversies with DG XI. DG VII (Transport), in contrast, was hardly involved in the matter. This situation reflects the persistence of a strongly economic focus, especially on issues of product harmonisation.

Not surprisingly, the role of the EP was very limited throughout the case study. Only in a single instance – in the 'clean' car process – owing to fairly specific circumstances, was it able to put its mark upon the negotiations. The Dutch national parliament may have had an indirect influence through its role in the establishment of domestic acidification policy (Hajer, 1993), but it was not directly involved in the preparation of the Dutch Government's stance in Brussels. In other Member States, parliaments did not regularly intervene in the bureaucratic preparation of EC standpoints either. Only in highly politicised cases did national parliaments sometimes directly address international and EC air pollution policy, for instance in Germany in the beginning of the 1980s (Boehmer-Christiansen and Skea, 1991: 104). In 1984, the UK's House of Commons Environment Committee urged a less defensive approach to European acidification policy, but the effect was limited (Boehmer-Christiansen and Skea, 1991: 211–212). It appears that in France, the issue of air pollution and acidification was kept entirely within the executive (Roqueplo, 1988; Héritier *et al.*, 1994). This again stresses the transgovernmental, strongly bureaucratic character of EC environmental policy making. The low degree of democratic control over Community policy at the domestic level may have the effect of (further) enhancing the discretionary power of national sectoral ministries to develop their own EC policies, either on the basis of established domestic positions and interests or as a result of a form of supranational policy co-ordination among national bureaucrats. Although the latter might be facilitated by the 'democratic deficit' at the EC level, the case study suggests the prevalence of the former, domestically rooted variant.

As regards private actors, national legislation in the Netherlands on the five issues in the case study was prepared in close collaboration with the branch organisations and companies involved. The only (partial) exception was the large combustion plants issue, where for instance the electricity producers and the employers' organisation VNO were initially kept at a distance by the Ministries of VROM and EZ. This was explained by the interdepartmental differences of opinion about the general direction of Dutch acidification policy (chapter 7). Intensive consultations with industry took place in later phases of the preparation of the BEES, however. Similar patterns of co-operation and negotiation with industrial actors in the domestic context can be observed in other countries and are in line with more general analyses of private-interest representation in Western Europe (e.g. Heisler and Kvavik, 1974; Richardson, 1982; G. Smith, 1990).

The involvement of Dutch industry in EC policy making was generally more intense in the 1980s than in the 1970s. The issues of the sulphur content of gas oil and particularly air quality did not attract much interest from Dutch industrial actors. They were somewhat more alert on the heavy fuel oil proposal, but the issues of car emissions and large combustion plants were followed most consistently, leading in some cases to active lobbying. This can easily be related to the greater and more direct economic impact of the more substantial EC legislation in the 1980s. With regard to the strategy chosen for lobbying, however, an interesting phenomenon can be observed. Throughout the period covered by the case study umbrella organisations, such as CONCAWE, UNIPEDE and CCMC/ CLCA, played a role in the direct articulation of the interests of Dutch industry in Brussels, mainly by means of comments on draft legislation and on negotiations and through consultations with the Commission. Particularly with the more far-reaching issues of the 1980s, however, the activities of the umbrella organisations were not always considered adequate by their Dutch members. The Dutch branch organisation RAI and Volvo Car in the 'clean' car issue as well as the Dutch refineries in the large combustion plants issue held minority positions in their respective umbrella organisations. As a consequence, the efforts of CLCA, CCMC and CONCAWE in Brussels were of little use (or were even counterproductive) for RAI, Volvo and the refineries. As direct access to the Community institutions was not sought, they were – effectively – represented at the EC level only through the Dutch Government. Particularly in the 'clean' car issue, the abiding dominance of the strategy of industrial lobbying at national rather than the EC level has also been observed in other countries (Arp, 1991: 16, 31–32; McLaughlin and Jordan, 1993). Similarly, the energy companies in the two countries representing the extremes in the large combustion plants controversy, Germany and the UK, mainly worked through their respective national governments (Boehmer-Christiansen and Skea, 1991, chapters 10 and 11; Héritier *et al.*, 1994: 210–212). Dutch companies involved in the large combustion plants issue, which were not in minority positions among their European counterparts, were confronted with the weakness and internal division of their respective umbrella organisations (UNICE, UNIPEDE) and put more emphasis on activities at the national level.

These findings give rise to the surmise that more substantial Community legislation in the field of the environment, involving larger economic and trade interests, may lead to the weakening rather than the strengthening of the role of umbrella organisations and thus to a greater relevance of the indirect, national route. This conclusion is in contrast to a number of recent publications (Greenwood *et al.*, 1992; Mazey and Richardson, 1993a) claiming that the more frequent use of qualified majority voting in the Council may stimulate the direct participation of private actors, through Euro-groups, in policy processes in Brussels. Although their point is in principle convincing and in line with the argument developed below that the legal resources of the Council are the central power basis of the Member State governments, the case study suggests that at least in more controversial issues the divergence of interests and opinions in Euro-groups may outweigh the effect of the change of the voting rules and once again throw private actors back into the arms of their respective national governments when they wish to influence decision making.

Dutch environmental organisations, notably SNM, recognised the importance of the EC for environmental policy making at an early stage. In 1974, SNM was one of the founders of the EEB. It regarded the EEB as the principal channel for influencing EC negotiations and it was usually among the driving forces behind the EEB's efforts. Nevertheless, the EEB's influence on air pollution and acidification policy was limited. In the 1970s, other subjects were given priority and the EEB's contributions to the negotiations over air quality standards and the sulphur content of fuels correspondingly small. More attention was paid to the 'clean' car and large combustion plants issues, but activities were still largely limited to written (and often rather late) comments. The national strategy was rarely deployed by SNM, simply because the positions of the Dutch delegations in Brussels generally were already on the 'green' side of the balance in the Council of Ministers. Direct lobbying by the EEB, although limited, was then seen as more effective.

With regard to the Netherlands, a similar conclusion was reached by Hey and Brendle in their extensive study of environmental organisations in the EC (1994: 269–276). Situations in other countries differed, however, depending mainly on the specific national styles and strategies of environmental movements (Hey and Brendle, 1994; Héritier *et al.*, 1994). German environmental groups, for instance, are rooted in a more action-oriented, confrontational tradition. As a result they did not, until recently, develop close relationships with either the national or the EC bureaucracy. British environmental organisations generally have a more pragmatic approach and nature conservation interests in particular are strongly represented in Brussels, both in the framework of the EEB and individually. As Hey and Brendle emphasise, however, this should not be seen primarily as an expression of a strong interest in EC environmental policy *per se*, but rather as an attempt to influence 'backward' British policy by blowing the whistle in Brussels. In France, a strong local focus prevails among environmental groups, with only a limited degree of organisation at the national level. Interest in European affairs among environmental organisations has undeniably increased since the late 1980s, as evidenced by the growing numbers of both Brussels-based lobby bureaux and European officers in national groups (Rucht, 1993; Hey and Brendle, 1994). The considerable variations in national traditions of environmental action and lobbying, however, make it difficult to discern overall patterns in the way this trend is currently materialising.

In sum, the consistently central position of the Ministry of VROM in the Netherlands, even in cases where strong industrial interests stimulated the active involvement of the Ministry of EZ (large combustion plants), in contrast with the more competitive relationship between DG XI and DG III in the Commission, particularly in cases directly affecting intra-Community trade, supports the conclusion above that economic aspects of environmental problems continued to play a more influential role at the Community level than at the Dutch domestic level. Additional evidence from other countries point to basically similar conclusions for Germany, but in the UK and the southern Member States, for instance, the balance may be different. Furthermore, in the case of acidification, the maturation of EC policies indeed led to greater interest and involvement of transnational actors. This did not reduce the importance of the indirect vis-à-vis the direct route for lobbying. On the contrary, it seems that the inability to reach agreement in umbrella organisations over more substantial – often more controversial – issues forced industrial actors to resort to their national government.

Vertical interdependence
Vertical interdependence describes the power dependence among the actors in a policy network. Resource dependencies are continuously reproduced and adapted in the interaction in the network. The study of the distribution and exchange of resources in decision making can therefore shed light on the shifts in resource dependencies between actors at the national and the EC level that may occur in relation to the Europeanisation of environmental policy. General expectations regarding the character and direction of such shifts were developed in chapter 3 and will serve as the basis for the following discussion.

Legal resources with respect to EC environmental policy making are distributed very asymmetrically. Before the coming into force of the Single Act, the Community's powers to act in the environmental field were not formally laid down. This gave the Commission in particular, as the initiator and main mover behind EC policies, a weak position vis-à-vis the Member States. Legal competence had to be 'conquered' almost case by case. The case study, however, suggests that the Commission could mobilise two alternative types of legal resources against the Member States, in practice usually in combination with other kinds of resources.

The first type was the gradual accumulation of competences and the use of competences once acquired as a resource in negotiations about further steps. In the case of air pollution this process started with the establishment of product norms for gas oil and motor vehicles and the formulation of air quality standards. With regard to product norms, the Community's authority to act was hardly contested in view of their obvious relevance to the functioning of the internal market and the long-established role of the EC in removing trade barriers. The fragility of the legal basis, however, was illustrated by the ease with which the attempt to regulate the sulphur content of other fuels was wrecked by almost all Member States. The decision-making process, particularly for the directive setting air quality standards for sulphur dioxide and particulates, was long and difficult, but the matter of competence was rarely discussed explicitly. It may, however, have had a background role, as it was argued that some Member States accepted the 'smaller evil' of air quality standards in order to shun more substantial measures (chapter 5; see also Wetstone and Rosencranz, 1983). In the mid-1970s, the Commission had stated its wish to acquire competences in the field of air pollution. The air quality directives were regarded by the Commission only as a first step in this process (see EAP 1977–1981: 13ff.). In fact, the *prospect* of a future extension of the Community's legal powers (through the Member States' wish to avert this 'danger') may have helped to establish a more limited competence. With the radical change in the German approach to air pollution problems in 1982 and their pressure for a Community policy parallel to the GFAV, the establishment of emission standards came within reach. After the failure of a premature attempt to introduce such standards immediately, a more gradual approach was chosen. Pressed on the one hand by Germany, which wanted rapid and substantial steps, and on the other hand by the majority of the other Member States, which did not want to accept emission values at the time, the Commission piloted a framework directive through the Council. Apart from the rather vague requirement of the use of the 'best available technology not entailing excessive costs' and some requirements regarding licensing procedures, the directive (84/360/EEC) mainly confirmed explicitly the Council's authority to set emission standards by unanimous vote, which in principle would have been possible under Articles 100 and 235 of the Treaty anyway. As a political statement, however, the framework directive could be used as a 'can opener' for the later large combustion plants directive. Later, emission standards were also set for air pollution from other source categories such as waste incinerators (89/369/EEC and 89/429/EEC). It should be added, though, that any existing competence as a resource in negotiations probably has only a limited range of effect. For instance, the possibility of setting EC-wide emission standards in the field water pollution, formally laid down in the 1970s (76/464/EEC) and first brought into practice in 1982 (82/176/EEC), was not considered to be of any relevance to air pollution.

A second type of legal resources sometimes used by the Commission, and also by Member States who wished to influence the transfer of competence from the national to the EC level, was the embeddedness of issues in broader international agreements or policies. Mostly, the aim was to stimulate EC involvement in the matter, except in the case of ammonia. As argued in chapter 5, the reference to the highly reputed WHO standards made by the Commission and, among others, the Netherlands facilitated both the acceptance of EC air quality standards in principle and the inclusion of stricter guide values in the directive. With regard to the 'clean' car, the Community's existing role in preparing common positions for the ECE negotiations added to the strong economic arguments for an EC competence in this field. In the large combustion plants issue, the Commission originally aimed at implementing a thirty per cent reduction of all sulphur dioxide emissions in 1993 relative to 1980, which had been laid down in the 1985 Protocol to the ECE Convention on Long-Range Transboundary Air Pollution (see chapter 7). In the first instance it hoped to make the EC an official party to the Protocol; later it attempted to reach the objective 'through the backdoor' of the large combustion plants. The former was thwarted by Member States who did not want to commit themselves to a reduction of thirty per cent, whereas the latter was looked upon critically by the more progressive Member States who did not want to have their reductions of more than thirty per cent used to boost the EC average to the advantage of the partners who lagged behind. The Commission's attempt to use the commitment to the ECE agreement to stimulate EC policy thus failed in both respects. Only the technical point of the reference year, 1980, originally appearing in the ECE agreements, was eventually adopted in the EC directive.

Reference to the ECE was used in a more negative sense in the ammonia issue. In its international efforts with regard to ammonia, the Dutch Government officially claimed to pay attention both to the EC and the ECE level, but in practice was active only at the ECE. At the Community level, at the same time, the lack of reliable international data on the transport and effects of ammonia (to be provided preferably by the respected ECE Co-operative Programme for Monitoring and Evaluation of Long-Range Transmission of Air

Pollutants in Europe, EMEP) was mentioned as one of the reasons not to act. It was thus implied both by the Netherlands and by the Commission that the ECE was to be regarded as the primary framework for international initiatives on the issue. As the development of substantial ECE policies in the field of ammonia are quite unlikely in view of the organisation's broad and highly heterogeneous character, this strategy will probably have the (desired) effect of leaving the matter essentially at the national level.[3] Considering those findings, a preliminary conclusion may be that the impact of the use of international embeddedness as a resource in EC negotiations varies and at first sight seems to be greater in the 1970s.

In comparison with the Commission, the Member States had very powerful legal resources at their disposal. Until 1987, the unanimity rule in the Council assigned them a de facto right to veto. Even if this right was not actually used, it lent substantial force to Member States' objections to draft directives as a whole (for instance the heavy fuel oil proposal) or to particular elements (for example Spain's protests against the large combustion plants directive; see chapter 7). The crucial importance of this resource was illustrated by the 'unblocking' of the so-called Luxembourg compromise with regard to car emission standards after the coming into force of the Single Act (see chapter 6). As a case of product harmonisation, the issue of the 'clean' car was taken along in the 'basic programmatic agreement' about the Single Market project. For the large combustion plants, in contrast, unanimity continued to be the rule, which accounts to a large extent for the considerable concessions that had to be made before a final agreement could be reached. It should be noted, however, that the voting rule in the Council implied only a negative power: the power to *block* decisions. In the first place, in an integrated, multi-issue framework like the EC, this set limits to the use of this resource. As will be argued below, the perception of fragmented linkage, that is, the wish not to frustrate the Community process as a whole in view of future gains, can for instance help to explain why the large combustion plants directive was adopted at all. In the second place, the Member States' de facto veto power was ill suited to the more positive purpose of stimulating EC measures.

Apart from exerting political pressure on the Commission formally to initiate the making of a directive, as for instance done by Germany with regard to the large combustion plants, the case study suggests the introduction of domestic legislation as the major way for a Member State to provoke Community legislation. Without giving rise to significant conflicts, this route was followed in the case of the gas oil directive. Here the emergence of domestic regulation in an increasing number of Member States and the implications for the functioning of the internal market was instrumental in bringing forth a Commission proposal in this field. In a more deliberate and conflictual way the method of *Alleingang* was applied by Germany with respect to the 'clean' car. It can be argued that the option of unilateral action exploits legal resources: the Community's treaty-based competence to ensure the functioning of the internal market and the Member States' capacity to challenge this competence by creating barriers to free trade or competition. In view of this juridical aspect, the probability of being subject to and then winning a possible Court case may be relevant to the effectiveness of unilateral action. It is no coincidence, however, that in the case study the method of unilateralism played a role only in relation to the harmonisation of product norms. This points to the importance of economic resources as well, particularly the capacity to 'hurt' other Member States by the unilateral introduction of measures. For instance with regard to the large combustion plants – which did not involve product harmonisation – this possibility did not exist: unilateral installation of expensive anti-pollution equipment in power stations in Germany would not harm other countries. The economic interest of the other Member States was evident, in contrast, in the 'clean' car case. In 1983–1985, the Germans carefully increased the pressure on their EC partners by making detailed preparations for the unilateral introduction of catalytic converters and unleaded petrol. Even though most insiders were aware that actual implementation was unlikely, Member States had to take the threat seriously because of the enormous economic consequences of a European car trade war. Comparable unilateral action by the Netherlands and Denmark had a considerably smaller impact in view of the smaller importance of their domestic markets for the European car industry.

In the case of the unilateral introduction of measures, the central role of the Member State governments is obvious, as they are the ones who enact such measures. Which economic resources can be mobilised by public actors is, however, closely related to their interaction with the industrial sectors at stake. Chapter 3 raised the expectation that the greater interference with social and economic life in the Member States of increasingly substantial EC environmental policies would bring more momentous resources into play in EC policy making, particularly in the economic field. Generally speaking, this was no doubt the case. The issues of air quality and gas oil in the 1970s gave rise only to limited conflicts with industrial interests. The more controversial issue in this period, the regulation of the sulphur content of other types of fuel, was easily averted. In the issues of the 1980s, in contrast, considerable industrial interests were at stake and played a major role in the negotiations. In the context of this study it is particularly important to examine which actors at which level of governance were actually able to mobilise different types of resources to defend those interests, and to what extent the processes in the 1970s differed from those in the 1980s in this respect.

As argued above, economic aspects were central in the perception of environmental issues at the EC level. Throughout the case study, the initiation of policies was strongly related to the perceived need to harmonise conditions of trade and competition in the light of the functioning of the internal market. Similarly, the cases of non-policy with regard to heavy fuel oil, coal and ammonia could be related to the absence of the perception of this need. The background to this situation was an interest in the generation of income and prosperity that was widely shared, at least among governments and industry. At the rather general level of the interests of an entire industrial sector, references by EC-wide umbrella organisations to their members' contribution to economic production were usually effective, as they were in line with this basic orientation of the Community. Examples were the objections expressed by CONCAWE with regard to the heavy fuel oil proposal that enhanced the protest of a number of Member States against the draft (chapter 5) and the evident importance of common emission standards for the European car industry as a whole (chapter 6). As soon as more specific interests were at stake, for instance of an individual firm or of a limited group of companies in one country, however, the mobilisation of economic resources directly at the EC level turned out to be more difficult. In the first place, divergence of interests within Euro-groups often gave rise to internal conflicts and ineffectiveness, the latter at least from the point of view of the dissenting minority. In the second place, such divergence of interests tended to be reproduced in the Council, as Member States were forced to take sides as well. In that case, in view of the crucial role of the Council in the EC political process and the legal resources available to Member States to influence and even block decision making, industrial actors had to fall back on their respective national governments, as indeed occurred with regard to the 'clean' car as well as the large combustion plants. This implies that economic resources could be mobilised by industrial actors predominantly in the domestic context *preceding* EC negotiations. In the Netherlands, but also for instance in Germany, this in practice usually meant that the exchange of economic (and other) resources between public and private actors centred around the making of domestic policy, on which the standpoint of the government delegation in Brussels was subsequently based.[4]

The preference of private actors for the national strategy, particularly regarding controversial issues, had consequences for the relationship between Euro-groups and their members. Umbrella organisations strongly depend on their members for informational and organisational resources. In practice both types of resources are connected: with limited money and staff, Euro-groups are less able to collect their technical expertise, statistical data, and so on, themselves. If private actors at the national level consider the activities of their umbrella organisations ineffective, however, they may expected to be less prepared to invest considerable amounts of their scarce resources. This was observed with regard to industrial actors in the context of the 'clean' car and the large combustion plants. As shown in the case study, Dutch industry was far from deeply involved in the activities of, for instance, CCMC/CLCA, CONCAWE, UNICE, UNIPEDE or EFIEC. The reason for this was the divergence of Dutch interests and opinions from those of these organisations, coupled with the rule of consensus prevalent within most Euro-groups.

For environmental umbrella organisations, during most of the case study period notably the EEB, the problem was less a divergence of interests, but primarily the minor role at the Community level of one of the environmental movement's principal resources: political legitimacy. Indeed, the issues of the 'clean' car and the large combustion plants raised more public interest than the highly specific, technical issues of the 1970s, but this was probably related to the high public and political salience of the issue of acidification rather than to a supposed maturation of EC environmental policy. Moreover, the public involvement in the issues mentioned was restricted to some northern Member States and had an impact mainly at the domestic level. As a result, public support could be used as a resource by environmental organisations only vis-à-vis their national governments. Particularly the German role in the 1980s, its forceful plea for rapid and effective action and its wish to take home 'visible' results from Brussels, can only be understood against this background. In order to influence decision making at the EC level directly, meanwhile, the EEB had to rely largely on informational resources. The vital importance of this type of resource, particularly in technically complicated issues, was illustrated by the case of the 'clean' car.[5] Only here did the EEB have sufficient in-house technical knowledge to be taken seriously by the other parties. Regarding all other issues in the case study, expertise was provided by national member organisations such as SNM. However, as this information usually had a more general background character in the first place and was not immediately available in Brussels in the second place, the EEB was unable to give quick and adequate reactions on ongoing negotiations, for instance in the form of new policy alternatives.

Whereas the power of industrial Euro-groups can be primarily related to the controversial nature of the issue at stake among their members, the environmental organisations appear to have been caught in a vicious circle of weakness and ineffectiveness. The limited impact of the EEB on EC decision making made it unattractive for its national members to provide the necessary (informational and organisational) resources, which in turn further handicapped the Bureau in its work. The central role of the Dutch SNM, which showed an early and outspoken interest in international co-operation, in preparing the EEB's positions may be interpreted as an attempt to break this vicious circle. Success was limited, however.

The overall picture emerging from this analysis of vertical interdependence is that of the growing importance of the Member State governments as mediators of economic interests in relation to the increasing substance and impact of EC acidification policy. The relatively small and 'innocent' issues of the 1970s left room for the mobilisation of a variety of resources, including for instance embedding an issue in broader international agreements, and in some cases the limited but direct involvement of industrial umbrella organisations. The more substantial interests that were at stake in the issues of the 1980s, on the contrary, generated more profound conflicts both among countries and within industrial sectors, and tended to focus the attention on the actors who had eventually the most powerful resources at hand: the national governments in their capacity as members of the Council. This observation is in line with the conclusions of the foregoing sections on policy focus and membership. In this situation, domestic agreement among public and private actors about the standpoints to be taken in the Council and often, as generally in the case of the Netherlands, about domestic policies as well, became almost a prerequisite for entering EC negotiations.

Horizontal interdependence
Horizontal interdependence refers to relations of resource dependence of the policy network under consideration with other policy networks, in this case either within or outside the environmental policy field.[6] What is usually called the co-ordination of different policy goals, or the 'integration' of environmental considerations into other policy fields, in practice usually entailed the balancing of conflicting claims on resources. It was expected that the importance of this kind of resource dependencies would grow with the increasing volume and impact of EC environmental policy.

The conflict of claims on scarce resources was particularly obvious in the instances in the case study where linkage with other policy fields occurred. In the issues of the sulphur content of fuels and the large combustion plants, specific provisions in the proposed legislation were perceived to interfere directly with goals of energy policy and social and regional policy. Interestingly, references to the economic resources at stake in these substantive connections were exclusively made by individual Member States and supported by their power to block adoption of the directives in question in the Council. With regard to the sulphur content of heavy fuel oil and solid fuels, a number of Member States made clear that they would use this power if necessary and thus prevented further work on the drafts. In the case of the large combustion plants, Spain succeeded in wresting considerable concessions from its partners in this way. The Commission, in contrast (and with respect to the combustion plants maybe in an attempt not to play too much into the hands of Spain and its allies), made hardly any effort to link the fuel and combustion plants issues to EC policies in the fields of energy and regional development.

Fragmented linkage also involves the exchange of resources between a specific issue and other policy areas, but here, one could say, the latter are not specified in substance and time. In other words, fragmented linkage is based on an actor's perception of general political embeddedness of the policy issue in question in the EC as a whole and the anticipation of long-term benefits which – from the nature of the Community – may be assumed to be often of an economic character. It is difficult to pin down the precise impact of fragmented linkage as there are often other, more specific factors that account for the Member States' willingness to embark upon a common policy. Nevertheless, the case study provided two instances where fragmented linkage had a demonstrable effect. In the case of air quality standards, the wish not to frustrate a Community process started by the Commission and supported by only a few Member States can help to explain the co-operative attitude of the other parties, who had little interest in such standards.[7] Fragmented linkage also appears to have played a role in the issue of the large combustion plants. There can be no doubt that the strong German pressure and the rapid support from the Commission and some other northern countries made it difficult for the others not to respond. It should be remembered, however, that in a number of Member States acidification was not perceived as a serious environmental problem until well into the 1980s. The willingness to negotiate the issue and the agreement with the final (considerably weakened) version of the directive may therefore be interpreted as a political concession to Germany and its northern European partners for the sake of the relations in the Community in a more general sense (a similar interpretation to that of Boehmer-Christiansen and Skea, 1991: 249).

Different forms of linkage played a role between issues within the environmental field. First, a conflict about the allocation of economic resources was, as it were, constructed by France in its tactical linkage of the large combustion plants and 'clean' car issues in June 1988. A general substantive connection between the two issues, both related to acidification, of course existed, but no reference to this was actually made. France simply used its legal power to block the large combustion plants directive to force a concession in the small car negotiations. The occurrence of tactical linkage in this period might be related to the greater issue density in the Environment Council in the 1980s, which created more opportunities for the coupling of issues. It should be noted, however, that also at that moment the coincidence of two major environmental issues in the final stage of decision making was the exception rather than the rule.[8] Secondly, a genuinely substantive connection between the emission of ammonia, the problem of acidification, and nitrate policy[9] was recognised and to some extent taken up in domestic policies in the Netherlands, but not at the EC level (with the incidental exception of the EEB – see chapter 7). As argued, Dutch actors had strategic reasons not to stimulate the rapid establishment of such linkages. The introduction of unleaded petrol in the early 1980s, finally, constituted a case of substantive linkage without entailing resource conflicts. On the contrary, the congruence of the German wish to create the conditions for the use of catalytic converters and the British concern about the health effects of lead produced an unexpected (and rather short-lived) coalition between the two countries on this point (chapter 6).

Considering these findings, the ad hoc quality of the issue linkages at stake throughout the period covered by the case study is striking. Horizontal dependencies were mostly perceived in relation to specific elements of (draft) directives. In negotiations this led to specific concessions or even to the withdrawal of the entire proposal. No balancing of resource claims at a more encompassing level took place, however, for instance between car emission and transport policies, between the reduction of emission from large stationary sources and the principles of EC energy policy, or between nitrate policy, ammonia emissions and the Common Agricultural Policy. Moreover, as far as linkages were established, this originated at the level of the Member States. On the basis of their perception of interference with – mostly domestic – policies on other issues or issue areas, national governments went to Brussels with sets of requirements, for instance regarding the fuel mix or the projected increase in energy production. Those requirements usually did not leave much room for bargaining, and functioned as prior conditions rather than starting points for the negotiation process. Horizontal interdependence thus tended to have a rather static character.

The dominance of issue linkage at the national level may be in part explained by the lack of comprehensive and concrete EC policies in, for instance, the fields of transport and energy. This can also account for the absence of spill-over from those fields to the environmental issue area.[10] In fact the well developed Common

Agricultural Policy would be the most obvious candidate for 'pulling' other issues to the EC level, but, for example, the ammonia issue was quite deliberately restricted to the national level. The finding that issue linkage takes place primarily in a domestic context could also be related to the continuously strong national focus of acidification policy, which also came to light in the previous sections. If the basic features of such policies were established domestically, it should be no surprise that horizontal resource dependencies were defined and handled mainly at this level and subsequently functioned as often rather restrictive conditions for policy making in Brussels.

The transfer of sovereignty, or the strength of national environmental policy

Throughout this study, for practical reasons, the group of EC measures relating to pollution by acidifying substances has been referred to as EC acidification policy. It may be questioned, however, whether an 'acidification policy' as such exists at the Community level. The case study and the above discussion showed a number of directives and drafts that were only loosely related and motivated mainly by issue-specific, mostly economic factors. Horizontal relations with other issues regarding acidification, environmental policy in general or other policy fields were established predominantly at the national level. Moreover, at least for the Netherlands, it appeared that the majority of basic decisions in acidification policy were made between public and private actors domestically, which then provided a firm basis for negotiations in Brussels. Only minor encroachments upon those domestic agreements had to be accepted. This was true for the 1980s even more than for the 1970s. EC measures with respect to acidification thus never became an integrated part of Dutch policies in this field, but instead continued to be in essence an additional stage *after* domestic decision making. Finished products were carried to Brussels, as it were, rather than the tools and materials necessary to make them. In the present section this general conclusion will be further elaborated, leading to an interpretation in terms of a differentiated shift of sovereignty. It will also examine to what extent this analysis, based on empirical evidence from the Netherlands, can be extended to other Member States.

*The Dutch case: improving the conditions for domestic
environmental policy*

In the 1970s, Dutch national legislation preceded Community
negotiations about the same issue. The notification of the Dutch
Decree on the sulphur content of fuels was claimed to be one of the
sources of inspiration for the Commission proposal in this field (see
chapter 5) and the first advisory air quality standards had already
been set in the Netherlands, in 1971. In the 1980s the EC started to
catch up. The large combustion plants proposal relatively quickly
followed the German GFAV. Even then, however, the Dutch domestic
decision-making process about the BEES and negotiations in the
Community hardly intermingled. Once agreement on the outline of
the BEES had been reached, the Dutch Government carefully kept to
this. Before then, it behaved rather passively in Brussels and left the
role of initiator to Germany. This in fact points to the continuous
relevance of the observation made by Moltke in 1979 that domestic
environmental decision making is generally regarded as 'pre-, not to
say extra-European' (Moltke, 1979: 85). Only the 'clean' car case
was different: the Netherlands, with the modest size of its market
and its small domestic car industry, was hardly in a position to take
action independently of the EC partners. This did not prevent Dutch
public and private actors from pulling strongly together, however,
largely owing to strong differences of opinion in the relevant
umbrella organisations.

   This raises the question of why an environmentally progressive
country such as the Netherlands should be interested in an EC
environmental policy at all. It goes without saying that measures
regarding air pollution at the national level were taken for
environmental and not for economic reasons. The wish to reduce or
to remove the competitive disadvantages created by those measures
was, however, the primary motivation for advocating Community
policies. Dutch industry in principle shared this interest, but,
particularly in the 1980s, the fact that it had previously committed
(or at least reconciled) itself to comparatively strict domestic policies
manoeuvred it into a minority position among industrial actors from
other Member States. This in turn reinforced the harmony between
Dutch public and private actors and the latter's reliance on the
Government's willingness, if necessary, to use its resources in the
Council. From the available literature an essentially similar picture
emerges for Germany.

This is not to say that environmental aspects were of no relevance at the EC level at all. For the Netherlands, however, the possible reduction of transboundary pollution as a result of EC policies was seen in the context of established domestic policies, that is, with a view to the realisation of national deposition targets. In fact even the Dutch *Alleingang* with regard to the 'clean' car in 1988/89 was defended domestically with reference to national environmental policy goals. Notwithstanding the evidently transboundary character of this issue in all respects, the strengthening of European environmental policy was not regarded as a relevant argument here.

For public actors at the Community level, and particularly the Commission's DG XI, the perception of environmental problems on a genuinely European scale was more important. In the Environmental Action Programmes and in a limited number of more specific documents, including one on acidification (COM(83)721), the Commission attempted to develop a comprehensive view as a basis for a coherent EC environmental policy, but this did not prevent the initiation of EC policies continuing to be based largely on other, particularly economic interests of the Member States. If such interests were absent or if economic interests countervailing common action dominated, the Commission's efforts were in vain (heavy fuel) or the issue was not taken up at all (ammonia).

Economic versus ecological sovereignty
Summarising the argument so far, the broadening of EC acidification policy in the 1980s was nourished by the specific effects of national policies on economic life in some of the Member States rather than by its own dynamic. From an environmental point of view, the development of EC acidification policy thus remained fragmented and primarily followed the logic of the internal market. This observation underlines the continual importance of the general spill-over process from the original core activity of the EC, internal market policy, to environmental policy, long after the crisis of the late 1960s (see chapter 2). The predominance of the internal market focus was illustrated by the fact that the Single Act prescribed the qualified majority rule only for measures directly related to the functioning of the common market (Article 100A). Genuinely 'environmental' policies remained under the unanimity rule (Article 130S) and thus, for the time being, outside the most far-reaching step in the deepening of European integration in this period (see further

chapter 10). The observation also suggests that the role of DG XI was in practice hardly more than that of a joint secretariat, essentially not unlike the secretariats of specific international treaties, but covering a much broader range of subjects and limited in its scope not so much by a restricted mandate as by its being subordinate to the more powerful demands of the internal market.

It thus appears that the perception of international interdependence in the economic dimension was considerably more influential than that in the ecological dimension. The Netherlands in fact gave up few of its powers to determine (or at least to set objectives regarding) the ecological quality of its territory, that is, its sovereignty in the ecological dimension. The Community then mainly served to improve the conditions for controlling environmental problems at the domestic level. The transfer of sovereignty, in other words, remained essentially limited to the economic dimension and entailed the review of the ordering of the market after the establishment of national environmental objectives and policies. The analysis of the build-up of EC environmental policy in terms of different dimensions of sovereignty thus adds a crucial nuance to the established, public-choice oriented interpretation of national governments' willingness to engage in common policies. Moravcsik (1993: 507), for instance, points out that EC institutions strengthen the power of governments in two ways: first, by increasing the efficiency of interstate bargaining (see also Keohane, 1984), and secondly by reinforcing the positions of national political leaders vis-à-vis domestic interest groups. In the present study, the latter factor appeared to be largely irrelevant. Instead, the study suggested that the question of either preservation or pooling of sovereignty involves the interaction of complex political processes at both levels of governance, in which the responses of various actors in different dimensions of sovereignty may counterbalance each other.

It should be realised, however, that the preponderance of the pooling of economic sovereignty over the pooling of ecological sovereignty is probably not due only to the embeddedness of environmental policy in the basically economic orientation of the EC as such or to the consistent dominance of national economic over national environmental interests. An additional factor is the impossibility of 'translating' the challenge of sovereignty in the ecological dimension, such as the impairment of environmental quality by transboundary air pollution, into 'ecological' resources that can be mobilised to exert pressure in international negotiations. As far as interest in EC environmental measures was ecologically motivated, therefore, it had to be expressed in terms of the other dimensions of sovereignty and interdependence. As military power was excluded by being disproportionate, both for the EC context and for familiar environmental issues such as acidification, this had to entail resources drawn from either the economic or the political dimension. As analysed above, Germany's use of its economic power to force the EC partners to accept the introduction of unleaded petrol and catalytic converters in cars was motivated by the wish to mitigate the economic effects of domestic legislation in this field as well as by the ecological argument of reducing the 'import' of pollutants. In most cases, however, as pointed out, the latter kind of arguments were at best of secondary importance.

The Dutch case in a broader perspective

The thesis of a limited shift of sovereignty in the ecological as compared with the economic dimension seems to be convincing for the Netherlands, but would it also apply to other Member States? This is questionable. If the evolution of environmental objectives and policies at the national level and their effect on economic life were indeed the principal factors behind the growth of EC environmental policy, it is obvious that this could be true only of a few countries in which domestic policies preceded EC legislation and who were thus able to initiate or stimulate EC efforts. The Netherlands generally belonged to this group, usually together with some other environmentally more progressive Member States, notably Denmark and Germany since the early 1980s.[11] Other countries, such as the UK, France and the Mediterranean Member States, however, often had not (or not yet) established elaborate national policies that could act as a basis for bargaining and were confronted with policy initiatives at the EC level, including the environmental objectives underlying them.[12] This particularly applied to acidification, which was perceived as a minor problem in the southern Member States. Specific policies in this field hardly existed in those countries. As a result, they themselves had neither economic nor environmental interests in EC acidification policies, which accounts for their predominantly reluctant attitude and their attempts to slow down, to temper and to propose exemptions (see La Spina and Sciortino, 1993).

In fact the question arises of why the complete rejection of proposals remained limited to the heavy fuel case. This can be explained only by economic and political pressure from the other Member States. Economic pressure was exerted most openly by Germany with regard to the 'clean' car. The prospect of a splitting of the European car market with the threat of *Alleingang* by the most powerful actor in that market was no doubt the most important reason to keep the negotiations going, despite crises. A similarly strong economic interest in Community harmonisation did not exist in the case of the large combustion plants. On the contrary, unilateral measures would here only damage the country that introduced them. The considerable concessions, granted particularly by the German presidency in the last phase of decision making, are consistent with this view. It is almost certain, however, that an international agreement between a comparable group of States would never have been reached at all outside the context of the EC, with its strong basis of political commitment and long-term reciprocity.

As this phenomenon of fragmented linkage in the Community refers mainly to the economic dimension, it can be argued that the environmentally less progressive Member States were taken along in common environmental policies mainly on the basis of (the perception of) economic interdependence. For those countries, the EC led to new policies that would otherwise not have been initiated, or at least not in that way and at that time. This process, which may be labelled the geographical spill-over of environmental policies, is undoubtedly a form of interference with national sovereignty, not only in the economic but also in the ecological dimension.[13]

Conclusion

This book started with the question of to what extent the increasing involvement of the EC in environmental policy was leading to a stronger interrelation between national and Community policy making and, possibly, to a shift of sovereignty in this field. Is the environmental policy really being 'taken over' by the Community, or is it not? The answer appears to be both yes and no, or rather: it depends on the perspective.

It cannot be denied that the EC has built up substantial powers in the environmental policy field that were formerly located exclusively in the domain of national sovereignty. The study showed, however, that this process was inextricably bound up with the pooling of sovereignty in the economic dimension. The motor behind the development of EC air pollution policy was hardly the perception of interdependence in the ecological dimension. Instead, the economic consequences of national environmental policies were perceived in the context of growing economic interdependence and the EC's tried and tested response to this. In this sense, it was argued, the findings confirmed the enduring importance of the process of general sector spill-over from internal market to environmental policy.

But what did this mean in practice? It appeared that, *effectively*, the environmental policy powers of the Member States that initiated the EC process were hardly affected. The political process of discussing and establishing policy goals and measures between public and private actors remained essentially at the domestic level. Exactly because they determined the agenda and the terms of EC negotiations, governments of countries such as the Netherlands and Germany were able to exploit the EC to strengthen and facilitate their national environmental policies, which themselves remained largely untouched. For those countries, in short, the Europeanisation of environmental policy did not pre-empt or replace national policy in this field. It rather entailed the establishment of an *additional* level of governance, as it were 'on top of' domestic environmental policy making and improving the control of its economic aspects in particular. Arguably, sovereignty in the ecological field was substantially limited in practice only in Member States that followed rather than initiated the EC initiatives.

Note

1   This is not to say that national economic interests were neglected, as is illustrated by the willingness of the Dutch Government to defend, if necessary, the 1.4-litre limit for small cars in the interest of Volvo Car (see chapter 6).

2   The strong interest of other Member States in a common policy concerning car emissions in fact gave the Germans the forceful political instrument of the threat of *Alleingang* (see the discussion below).

3   This kind of policy, with an element of *divide et impera*, is not uncommon in international (environmental) politics. See for instance the preference of Italy and some other West European countries for the United Nations Environment Programme instead of the OECD as a framework for international policies concerning chlorofluorocarbons in the 1980s (Kakebeeke, 1993: 28–29).

4   In other Member States, particularly those where domestic environmental policy is not so often ahead of EC initiatives, the preparation of EC standpoints may be not as closely related to (the making of) national measures as in the Netherlands or Germany. This does not, however, affect the basic argument that national governments in many cases act as an intermediary in defending industrial interests in Brussels.

5   Informational resources were also important as a bargaining resource for public actors. One of the reasons why the Netherlands was taken seriously by the big car-producing countries in the 'clean' car negotiations was the technical expertise available in the Ministry of VROM. Denmark's positions, in contrast, were often considerably less well regarded, not only because of their relatively radical character, but also because of their reportedly weak technical basis.

6   As explained in chapter 3, the balance between the ecological and economic (internal market) aspects of environmental problems is considered to be the central element of the policy focus of the EC environmental policy network (discussed above). The present section deals with relations between environmental issues, with other sectoral issue areas, and with the EC process as a whole.

7   The other part of the explanation was that air quality standards were relatively innocuous, especially when compared with the alternative of emission standards, which was gradually appearing in Commission documents and some national policies, notably in the Netherlands. In contrast, the heavy fuel oil proposal, which was economically more significant, was rejected by a number of Member States despite the possible impact of fragmented linkage (see chapter 5).

8   Tactical linkage between completely different issues dealt with in different Councils did not occur in the case study and may in fact be considerably less likely, except for major, highly controversial issues which have been 'elevated' to the level of the General Council (of Foreign Ministers) or even the European Council (of Heads of State and Government). This seldom happens to environmental issues, however. The diffuse and untraceable package deals between air pollution and totally different issues in the EC arena suggested by Roqueplo (1988: 139–140) are better included under the heading of fragmented linkage (see above).

9   Besides the fact that the issues of ammonia and nitrate were both primarily related to the livestock industry and, if taken seriously, demanded considerable investment in this sector, there was the classic problem of the shift of environmental pollution from one medium to another, in this case from the air to ground and surface water, or vice versa.

10   Spill-over processes from EC environmental policy to other issue areas were not expected anyway, in view of the difficulties in 'integrating' environmental considerations into other fields (see chapter 3), and did not occur. The spill-over process at a more aggregated level from internal market policy to environmental (and other post-industrial) policy goals will be discussed in the next section.

11   In order to be effective in the Community context, the 'lead' countries would have to share basic interests in the environmental policy field and not

cut one another's throats in Brussels. In air pollution issues, Germany, the Netherlands and Denmark appeared to agree on essential points, but close co-operation was usually prevented by differences in priorities and strategies. The shape and importance of coalitions in EC policy making deserve further study, especially in view of qualified majority voting in the framework of the Single Act and the 'Maastricht' Treaty (see chapter 10).

12 In addition, Member States such as Germany and the Netherlands sometimes came upon provisions in EC proposals that did not correspond with existing national policies. The Netherlands, for instance, had to deal at least twice with proposals that were in conflict with national policy: the limit of 0.2 per cent sulphur content instead of 0.15 per cent in the revision of the gas oil directive in 1987 and the absence of a special refinery regime in the large combustion plants draft. In addition, several compromises had to be accepted during the 'clean' car process. Concessions in the ecological field in the shape of laxer environmental standards (gas oil, 'clean' car) were eventually made in order that any sort of agreement about harmonising standards could be reached at all. In contrast, the Dutch Government firmly held to the important economic point of the refinery regime until an exemption had been obtained. This once more underlines that EC policy was perceived as a means to mitigate negative economic consequences of domestic environmental measures rather than as a response to the perception of interdependence in the ecological dimension.

13 This interpretation is supported by many analyses of environmental policies in the southern Member States that stress the importance of EC environmental legislation as the main driving force behind national policy programmes in this field. See, for instance, Bennett (1991) for the specific field of air pollution; La Spina and Sciortino (1993), Aguilar Fernández (1993) and Pridham (1994).

10

Epilogue: constants and shifts in EC environmental policy making

Introduction

This study focused on environmental policy making on the borderline between the State and the EC. It turned out that the Europeanisation of environmental policy was not a simple, unremitting process. As far as the policy field could be observed to be 'moving' to Brussels, it was for quite specific, often predominantly economic reasons and with a firm domestic background. While the previous chapter developed and elaborated this conclusion on the basis of the empirical findings, one may wonder what these insights actually tell us about the practice of environmental policy making in the EC. This question is of particular interest against the background of the observation made earlier (chapter 2) that the output of theorising about the 'day-to-day' policy process in Brussels has so far been fairly limited. It is not my ambition to develop a full theory of EC environmental policy making here, but in the form of four propositions about what I see as basic characteristics of the process, I hope to add some elements to the debate.

Before doing so, however, it is useful to evaluate in some more detail to what extent the empirical material collected in this study allows for more general conclusions. With the advantage of hindsight I will attempt to assess the ways in which the choice of the particular field of air pollution and acidification has coloured the results of the case study.

A chapter like this, finally, provides an opportunity to look ahead and to venture some thoughts on the future development of the research object. In the final section I will address the effect that the drastic shifts in European political relations may have on environmental policy making in the EC or, rather, the European Union (EU).

Central issues are the implications of the institutional changes brought about by the 'Maastricht' Treaty and the consequences of the extension of the Union to fifteen and possibly more Member States, which in turn may lead again to, probably more far-reaching, political and institutional responses.

The case study approach in retrospect

As pointed out before, the case study which forms the core of this book had two major limitations: the restriction of the subject matter to policies in the field of air pollution and acidification, and the concentration on the relationship between the EC and one Member State, the Netherlands. In what sense did this produce a bias in the outcomes of the study and does it offer opportunities for generalisation to EC environmental policy in a wider sense?

The case study was about the issue area of acidification, but in fact consisted of five relatively distinct policy issues. Their common feature was the preoccupation with the group of pollutants responsible for the problem of acidification (sulphur dioxide, nitrogen oxides and ammonia) and the relevant group of sources. In the introduction to the case study (chapter 4), it was argued that this disaggregate approach was necessary, because the making of individual directives was assumed to be by far the most important locus of interaction between actors in EC environmental policy. This raises two questions, first about the adequacy of this approach, and secondly about the extent to which it is possible to draw more general conclusions on the basis of this case study.

The question about the adequacy of the approach on the basis of individual directives has to be considered with some caution, as the findings of this study may be biased by this very approach. Nevertheless, the case study appears to provide sufficient and convincing evidence that linkage between issues was generally ad hoc and that attempts to bring about a more comprehensive view of environmental policy making at the Community level were made mainly by the Commission and had only a limited impact. Considerations related to European integration in a broader sense proved to be relevant in certain situations and for some countries, but as far as acidification was concerned hardly at all for the

Netherlands. This indicates that the level of aggregation beyond that of individual directives was indeed of relatively minor importance. Actors, in short, came to Brussels for concrete policies and not for broad plans and programmes.

As a consequence, one might say, the development of EC acidification policy remained essentially a 'bottom-up' process, consisting of the 'accumulation' of specific measures. Thus, changes in the character of the accumulated measures and the processes leading to those measures did not just reflect but were themselves the substance of the development of the broader policy field. The problem of the generalisation of the outcomes of the present study then comes down to the question of whether the changes observed in the issues constituting the field of acidification are representative of shifts in other areas of environmental policy. This question can only be answered with the help of additional empirical research, but two factors may have coloured the findings.

First, the problem of acidification attracted considerable attention in some Member States in the 1980s. This was not as strongly the case for topics such as waste, water pollution or industrial hazards. The strong domestic concern about acidification, particularly in Germany but also in the Netherlands, may have reinforced the observed tendency to formulate national policies without gratuitous delay, that is, in advance of (negotiations about) EC legislation. This circumstance may also have strengthened relationships and loyalties between domestic actors, which continued to play a role when the issue was taken up at the EC level. Together with the controversial nature of the issue, this may have added, for instance, to the weak performance of umbrella organisations. It should be added, however, that the pre-existence of domestic policy networks in itself is in no way unique to acidification. At least as far as the Netherlands is concerned, domestic policies and consequently domestic policy networks were already in place in almost every environmental policy area before the EC got involved.

As a second specific characteristic, acidification had an evidently transboundary character, equalled only by a few other environmental issues, such as climate change, pollution of large international water courses and transfrontier shipment of waste. This factor can in fact be argued to have an effect opposite to that of the first one, as it would logically stimulate carrying the issue to the international level. Given that the ecological aspects of acidification were dealt with internationally only to a limited extent, in other words, this may be expected to be even less so for issues with less obviously trans-boundary features.

The relatively strong domestic attention to acidification in the Netherlands, Germany and some other countries, in sum, may have caused a certain bias with regard to the involvement of domestic actors. In general, however, there is little reason to assume that the principal findings of this study do not hold for other environmental policy fields as well. For instance, the predominantly economic policy focus at the EC level and the ad hoc quality of horizontal linkages appear as properties of the policy system under consideration rather than being restricted to one specific issue. The increasingly central role in the process of the Member State governments as holders of decisive legal powers in the Council may also be expected to be a more general trend, since the driving force behind this trend, the growing substance to EC involvement during the 1980s, could also be observed in other areas of environmental policy (see chapter 1).

Apart from the subject matter, the necessary focus on one Member State narrowed down the scope of the case study. In the previous chapter it was pointed out that some of the conclusions are probably not valid for all EC countries. In particular, the observation that the shift to the EC level of sovereignty in the ecological dimension was very limited compared with that in the economic dimension is likely to be specific to the Member States with relatively well developed and institutionalised environmental policies, including the Nether-lands but also Germany and Denmark. Since 1995, Sweden, Finland and Austria may be added to this group. To obtain a more complete picture of the process and the impact of the Europeanisation of environmental policy, further research should be conducted, particularly in the Member States that follow rather than initiate EC efforts in this field. In order to test the findings of this study, in addition, similar investigations in Germany, Denmark or the new Member States would be interesting.

A second bias related to the selection of the Dutch case may be caused by the country's attitude to the EC and EC policy making in general. Generally speaking, the Dutch Government has always been one of the strongest proponents of European integration, as last illustrated by its (unsuccessful) attempts to give considerable 'federalist' accents to the 'Maastricht' Treaty. In day-to-day acidific-ation policy, however, ideological aspects appear to have played a very small role; the Dutch approach here might be characterised as 'positive-pragmatic'. In countries such as France, the UK, Spain or Denmark, in contrast, where the pros and cons of European integration are traditionally much more subject to public debate, ideological and strategic positions in this respect are probably more prominent, especially in relatively specialised policy fields such as the environment. When conducting a similar study in other Member States, this should be reflected in a more detailed elaboration of the concept of fragmented linkage.

Finally, it has to be realised that the Netherlands is only a medium-size Member State that does not have the same political weight and impact in Brussels as for instance Germany or France. This observation strongly supports the findings of this study. Since the Netherlands has a relatively limited ability to push through its own strategies and solutions in Brussels, this underlines that the persistence of ecological sovereignty at the national level is a feature of the two-level policy system itself rather than a matter of power among the Member States.

Implications for understanding the EC environmental policy process: four propositions

This study set out to examine the interaction and intertwining of the national and the Community level in environmental policy making. The conclusion drawn in the previous chapter was that the inter-twining of the two levels did not proceed as quickly and as fully as one might have expected. At least from the point of view of Member States with relatively developed national environmental policies, the challenge to sovereignty in the ecological dimension, that is, the gradual erosion of the power to determine the (ecological) quality of the national territory as a result of increasingly transboundary environmental impacts, led to little pooling of sovereignty in this dimension. Instead, environmental objectives and policies continued to be established largely at the national level and, generally speaking, only their consequences in the economic dimension (i.e. in relation to the growing intertwining of national economies) gave rise to common measures. This was interpreted as illustrating the continual importance of the process of sector spill-over from internal market policy to the adjacent policy field of the environment. This conclusion basically answers the questions posed at the beginning of this book, but the question immediately following from it is, under what circumstances and in what way will this spill-over take place? Or, more pragmatically, what does it mean for the 'day-to-day' practice of environmental policy making in Brussels?

It seems to me that the findings of this study can be turned into four simple but fundamental propositions which may help to understand the process and outcomes of negotiations about environmental issues in the Community. They are intended as starting points for discussion and further research rather than as definitive conclusions. The propositions are:

(i)   The Member State level still makes sense in the analysis of EC environmental policy making.

(ii) Existing national policies play a crucial role in the design of EC environmental measures.

(iii) Apart from issue-specific factors, the sense of political commitment and long-term reciprocity (fragmented linkage) prevalent in the EC is needed to explain the progress of EC environmental policy.

(iv) EC environmental policy making is essentially about economics.

The first proposition prepares the ground for the other three. The case study suggests that domestic policies continue to be important as points of departure, both in the initial phase and in the decision-making phase of EC environmental policy. The balance between the Member States and the supranational institutions of the Community might turn out somewhat differently for other policy areas within the environmental field. Further systematic empirical research would give more insight into this question. Moreover, it should be remembered that this relationship is a highly dynamic one. The recent developments in the field of air pollution indeed point to certain changes. While for instance the issues of the regulation of sulphur emissions from the oil industry (see chapter 7), the monitoring and evaluation of air quality and the incineration of hazardous waste were strongly inspired by national policies or pressure from Member States, the initiative and content of some other proposals (for instance those on integrated pollution prevention and control, and on industrial emissions of volatile organic compounds) appear to have followed partly from efforts on the part of the Commission to establish a more comprehensive 'programme' for the policy area (Héritier *et al.*, 1994). The initial phase of the EC's climate policy was also characterised by a leading role of the Commission (Jachtenfuchs and Huber, 1993; Huber, forthcoming), but it should be noted that the issue was subsequently held up by the Council for a number of years. In the important issue of waste packaging materials, on the other hand, the emergence of divergent national legislation was instrumental in bringing about EC initiatives (Porter and Butt Philip, 1993). The picture may be somewhat less unambiguous than suggested in earlier chapters, in short, but I think it is still safe to assert that in the context of the day-to-day process of EC environmental policy making, the nation state remains a major and in many senses decisive arena for developing new policies and for balancing various societal forces and interests.

Regardless of the question of whether national policies really served as the basis of any particular Commission initiative, as in most of the case study issues, or if the connection was slightly more diffuse, it is clear that few policy problems are taken up by the Community which are not yet covered by (draft) legislation in at least one or a small number of Member States. This study indicated that such 'pre-existing' domestic policies have a· very strong tendency to become virtually immovable points of reference for the Member State's input in Brussels. The reason for this is obvious: EC directives which are as close as possible to existing national regulation not only facilitate the administrative process of implementation, but also render it unnecessary to renegotiate carefully constructed domestic compromises about the form and content of the measures.

The situation of certain countries that already have or are developing their own policies with regard to an issue just being taken up by the Community and others not having such policies results in a division between the Member States which may be very important for the process of policy making. Since they have developed their own policies, the former group of countries may be expected to have a perceived 'domestic' interest in policy responses to the environ-mental problem in question. As demonstrated, EC legislation is in that case regarded as relevant primarily because it may help to take away the competitive disadvantages of unilateral measures, but at the same time it should not interfere too much with the domestic approach. The second group of countries has essentially the same economic interest in the proper functioning of the internal market. Somewhat simplistically, however, it can be assumed that they do not have a particular interest in the environmental aspects of the issue. Competitive effects of national policies being absent, in other words, they are likely to be against EC involvement or, if this cannot be avoided, to press for the lowest possible common standards. Between these two extremes, there are often some countries that have a more 'neutral' stance and, within certain limits, do not object to international measures, without initiating them themselves (see Héritier *et al.*, 1994: 126–127, presenting France as a typical example of what may be called the 'benevolent followers'). Especially in cases of qualified majority voting, the exact position of those countries can be crucial.

Considering this basic division among the Member States, which I think can be identified in varying compositions in almost every instance of EC environmental policy making, it may be wondered how the EC environmental policy field has been able to grow so quickly. This is in fact the question of why and under what circumstances the general spill-over process from internal market to environmental policy actually takes place. There appear to be two types of forces at work here, both discussed in the previous chapter. The first type entails issue-specific forces, most important of which is the economic pressure to harmonise divergent national standards. This particularly applies to divergent product standards, which may directly inhibit intra-Community trade. As illustrated by the 'clean' car, countries which are sufficiently able to 'hurt' other Member States can actively make use of this by establishing (or threatening) unilateral standards. In addition, Member States can exert political pressure on the Commission or on other countries, as for instance Germany did in the large combustion plants case. The latter kind of pressure, however, cannot be separated from the political context in which it is exerted. In this regard, as pointed out at the beginning of this book, the EC is unique, as the scope and intensity of co-operation produces a strong sense of long-term reciprocity. The air quality standards of the early 1980s and the large combustion plants directive are probably just two of many pieces of EC environmental legislation that would not have been possible without the Member States' basic conviction that making a certain amount of concessions in the context of the Community in the end does pay.[1] Fragmented linkage, thus, is the second type of force necessary to explain EC involvement in environmental policy, both at the level of individual measures and at the aggregate level of sector spill-over. This is expressed in the third proposition.

The fourth proposition refers to the negotiation process itself. It has already been pointed out that the major interest shared by all Member States in EC environmental policy making is in fact an economic one: the avoidance of barriers to trade and unequal conditions of competition. Once an issue has been taken up by the Community, therefore, it should not be surprising that the Member States' bargaining positions are primarily based on a constellation of economic interests and that negotiations are conducted primarily in economic terms. This tendency is enhanced by the circumstance that environmental goals can be formulated and pursued at the EC level, but that 'ecological' resources to lend force to demands in this field do not exist (see chapter 2). Among other things, this insight can help to explain the watering down of proposals in compromises, which often occurs in the final, decisive phase of EC negotiations, for instance in the large combustion plants case. Because of the lack of specific 'ecological' resources, bargaining leverage needed for a compromise on one aspect of the issue can in practice only take the form of relaxation of requirements and lowering of costs on another aspect. The consequences of this can be particularly dramatic in the case of unanimous voting in the Council. Unwilling Member States are then able to use their de facto power of veto on substantive issues for improving their distributive positions (Scharpf, 1985, 1988). In the case of the large combustion plants, through tactical linkage, this negative 'negotiation spiral' in the end even involved a wholly different issue, the 'clean' car.

The recent treaty revisions and the more frequent use of qualified majority voting in the Council have changed the legal resources available to the Member States and thus considerably limited the opportunities for following the above 'blackmail' strategy. Instead of being able to block the adoption of measures individually, Member States under qualified majority voting have to join forces to pressurise the decision-making process. It should be noted, though, that this is true both for countries that consider proposed measures too lax and for those that consider them too strict, that is, too demanding for their national economy. As the Member State representing the most radical position in the discussions has to look for allies in the Council, qualified majority voting has the general effect of moderating the extremes of the bargaining process and broadening the margins of common decisions. This was illustrated by the 'clean' car case: whereas Denmark and Greece were able to paralyse the Luxembourg compromise in 1985, they had to give up their resistance and accept the solution designed by the other parties after the coming into force of the Single Act.

The partial abandonment of the veto in the environmental field and the increased need for coalition building following the Single Act and the 'Maastricht' Treaty may at first sight seem to affect seriously the pivotal role of individual Member States in the process and to herald the genuine erosion of national sovereignty. In the next, final section of this chapter, which attempts to look ahead to the future development of EU environmental policy, this argument will be further developed. It will be contended, however, that other tendencies may counterbalance these shifts. In view of that, I claim, the basic tenor of the four propositions presented here can as yet be maintained.

The European Union: the future development of environmental policy

The 'Maastricht' Treaty, European Union,[2] enlargement in the northern and maybe the eastern direction: the process of European integration may receive more criticism today than at the end of the 1980s, but it has certainly not lost its dynamism. Institutional modifications and the establishment of a new balance of power between fifteen or more Member States will inevitably affect the course of the environmental policy field. Will the connection between the two levels of governance in the environmental field continue to be fragmented and essentially market oriented, or will the developments of the 1990s force Member States to make a more fundamental choice between national policy making and 'the way to Brussels'? This section will attempt to spy out the land in the light of the findings of this study, starting with the ramifications of the treaty revisions.

The Single Act and 'Maastricht'
In the Single Act, which entered into force in 1987, qualified majority voting was introduced for legislation directly related to the

establishment and functioning of the internal market (Article 100A). Apart from that, the Single Act introduced a legal basis for taking measures primarily aimed at the protection of the environment, but here unanimity remained the rule (Article 130R–T). The distinction between two types of environmental measures that could already be observed in the 1970s (see chapter 1) was thus confirmed in the Single Act. The fact that the 'qualitative leap' in the pooling of sovereignty implied by majority voting (Weiler, 1991; also chapter 2) was reserved for the category of immediately trade-related measures indicates that the perception of the Member States' increasing interdependence in the ecological dimension was not among the driving forces behind this step. Genuinely 'environmental' measures continued to be explicitly the domain of national sovereignty. The shift of political sovereignty implied by the Single Act, in other words, although in itself directly relevant to environmental policy, only took place in the wake of the perception of increasing economic interdependence.

The 'Maastricht' Treaty on European Union, in force since the end of 1993, extended qualified majority voting to issues not immediately related to the functioning of the market, including most of the 'genuinely' environmental measures, under Article 130S. It may be argued that this step rather than the Single Act in principle opened the way for the transfer of sovereign powers in the ecological dimension not directly related to interests of trade and competition, and unimpaired by the continuous threat of the de facto power of veto of each Member State. More concretely, it would mean that any Member State could be forced to accept ecological policy goals and norms against its will. As argued, this was in practice already the case for the Member States that had not yet installed domestic policies when EC measures were adopted, but now they would have considerably fewer resources to wrest economic compensation during the negotiations or on the longer term. In addition, the environmentally more advanced Member States could now more easily be confronted with common environmental policies not conforming to their own domestic models.

This development could be regarded as a corollary of the growing interdependence in the ecological dimension: it would reflect the Member States' perception that the latitude for independently determining domestic ecological quality is gradually shrinking because of increasing flows of pollution, polluting products, technologies and so on across boundaries.[3] The Fifth Environmental Action Programme (EAP 1993–2000), proposed by the Commission in 1992 and approved by the Member States in February 1993, had anticipated this change. More than its predecessors, it attempted to formulate integrated environmental policy objectives at the Union level.

Nevertheless, it may be doubted whether the 'Maastricht' Treaty and the Fifth Action Programme will indeed constitute the basis of a new phase in the pooling of ecological sovereignty in the EU. By extending qualified majority voting to fields other than the historical core activity of the Community – the establishment of the internal market – 'Maastricht' further strengthened decisional supranationality (Weiler, 1982; see also chapter 2) and implied a new and fundamental step in the process of European integration, only a few years after the Single Act. Whereas the abandonment of unanimous voting in the earlier treaty revision occurred in the relatively clear-cut context of the '1992' project, the new modifications were much more open ended. Although some types of measure were explicitly excluded from qualified majority voting, particularly in the new text of Article 130S, the crucial resource of the Member States in bargaining over common measures was put in jeopardy. Concern about the shift in the balance between national and EU powers had surfaced during the negotiations (Dehousse, 1992). In order to restore the equilibrium, a general reference to the so-called subsidiarity principle was added to the basic principles of the Treaty:

> In areas which do not fall within its exclusive competence, the Community shall take action, in accordance with the principle of subsidiarity, only if and in so far as the objectives of the proposed action cannot be sufficiently achieved by the Member States and can therefore, by reason of the scale or effects of the proposed action, be better achieved by the Community.
>
> (Article 3B)

These lines did not take away growing uneasiness about the impacts of 'Maastricht', however. The rejection of the Treaty in the first Danish referendum in 1992 and the laborious process of ratification in other Member States such as France and the UK marked the start of a broad and fundamental debate about the role of the EU vis-à-vis the Member States. The meaning and implications of the notion of subsidiarity played an important role in this debate. Being one of the 'new' areas in which the Community's competences had most dramatically increased in the years before, environmental policy acted as one of the focal points. Existing legislation was also discussed. In December 1993, for instance, the President of the Commission, Jacques Delors, proposed the simplification of twenty-eight directives, several of which dealt with the environment,[4] and even the 'renationalisation' of issues was suggested (Brinkhorst, 1992). Since then, the subsidiarity debate has gradually come to be seen not exclusively as a backdrop to the integration process but also as a step towards a new balance in decisional supranationality. A generally more critical stance to granting policy powers to the EU would then be set off against the increase in the supranational quality of decision making in the Council. It can hardly be denied, though, that 'Maastricht' has left profound marks in the Union's political landscape. It brought about a serious reconsideration of the scope of the EU's activities and a considerably more reticent approach on the part of the Commission. Even more than in other periods, therefore, the initiative to shift more sovereign powers in the ecological dimension to the Union level must now come from the Member States. This study, however, has highlighted the Member States' consistent tendency to make basic ecological choices domestically. In the present situation, it is not likely that this will soon start to change.

Environmental policy making in an enlarged Union
Although the influence of 'Maastricht' on the transfer of ecological sovereignty may be argued to be limited, the (re)introduction of qualified majority voting will in practice undeniably have a substantial impact on decision making in the Council. The increased need to form coalitions with other countries has been referred to. Particularly in this field, the consequences of the other major change of the recent and coming years may be most immediately felt: the accession of new members.

The composition of the Union in relation to the number of votes required for a blocking minority is crucial for the outcome of qualified majority voting. From this point of view, it may be argued that the accession of Austria and the Nordic countries Sweden and Finland will shift the balance in the Council to the more environmentally oriented side. As all those countries have relatively well developed and institutionalised national environmental policies, it should become easier to mobilise a group of countries willing to

block EU legislation that it considers too undemanding. The dispute
about the exact voting requirements after accession of Austria and
the Nordic countries that arose in March 1994 makes clear that the
possible consequences of a new balance in the Council were
recognised by the existing Member States. Spain and the UK, the
principal instigators of the controversy, insisted on retaining the old
threshold of twenty-three (instead of twenty-seven) votes for a
qualified minority, in spite of the increase in the total number of
votes in the Council from seventy-six to ninety. Not raising the
threshold would continue to enable the blocking of any Council
decision for instance by Spain, the UK and one other Member State,
or by the Mediterranean states.[5]

As noted earlier, the power to block decisions is essentially a
negative one. In order to stimulate EU activity, other strategies are
required. In this study, the introduction of domestic legislation was
identified as the main way of provoking common measures,
particularly if product standards are involved (chapter 9; for a
similar view, see Jänicke, 1990: 230). So far, the forerunners in the
environmental field have been mainly individual States, particularly
Germany. For instance the Netherlands has been considerably less
'activist' in this sense, which is at least partly related to its
considerably lower capacity to 'hurt' Member States (other than
itself) by unilateral measures. The accession of the Nordic countries
and Austria may widen the opportunities for the formation of
'forerunner *groups*'. The formation of such groups would take away
part of the competitive disadvantage of single-country initiatives and
at the same time probably carry more weight in the EU context. A
strategy coming close to the one outlined here has been attempted,
for instance with some success by the Netherlands with regard to
refinery emissions (chapter 7), but co-operation at a sub-EU scale as
a pre-stage for genuinely common measures also appears to be in line
with a more general tendency towards more differentiation inside the
Union.[6]

In the wake of the controversies following 'Maastricht' and for
instance the difficulties encountered by many Member States to
comply with the requirements of the European Monetary Union, the
recurrent idea of a 'two-speed Europe' ('*Europe à deux vitesses*') was
once again raised.[7] It would allow Member States to work at
different speeds towards a commonly shared final goal. This
approach had been applied before, in the large combustion plants

directive, which required strongly divergent efforts to reduce emissions of sulphur and nitrogen oxides until 2003 and 1998, respectively. As a single common goal was not defined in the directive; it even tended to genuine differentiation of policy goals rather than *deux vitesses.*

Does the 'two-(or-more-)speed' approach constitute a likely perspective for environmental policy making in the EU? On the one hand, it may be expected that the Nordic/Austrian accession will further emphasise the cleavages with regard to environmental policy in the Union. The pressure to create effective, relatively stringent common measures will increase, but less willing Member States will be able to resist such pressure, practically to the same extent as before. If it turns out to be impossible to establish policies that meet the wishes of the more 'environmentalist' northern countries, this will strengthen the inclination of the latter to maintain stricter domestic standards and to cherish national sovereignty in the ecological field. The result will be a multi-speed Europe, either in a formalised way following the example of the large combustion plants or in an informal way. Particularly in the latter case, the group of ecologically more progressive countries may (but will not necessarily!) function as forerunners in the sense sketched above. On the other hand, there are economic as well as juridical limits to the application of stricter national standards. In principle only product standards require full harmonisation in order to warrant free trade, but competitive disadvantages may force countries to refrain from differentiation of emission norms or environmental quality standards as well. As the north-western Member States are important mutual trading partners, part of this problem would be overcome by forming 'forerunner coalitions', but by no means all of it. What degree of competitive disadvantage the forerunners are willing to bear will depend on the interests of the specific industrial sector in question in relation to the perceived seriousness of the environmental problem.[8] Unless differentiation – be it with a fixed time horizon or not – is formally laid down in EU legislation itself, the Treaty may also set limits to unilateral action. In this context it should be kept in mind that not only divergent product standards but also other types of measures may lead to direct or indirect barriers to trade. The Danish bottle case showed that 'the Internal Market does not preclude differences between environmental standards in the Member States' as long as they are not 'disproportionate' (Koppen, 1993). However, the interpretation of the 'proportionality' of different kinds of measures under various legal conditions has to be further clarified in subsequent cases and it is not at all certain that the Court will maintain its relatively flexible approach to Member States that want to be 'cleaner than the rest' (Koppen, 1993).

Whether environmental regulation in the EU does move towards a multi-speed model will eventually depend on the divergence between the Member States with regard to environmental objectives and standards and the extent to which such divergence is felt to be a problem in relation to other goals of the Union. The principal factors behind this are: the priority given to environmental issues in the 'greener' Member States, the progress of economic integration, and above all the future enlargement of the Union. On the basis of these factors, three possible scenarios can be sketched.

The first scenario is that changes in the three underlying factors remain limited. The backlash in the integration process after 'Maastricht' will continue to be felt. The accession of the Nordic countries and Austria may increase the diversity between the Member States, but tensions between divergent domestic environmental objectives and internal market policies can be accommodated with reference to the subsidiarity principle and with the help of existing constructions. In that case, the present combination of formalised and informal differentiation giving rise to a variety of economic and juridical struggles and 'forerunner effects' will continue.

In the second scenario, the problems connected with divergent standards become more and more pressing. This may be due both to the Nordic/Austrian accession and to a new upswing of the economic integration process, or especially a combination of them both. Growing stresses will push environmental issues more to the centre of the Union's political agenda. One of the outcomes of this study was to show that environmental issues have been treated in the EC so far as somewhat isolated. If linkages with other policy fields were established at all, this was done mainly on an ad hoc basis and at the instigation of one or more Member States whose specific interests were threatened. At the level of individual directives this situation prevented a full balancing at the EC level of the fundamental interests underlying the problems at stake. At a more general level too, however, the isolation of environmental policy was – and still is – expressed by the fact that the field seldom reaches the highest political spheres in the EU, notably the major budgetary deliberations and the general strategic discussions in the European Council of Heads of State and Government. A higher priority to environmental issues, for the reasons given, might lead to a more prominent place of such issues in what may be called the 'big bargains' of the Union, for instance regarding agricultural, structural, internal market or monetary policy.[9] As the environmentally most progressive Member States are all located in the richer, northern part of the Union, environmental policy in this scenario would be linked particularly to the management of north–south relations within the EU. For instance, the structural funds could emerge as a framework for side payments to support environmental policies in the more hesitant southern Member States. Apart from a sharp increase in the perceived urgency of finding truly common solutions for environmental problems, this scenario would require a great willingness on the part of the northern Member States to pay for environmental improvement abroad. If embedded in the context of the structural funds, one can imagine such willingness to exist with regard to countries such as Greece, Spain, Portugal and Ireland. Negotiations about material support for the implementation of common environmental policies can, however, be complicated by the position of countries that are not subject to structural fund programmes but that do lag behind in environmental policy, notably the UK.

The third scenario is that the entire trend outlined here, including the first two scenarios, will be as it were surpassed by a further extension of the Union to include a number of Central and Eastern European States, such as Hungary, the Czech Republic, and Poland. This development would add to the diversity in the Union, not only in the ecological field but in the economic and almost all other policy fields as well. It is almost inevitable that the resulting tensions, combined with the increasing stress on the 'workability' of the Union's institutions (ISEI, 1993), will eventually lead to more fundamental adaptations and in particular to more formal arrangements around the differentiation of policies. This could take the far-reaching form of different types of membership or the explicit formation of a 'core group' in the EU, but one could also think of the more pragmatic solution of creating more room for deviating national policies in areas where the problems are most pressing, presumably including environmental policy. It remains to be seen if the latter should be done by changing the relevant Treaty provisions

(Article 100A, 130T, etc.) or at the level of the specific legislative acts of the Union.

Which scenario is most likely? The second scenario has considerable difficulties. In the first place it is questionable if the required rise of the political salience of environmental issues will take place. Apart from the perceived seriousness of trade barriers related to differentiation of environmental policies, this will depend on the cycles of environmental concern in general. Secondly, the problems associated with fitting environmental policy preferences into a politically acceptable redistribution of financial resources in the EU should not be underestimated. Over the next few years, therefore, the first scenario seems to be the most realistic. Particularly if the accession of Central and Eastern European States happens to be shelved – for whatever reason – EU environmental policy may be confronted with a protracted period of 'muddling through'. The more fundamental political and institutional answer to a multi-speed Europe, outlined in the third scenario, is likely to be provoked only by a further extension of the Union to the east. It should be realised, however, that in that case the outcome in the environmental field will once again be closely linked up with a multitude of political and economic factors. The third scenario, to be sure, would put environmental policy for a while at the mercy of a veritable storm in the process of European integration.

Notes

1   Strong domestic reasons, usually of an economic kind, may still lead Member States to block common measures, despite issue-specific arguments for such measures and despite fragmented linkage. The case study included the example of the sulphur content of heavy fuel oil. The Community's lasting inability to move on the climate issue may provide another.

2   As far as this section refers to the situation after the signing and coming into force of the 'Maastricht' Treaty on European Union, the latter name will be used instead of European Community.

3   A second, relatively minor element in the 'Maastricht' Treaty that might stimulate the transfer of ecological sovereignty to the EU level is the slight extension of the powers of the EP. Not the increase of its powers in the decision-making process itself (particularly the application of the co-operation procedure in most decisions under Article 130S), but rather its growing political credibility resulting from this increase, might enhance its role as instigator of supranational policies, including environmental ones.

4   See *The Environment Digest* (1993), nos 77–78: 17, quoting *The Guardian*, 13 December 1993, *The Independent on Sunday*, 12 December 1993, and *The Independent*, 14, 18 and 20 December 1993.

5   The diplomatic compromise that was eventually constructed at the summit in Ioannina (Greece) in March 1994 prescribed a prolonged attempt to reach agreement in the case of a minority of twenty-three to twenty-seven votes and thus hardly constituted a genuine solution to the problem. This illustrates the difficulty of achieving even a relatively small institutional adaptation. (Note that the figures referred to here were based on the planned accession of Austria, Sweden and Finland as well as Norway. After the membership of the last country had been prevented by a national referendum on 28 November 1994, the critical range for the blocking minority became twenty-three to twenty-six votes out of a total of eighty-seven.)

6   On the innovation of EU environmental policy and the possible role of a 'green' alliance, see: Andersen and Liefferink (forthcoming); Liefferink and Andersen (forthcoming).

7   Considerable attention was, for instance, attracted by an article by the French Minister of European Affairs, Alain Lamassoure, in *Le Monde*, 30 May 1994, advocating the formation of a 'core group' of Member States most strongly committed to the goals of European integration. The other Member States could join later, depending on their specific situations. Some months later, a similar suggestion was made in a discussion paper by the German Christian Democrats (CDU/CSU).

8   It is even conceivable that north-west European countries, perhaps under the influence of multinational firms, have an interest in *maintaining* differences in environmental regulation among the Member States, as this would enable the establishment of a high level of environmental protection domestically, accompanied by a concentration of environmentally more harmful production processes in countries with lower standards. In his thorough study of environmental regulation and competitive advantages, however, Leonard (1988) showed that a flight of investments to so-called 'pollution havens' rarely takes place in practice. For the vast majority of firms the costs and problems related to moving far outweigh the costs of adaptation to stricter environmental norms. If industries flee at all, it may be added, they will probably do so to countries where tightening of standards is not expected in the foreseeable future, rather than to reluctant EU Member States.

9   At present, environmental issues are mainly taken into account in those fields as conditions to specific policies or projects, for instance in the form of environmental requirements on infrastructural projects supported by the structural funds. They are, however, hardly part of the underlying programmatic agreements.

References

I Legislative texts

A The Netherlands (in alphabetical order)

Note: Stb. = *Staatsblad*; Stcrt. = *Staatscourant* (official journals of the Dutch government). Also published in: *Nederlandse staatswetten, editie Schuurman & Jordens*, WEJ Tjeenk Willink, Zwolle (several volumes).

Besluit emissie-eisen stookinstallaties (BEES; Decree emission requirements combustion installations), Stb. 1987, 164; and amendment: Stb. 1991, 354.

Besluit luchtkwaliteit zwaveldioxide en zwevende deeltjes (zwarte rook) (Decree air quality sulphur dioxide and suspended particulates (black smoke)), Stb. 1986, 78.

Besluit zwavelgehalte brandstoffen (Decree sulphur content of fuels), Stb. 1974, 549; last amendment, Stb. 1988, 408.

Circulaire inzake de eisen met de betrekking tot de uitworp van luchtverontreinigende stoffen door kolengestookte installaties, Stcrt. 1982, 192: 9.

Circulaire over de luchtverontreiniging door kolengestookte installaties, Stcrt. 1981, 174: 4 (summary).

Hinderwet (Nuisance Act), Stb. 1952, 274.

Meststoffenwet (Fertilisers Act), Stb. 1986, 598.

Wet Bodembescherming (Soil Protection Act), Stb. 1986, 374.

Wet inzake de luchtverontreiniging (Air Pollution Act), Stb. 1970, 580; last amendment, Stb. 1985, 655.

Wet verontreiniging oppervlaktewater (Surface Water Pollution Act), Stb. 1969, 536.

B European Community (in chronological order)

Note: OJ = *Official Journal of the European Communities*.

70/220/EEC, Directive of 20 March 1970 on the approximation of the laws of the Member States related to measures to be taken against air pollution by gases from engines of motor vehicles, OJ L76, 6 April 1970.

Amendments: 74/290/EEC, OJ L159, 15 June 1974.
                 77/102/EEC, OJ L32, 3 February 1977.
                 78/665/EEC, OJ L223, 14 August 1978.
                 83/351/EEC, OJ L197, 20 July 1983.
                 88/76/EEC, OJ L36, 9 February 1988.
                 88/436/EEC, OJ L214, 6 August 1988.
                 89/458/EEC, OJ L226, 3 August 1989.
                 89/491/EEC, OJ L238, 15 August 1989.
                 91/441/EEC, OJ L242, 30 August 1991.

73/404/EEC, Directive of 22 November 1973 on the approximation of the laws of the member states relating to detergents, OJ L347, 17 December 1973.

Amendments: 82/242/EEC, OJ L109, 22 April 1982.
                 86/94/EEC, OJ L80, 25 March 1986

74/290/EEC: see 70/220/EEC.

75/442/EEC, Directive of 15 July 1975 on waste, OJ L194, 25 July 1975.

Amendment: 91/156/EEC, OJ L78, 26 March 1991.

75/716/EEC, Directive of 24 November 1975 on the approximation of the laws of the member states relating to the sulphur content of certain liquid fuels, OJ L307, 27 November 1975.

Amendments: 87/219/EEC, OJ L91, 3 April 1987.
                 93/12/EEC, OJ L74, 27 March 1993.

76/160/EEC, Directive of 8 December 1975 concerning the quality of bathing water, OJ L31, 5 February 1976.

76/464/EEC, Directive of 4 May 1976 on pollution caused by certain dangerous substances discharged into the aquatic environment of the Community, OJ L129, 18 May 1976.

77/102/EEC: see 70/220/EEC.

77/312/EEC, Directive of 22 March 1977 on biological screening of the population for lead, OJ L105, 28 April 1977.

78/319/EEC, Directive of 20 March 1978 on toxic and dangeous waste, OJ L84, 31 March 1978.

78/611/EEC, Directive of 29 June 1978 on the approximation of the laws of the Member States concerning the lead content of petrol, OJ L197, 20 July 1978 (replaced by Directive 85/210/EEC).

78/659/EEC, Directive of 18 July 1978 on the quality of fresh water needing protection or improvement to support fish life, OJ L222, 14 August 1978.

78/665/EEC: see 70/220/EEC.

79/923/EEC, Directive of 30 October 1979 on the quality required of shellfish waters, OJ L281, 10 November 1979.

80/779/EEC, Directive of 15 July 1980 on air quality limit values and guide values for sulphur dioxide and suspended particulates, OJ L229, 30 August 1980.

82/176/EEC, Directive of 22 March 1982 on limit values and quality objectives for mercury discharges by the chlor-alkali electrolysis industry, OJ L81, 27 March 1982.

82/884/EEC, Directive of 3 December 1982 on a limit value for lead in the air, OJ L378, 31 December 1982.

83/351/EEC: see 70/220/EEC.

83/513/EEC, Directive of 26 September 1983 on limit values and quality objectives for cadmium discharges, OJ L291, 24 October 1983.

84/156/EEC, Directive of 8 March 1984 on limit values and quality objectives for mercury discharges by sectors other than the chlor-alkali electrolysis industry, OJ L74, 17 March 1984.

84/360/EEC, Directive of 28 June 1984 on the combating of air pollution from industrial plants, OJ L188, 16 July 1984.

84/491/EEC, Directive of 9 October 1984 on limit values and quality objectives for discharges of hexachlorocyclohexane, OJ L274, 17 October 1984.

85/203/EEC, Directive of 7 March 1985 on air quality standards for nitrogen dioxide, OJ L87, 27 March 1985.

85/210/EEC, Directive of 20 March 1985 on the approximation of the laws of the Member States concerning the lead content of petrol, OJ L96, 3 April 1985.
Amendment: 87/416/EEC, OJ L225, 13 August 1987.

85/337/EEC, Directive of 27 June 1985 on the assessment of the effects of certain public and private projects on the environment, OJ L175, 5 July 1985.

86/280/EEC, Directive of 12 June 1986 on limit values and quality objectives for discharges of certain dangerous substances included in List I of the Annex to Directive 76/464/EEC, OJ L181, 4 July 1986.

87/219/EEC: see 75/716/EEC

87/416/EEC: see 85/210/EEC.

88/76/EEC: see 70/220/EEC.

88/458/EEC: see 70/220/EEC.

88/609/EEC, Directive of 24 November 1988 on the limitation of the emission of pollutants into the air from large combustion plants, OJ L336, 7 December 1988.

89/369/EEC, Directive of 8 June 1989 on the prevention of air pollution from new municipal waste incineration plants, OJ L163, 14 June 1989.

89/429/EEC, Directive of 21 June 1989 on the reduction of air pollution from existing municipal waste incineration plants, OJ L203, 15 July 1989.

89/458/EEC: see 70/220/EEC.

91/441/EEC: see 70/220/EEC.

91/676/EEC, Directive of 12 December 1991 concerning the protection of waters against pollution caused by nitrates from diffuse sources, OJ L375, 31 December 1991.

93/12/EEC: see 75/716/EEC.

II Official documents

A The Netherlands (in alphabetical order)

Note: TK = Tweede Kamer (documents of the Second Chamber of the Parliament; with year of publication and number). Since 1985 certain official

documents were also issued in English; * indicates that the English edition has
been used as basis of reference in this study.

Bestrijdingsplan verzuring, TK 1988–1989, 18225, no. 31.*
IMP-Lucht (Indicatief Meerjaren Programma Lucht) 1976–1980, TK 1976–1977,
    14314, nos 1–3.
IMP-Lucht (Indicatief Meerjaren Programma Lucht) 1981–1985, TK 1982–1983,
    17600, hfst. XVII, no. 7.
IMP-Lucht (Indicatief Meerjaren Programma Lucht) 1984–1988, TK 1983–1984,
    18100, hfst. XI, no. 7.
IMP-Lucht (Indicatief Meerjaren Programma Lucht) 1985–1989, TK 1984–1985,
    18605, nos 1–2.
IMP-Milieubeheer (Indicatief Meerjaren Programma Milieubeheer) 1985–1989,
    TK 1984–1985, 18602, nos 1–2.
IMP-Milieubeheer (Indicatief Meerjaren Programma Milieubeheer) 1986–1990,
    TK 1985–1986, 19204, nos 1–2.
Milieuprogramma 1988–1991, TK 1987–1988, 20202, nos 1–2.
Milieuprogramma 1990–1993, TK 1989–1990, 21304, nos 1–2.*
NMP1 (Nationaal Milieubeleidsplan 1), TK 1988–1989, 21137, nos 1–2.*
NMP-Plus (Nationaal Milieubeleidsplan Plus), TK 1989–1990, 21137, nos 20–
    21.*
NMP2 (Nationaal Milieubeleidsplan 2), TK 1993–1994, 23560, nos 1–2.
Nota Energiebeleid, deel II: Kolen, TK 1979–1980, 15802, no. 7.
Nota Milieuhygiënische Normen 1976, TK 1976–1977, 14318, nos 1–2.
Notitie mest- en ammoniakbeleid derde fase, TK 1992–1993, 19882, no. 34.
Plan van aanpak beperking ammoniak-emissies van de landbouw, TK 1990–
    1991, 18225, no. 42.
Problematiek van de verzuring, De, TK 1983–1984, 18225, nos 1–2.
SO$_2$-Beleidskaderplan, TK 1979–1980, 15834, nos 1–2.
Tussentijdse Evaluatie Verzuringsbeleid, TK 1987–1988, 18225, no 22.
Urgentienota Milieuhygiëne, TK 1971–1972, 11906, nos 1–2.

B European Community
COM documents (in chronological order).

COM(73)530, draft of EAP 1973–1976, see below.
COM(74)158: draft of directive 75/716/EEC, see above.
COM(75)166: draft of Directive 82/884/EEC, see above.
COM(75)681, draft directive on the use of fuel oils with a view to reducing
    sulphur emissions (see also OJ C54, 8 March 76; withdrawn).
COM(76)48: draft of Directive 80/779/EEC, see above.
COM(83)173, draft of Directive 84/360/EEC, see above.
COM(83)338, Acid depositions, Communication from the Commission to the
    Council.
COM(83)704, draft of Directive 88/609/EEC, see above.
COM(83)721, Communication from the Commission to the Council
    concerning environmental policy in the field of combating air pollution.

COM(84)226, draft of Directive 88/76/EEC (amendment to Directive 70/220/EEC), see above.
COM(85)47, revised draft of Directive 88/609/EEC, see above.
COM(85)228, revised draft of Directive 88/76/EEC (amendment to Directive 70/220/EEC), see above.
COM(85)377, draft of Directive 87/219/EEC (amendment to Directive 75/716/EEC), see above.
COM(87)706, draft of Directive 89/458/EEC (amendment to Directive 70/220/EEC), see above.
COM(88)338, Environment and Agriculture, Communication from the Commission.
COM(88)708: draft of Directive 91/676/EEC, see above.
COM(89)257, revised draft of Directive 89/458/EEC (amendment to Directive 70/220/EEC), see above.

Other documents (in alphabetical order)
Note: OJ = *Official Journal of the European Communities.*

EAP 1973–1976 (Action Programme on the Environment), OJ C112, 20 December 1973 (draft: COM(73)530, also published in: OJ C52, 26 May 1972).
EAP 1977–1981 (Action Programme on the Environment), OJ C139, 13 June 1977.
EAP 1982–1986 (Action Programme on the Environment), OJ C46, 17 February 1983 (draft: OJ C305, 25 November 1983).
EAP 1987–1992 (Action Programme on the Environment), OJ C328, 13 August 1987.
EAP 1993–2000, *Towards sustainability*, OJ C138, 17 May 1993.
SEC(72)666, preliminary draft of EAP 1973–1976, see above (also published in: OJ C52, 26 May 1972).

III Books and articles

Ågren, C. (1994), 'The making of a protocol', *Acid News*, 1, February, 11–13.
Aguilar Fernández, S. (1993), 'Spanish pollution control policy and peripheral regions in the European Community', paper presented at the ECPR Joint Session of Workshops, Leiden, 2–8 April.
Aguilar Fernández, S. (forthcoming), 'Abandoning a laggard role: new strategies in Spanish environmental policy', in: J. D. Liefferink and M. S. Andersen (eds), *The innovation of European environmental policy*, Copenhagen: Akademisk Forlag/Scandinavian University Press.
Andersen, M. S. and J. D. Liefferink (eds) (forthcoming), *European environmental policy: the pioneers*, Manchester, Manchester University Press.
Allison, G. T. (1971), *Essence of decision – explaining the Cuban missile crisis*, Boston, Little, Brown and Company.

Andersen, S. S. and K. A. Eliassen (1991), 'European Community lobbying', *Journal of Political Research*, 20, 173–187.

Arp, H. A. (1991), 'Interest groups in EC legislation: the case of car emission standards', paper presented at the ECPR Joint Session of Workshops, Essex, 22–28 March.

Arp, H. A. (1992), *The European Parliament in European Community environmental policy*, Florence, European University Institute, EUI Working Paper EPU No. 92/13.

Arp, H. A. (1993), 'Technical regulation and politics: the interplay between economic interests and environmental policy goals in EC car emission legislation', in: J. D. Liefferink, P. D. Lowe and A. P. J. Mol (eds), *European integration and environmental policy*, London, Belhaven Press, 150–171.

Averyt, W. F. (1977), *Agropolitics in the European Community. Interest groups and the Common Agricultural Policy*, New York, Praeger Publishers.

Baldock, D. and G. Bennett (1991), *Agriculture and the polluter pays principle, a study of six EC countries*, London, Institute for European Environmental Policy.

Becker, K. (1988), *Der weite Weg nach Luxemburg, Bemühungen der BRD zur Verminderung der Schadstoffemissionen von Personenkraftwagen*, Berlin, Umweltbundesamt.

Bennett, G. (ed.) (1991), *Air pollution control in the European Community. Implementation of the EC Directives in the twelve Member States*, London, Graham and Trotman.

Bennett, G. (1992), *Dilemma's. The hard reality of environmental management*, London, Earthscan.

Bennett, G. and J. D. Liefferink (1989), 'Het milieubeleid van de Europese Gemeenschap, theorie en praktijk', in: G. Spaargaren, *et al.* (eds), *Internationaal milieubeleid*, 's-Gravenhage, SDU Uitgeverij, 45–62 (2nd ed., 1993, 39–58).

Benson, J. K. (1975), 'The interorganizational network as a political economy', *Administrative Science Quarterly*, 20, June, 229–249

Benson, J. K. (1982), 'Networks and policy sectors: a framework for extending interorganizational analysis', in: D. Rogers and D. Whitten (eds), *Interorganizational coordination*, Ames, IA, Iowa State University Press.

Bishop, A. S. and R. D. Munro (1972), 'The UN regional economic commissions and environmental problems', *International Organization*, 26, 348–371.

Boehmer-Christiansen, S. (1990), 'Vehicle emission regulation in Europe – the demise of lean-burn engines, the polluter pays principle ... and the small car?', *Energy and Environment*, 1 (1), 1–25.

Boehmer-Christiansen, S. and J. Skea (1991), *Acid politics: environmental and energy policies in Britain and Germany*, London, Belhaven Press.

Boehmer-Christiansen, S. and H. Weidner (1992), *Catalyst versus lean burn*, Berlin, Wissenschaftszentrum Berlin für Sozialforschung, WZB Paper FS II, 92–304.

Brinkhorst, L. J. (1989), 'Communautair milieubeleid, prioriteiten en per-spectieven', in: G. Spaargaren, *et al.* (eds), *Internationaal milieubeleid*, 's-Gravenhage, SDU Uitgeverij, 63–80.

Brinkhorst, L. J. (1992), *Subsidiariteit en milieu in de Europese Gemeenschap. Doos van Pandora of panacee?*, Leiden, Rijksuniversiteit Leiden, inaugural lecture.

Brownlie, I. (1990), *Public international law*, Oxford, Clarendon Press.

Brussaard, W. (ed.) (1993), *Hoofdlijnen van het agrarisch recht*, Zwolle, W. E. J. Tjeenk Willink.

Bulmer, M. (ed.) (1984), *Sociological research methods*, London, Macmillan.

Bulmer, S. (1983), 'Domestic politics and European Community policy-making', *Journal of Common Market Studies*, 21 (4), 349–363.

Bungarten, H. H. (1978), *Umweltpolitik in Westeuropa. EG, internationale Organisationen und nationale Umweltpolitiken*, Bonn, Europa Union Verlag.

Caldwell, L. K. (1990), *International environmental policy: emergence and dimensions*, Durham, Duke University Press (2nd ed.).

Cassese, A. (1986), *International law in a divided world*, Oxford, Clarendon Press.

Cawson, A. (1992), 'Interests, groups and public policy-making: the case of the European consumer electronics industry', in: J. Greenwood, J. R. Grote and K. Ronit (eds), *Organized interests and the European Community*, London, Sage, 99–118.

CEC (Commission of the European Communities) (1987), *Basisstatistieken van de Gemeenschap – 24e uitgave*, Luxembourg, Office for Official Publications of the European Communities.

CEC (Commission of the European Communities) (1988), *Basisstatistieken van de Gemeenschap – 25e uitgave*, Luxembourg, Office for Official Publications of the European Communities.

CEC (Commission of the European Communities) (1990), *Basisstatistieken van de Gemeenschap – 27e uitgave*, Luxembourg, Office for Official Publications of the European Communities.

Collie, L. (1993), 'Business lobbying in the European Community, the Union of Industrial and Employers' Confederations of Europe', in: S. Mazey and J. Richardson, J. (eds), *Lobbying in the European Community*, Oxford, Oxford University Press, 213–229.

Corcelle, G. (1985), 'L'introduction de la 'voiture propre' en Europe', *Revue du Marché Commun*, 287, 258–263.

Corcelle, G. (1986), 'L'introduction de la 'voiture propre' en Europe: suite et fin', *Revue du Marché Commun*, 295, 125–131.

Corcelle, G. (1989), 'La 'voiture propre' en Europe: le bout du tunnel est en vue!', *Revue du Marché Commun*, 331, 513–526.

Dahl, R. (1961), *Who governs?*, New Haven, Yale University Press.

Dehousse, R. (1992), *Does subsidiarity really matter?*, Florence, European University Institute, Working Paper LAW No. 92/32.

Dietz, F., J. van der Straaten and M. van der Velde (1991), 'The European Common Market and the environment: the case of the emission of NO$_x$ by motorcars', *Review of Political Economy*, 3 (1), 62–78.

Donkers, R. H. (1988), 'Die Niederländische Regierung und die EG-Umweltpolitik. Das Beispiel der EG-Politik zur Bekämpfung der Versäurung', in: K. Tudyka (ed.), *Umweltpolitik in Ost- und West-europa*, Opladen, Leske & Budrich, 213–228.

Donkers, R. (1989), 'De rol van Nederland bij de totstandkoming van Communautaire wetgeving en de praktische problemen bij de implementatie daarvan', in: T. M. C. Asser Instituut (ed.), *Europees milieurecht, verslag van de zeventiende zitting van het Asser Instituut Colloquium Europees Recht 4 September 1987*, 's-Gravenhage, TMC Asser Instituut.

Dos Santos, T. (1973) 'The crisis of development theory and the problem of dependence in Latin America', in: H. Bernstein (ed.), *Underdevelopment and development*, Harmondsworth, Penguin.

Dovland, H. and J. Saltbones (1986), *Emissions of sulphur dioxide in Europe in 1980 and 1983*, Lillestrom, EMEP/CCC, Report 1/86.

EC (European Communities) (1973), 'Agreement of the representatives of the governments of the member states meeting in Council of 5 March 1973 on information for the Commission and for the member states with a view to possible harmonization throughout the Communities of urgent measures concerning the protection of the environment', *Official Journal of the European Communities*, C9.

EC (European Communities) (1974), 'Agreement of the representatives of the governments of the member states of the European Communities meeting in Council of 15 July 1974 supplementing the agreement of 5 March 1973 on information for the Commission and for the member states with a view to possible harmonization throughout the Communities of urgent measures concerning the protection of the environment', *Official Journal of the European Communities*, C86.

EEB (European Environmental Bureau; author: E. R. Klatte) (1984), *Ten years of European Environmental Bureau (1974–1984)*, Brussels, EEB.

Eerens, H. C., et al. (1989), *Uitvoering besluiten luchtkwaliteit zwaveldioxide en zwevende deeltjes, stikstofdioxide en koolstofmonoxide en lood, rapportage over de jaren 1986, 1987 en 1988*, Bilthoven, Rijksinstituut voor Volksgezondheid en Milieuhygiëne.

Eliassen, A. (1978), 'The OECD study of long range transport of air pollutants', *Atmospheric Environment*, 12, 479–487.

EP (European Parliament) (1984), 'Resolutie tot besluit van raadpleging van het Europees Parlement over het voorstel van de Commissie van de Europese Gemeenschappen aan de Raad vor een richtlijn inzake beperking van de emissie van verontreinigende stoffen door grote stookinstallaties', *Official Journal of the European Communities*, C337, 446.

EP (European Parliament) (1985), 'Resolutie over het voorstel van de Commissie van de Europese Gemeenschappen aan de Raad vor een richtlijn inzake beperking van de emissie van verontreinigende stoffendoor grote stookinstallaties (COM(83)704) naar aanleiding van een gewijzigd voorstel van de Commissie (COM(85)47)', *Official Journal of the European Communities*, C175, 297.

EP (European Parliament) (1986), 'Resolutie over de nalatigheid van de Raad maatregelen te treffen tegen de luchtverontreiniging door grote stookinstallaties', *Official Journal of the European Communities*, C176, 171.

EP (European Parliament) (1989), 'Wetgevingsresolutie houdende advies van het Europees Parlement inzake het voorstel van de Commissie aan de

Raad voor een richtlijn inzake de bescherming van zoet water, kustwater en zeewater tegen verontreiniging door van diffuse bronnen afkomstige nitraten, *Official Journal of the European Communities*, C158, 487.

Frank, A. G. (1967), *Capitalism and underdevelopment in Latin America*, New York, Monthly Review Press.

Frouws, J. (1988), 'State and society with respect to agriculture and the rural environment in the Netherlands', in: J. Frouws and W. T. de Groot (eds), *Environment and agriculture in the Netherlands*, Leiden, Centrum voor Milieustudies Leiden, Mededelingen no. 47, 39–55.

Frouws, J. (1993), *Mest en macht. Een politiek-sociologische studie naar belangenbehartiging en beleidsvorming inzake de mestproblematiek in Nederland vanaf 1970*, Wageningen, Landbouwuniversiteit, Studies van Landbouw en Platteland 11.

Füllenbach, J. (1981), *European environmental policy: East and West*, London, Butterworths.

Garrett, G. (1992), 'International cooperation and institutional choice: the European Community's internal market', *International Organization*, 46 (2), 533–560.

Gezondheidsraad (1971), *Advies inzake grenswaarden SO_2*, 's-Gravenhage, Ministerie van Volksgezondheid en Milieuhygiëne, Verslagen en Mededelingen, no. 22.

Giddens, A. (1984), *The constitution of society*, Cambridge, Polity Press.

Giddens, A. (1985), *The nation-state and violence*, Cambridge, Polity Press.

Giddens, A. (1990), *The consequences of modernity*, Cambridge, Polity Press.

Grant, W. (1993), 'Pressure groups and the European Community', in: S. Mazey and J. Richardson, J. (eds), *Lobbying in the European Community*, Oxford, Oxford University Press, 27–46.

Grant, W., W. Paterson and C. Whitston (1988), *Government and the chemical industry*, Oxford, Clarendon Press.

Greenwood, J., J. R. Grote and K. Ronit (1992), 'Introduction: organized interests and the transnational dimension', in: J. Greenwood, J. R. Grote and K. Ronit (eds), *Organized interests and the European Community*, London, Sage, 1–41.

Haas, E. B. (1958), *The uniting of Europe. Political, economic and social forces, 1950–1957*, Stanford, CA, Stanford University Press.

Haas, E. B. (1964), *Beyond the nation-state. Functionalism and international organization*, Stanford, CA, Stanford University Press.

Haas, E. B. (1971), 'The study of regional integration: reflections on the joy and anguish of pretheorizing', in: L. N. Lindberg and S. A. Scheingold (eds), *Regional integration. Theory and practice*, Cambridge, MA, Harvard University Press.

Haas, E. B. (1975), *The obsolescence of regional integration theory*, Research Series no. 25, Berkely, University of California, Institute of International Studies.

Haas, E. B. (1980), 'Why collaborate? Issue-linkage and international regimes', *World Politics*, 32 (3), 357–405.

Haigh, N. (1988), 'The European Economic Community', in: B. Rhode (ed.), *Air pollution in Europe, a collection of country reports on air pollution* and national policies. Vol. 1: Western Europe, Vienna, Vienna Centre, Occasional Paper no. 4.

Haigh, N., et al. (1986), European Community environmental policy in practice, 4 vols, London, Graham and Trotman.

Hajer, M. A. (1993), The politics of environmental discourse: a study of the acid rain controversy in Great Britain and the Netherlands, dissertation, Oxford University.

Hawdon, D. (1988), 'Energy policy', in: P. Coffey (ed.), Main economic policy areas of the EEC – towards 1992, Dordrecht, Kluwer Academic Publishers, 99–131.

Heisler, M. O. and R. B. Kvavik (1974), 'Patterns of European politics: the "European Polity" model', in: M. O. Heisler (ed.), Politics in Europe. Structures and processes in some post-industrial democracies, New York, David McKay Company, 27–89.

Héritier, A., et al. (1994), Die Veränderung von Staatlichkeit in Europa. Ein regulativer Wettbewerb: Deutschland, Grossbritannien, Frankreich, Opladen, Leske & Budrich.

Hey, C. and U. Brendle (1994), Umweltverbände und EG. Strategien, politische Kulturen und Organisationsformen, Opladen, Westdeutscher Verlag.

Hoffmann, S. (1983), 'Reflections on the nation-state in Western Europe today', in: L. Tsoukalis (ed.), The European Community. Past, present and future, Oxford, Basil Blackwell.

Holsti, K. J. (1983), International politics. A framework for analysis, Englewood Cliffs, NJ, Prentice-Hall International (4th ed.).

Holzinger, K. (1994), Politik des kleinsten gemeinsamen Nenners? Umweltpolitische Entscheidungsprozesse in der EG am Beispiel der Einführung des Katalysatorautos, Berlin, edition sigma.

Hontelez, J. J. A. M. (1993), 'Internationaal milieubeleid en de milieubeweging', in: G. Spaargaren, et al. (eds), Internationaal milieubeleid, 's-Gravenhage, SDU Uitgeverij, 171–194 (2nd ed., 1993, 171–194).

Huber, M. (forthcoming), 'Leadership in the EU climate policy. Innovative policy making in policy networks', in: J. D. Liefferink and M. S. Andersen (eds), The innovation of EU environmental policy, Copenhagen, Akademish Forlag/Scandinavian University Press.

Huelshoff, M. G. (1994), 'Domestic politics and dynamic issue linkage: a reformulation of integration theory', International Studies Quarterly, 38, 255–279.

Hull, R. (1993), 'Lobbying Brussels: a view from within', in: S. Mazey and J. Richardson, J. (eds), Lobbying in the European Community, Oxford, Oxford University Press, 82–92.

ISEI (Interdisciplinaire Studiegroep Europese Integratie) (1993), Institutionele toekomstverkenningen. De plaats van Nederland in de Europese Gemeenschap (EG) bij toetreding van nieuwe leden, 's-Gravenhage, SDU Uitgeverij.

Jachtenfuchs, M. (1989), 'Die EG-Umweltpolitik nach dem vierten Aktionsprogramm', Ars Aequi, 38 (5), 183–188.

Jachtenfuchs, M. and M. Huber (1993), 'Institutional learning in the European

Community: the response to the greenhouse effect', in: J. D. Liefferink, P. D. Lowe and A. P. J. Mol (eds), *European integration and environmental policy*, London, Belhaven Press, 36–58.

Jänicke, M. (1990), 'Erfolgsbedingungen von Umweltpolitik im internationalen Vergleich', *Zeitschrift für Umweltpolitik und Umweltrecht*, 3, 213–232.

Jansen, M. and J. K. de Vree (1985), *The ordeal of unity: the politics of European integration 1945–1985*, Bilthoven, Prime Press.

Johnson, S. P. and G. Corcelle (1989), *The environmental policy of the European Communities*, London, Graham and Trotman.

Jordan, G. and K. Schubert (1992), 'A preliminary ordering of policy network labels', *European Journal of Political Research*, 21, 7–27.

Kakebeeke, W. J. (1989) 'Milieu als (inter)nationale prioriteit', in: G. Spaargaren, *et al.* (eds), *Internationaal milieubeleid*, 's-Gravenhage, SDU Uitgeverij, 27–44 (2nd ed., 1993, 19–37).

Kamminga, M. T. and E. R. Klatte (1994), 'Twintig jaar EG milieubeleid en het integratiebeginsel', *Milieu & Recht*, 1, 2–10.

Kapteyn, P. J. G. and P. VerLoren van Themaat (1987), *Inleiding tot het recht van de Europese Gemeenschappen*, Deventer, Kluwer (4th ed.).

Kapteyn, P. J. G. and P. VerLoren van Themaat (1989), *Introduction to the law of the European Community: after the coming into force of the Single European Act*, Deventer, Kluwer Law and Taxation Publishers.

Katzenstein, P. (1978), *Between power and plenty. Foreign economic policies of advanced industrial states*, Madison, University of Wisconsin Press.

Keohane, R. O. (1984), *After hegemony. Cooperation and discord in the world political economy*, Princeton, NJ, Princeton University Press.

Keohane, R. O. and S. Hoffmann (1990), 'Conclusions: Community policies and institutional change', in: W. Wallace (ed.), *The dynamics of European integration*, London, Pinter Publishers, 276–300.

Keohane, R. O. and S. Hoffmann (1991), 'Institutional change in Europe in the 1980s', in: R. O Keohane and S. Hoffmann (eds), *The new European Community. Decisionmaking and institutional change*, Boulder, CO, Westview Press, 1–39.

Keohane, R. O. and J. S. Nye (1977), *Power and interdependence. World politics in transition*, Boston, MA, Little, Brown and Company.

Keohane, R. O. and J. S. Nye (1987), 'Power and interdependence revisited', *International Organization*, 41 (4), 725–753.

Kooijmans, P. H. (1990), *Internationaal publiekrecht in vogelvlucht*, Groningen, Wolters-Noordhoff (2nd ed.).

Koppen, I. J. (1988a), *The European Community's environment policy. From the summit in Paris, 1972, to the Single European Act, 1987*, Florence, European University Institute, Working Paper 88/328.

Koppen, I. J. (1988b), 'De Europese Akte als Grondwet van het milieubeleid van de Europese Gemeenschappen', *SEW*, 10, 624–637.

Koppen, I. J. (1993), 'The role of the European Court of Justice', in: J. D. Liefferink, P. D. Lowe and A. P. J. Mol (eds), *European integration and environmental policy*, London, Belhaven Press, 126–149.

Krämer, L. (1987) 'The Single European Act and environment protection:

reflections on several new provisions in Community law', *Common Market Law Review*, 24, 659–688.

Krasner, S. D. (1978), *Defending the national interest: raw materials investments and US foreign policy*, Princeton, Princeton University Press.

Krasner, S. D. (ed.) (1983), *International regimes*, Ithaca, Cornell University Press.

La Spina, A. and G. Sciortino (1993), 'Common agenda, southern rules: European integration and environmental change in the Mediterranean states', in: J. D. Liefferink, P. D. Lowe and A. P. J. Mol (eds), *European integration and environmental policy*, London, Belhaven Press, 217–236.

Landbouwschap (1988), *Nota uitgangspunten milieuvraagstukken*, 's-Gravenhage, Landbouwschap.

Lasok, D. and J. W. Bridge (1991), *Law and institutions of the European Communities*, London, Butterworths (5th ed.).

Laumann, E. O. and D. Knoke (1987), *The organizational state. Social choice in national policy domains*, Madison, WI, University of Wisconsin Press.

Leonard, H. J. (1988), *Pollution and the struggle for the world product. Multinational corporations, environment and international comparative advantage*, Cambridge, Cambridge University Press.

Liefferink, J. D. (forthcoming), 'The Netherlands: a net exporter of environmental policy principles', in: M. S. Andersen and J. D. Liefferink (eds), *European environmental policy: the pioneers*, Manchester, Manchester University Press.

Liefferink, J. D. and M. S. Andersen (eds) (forthcoming), *The innovation of European environmental policy*, Copenhagen, Akademish Forlag/ Scandinavian University Press.

Liefferink, J. D., P. D. Lowe and A. P. J. Mol (eds) (1993a), *European integration and environmental policy*, London, Belhaven Press.

Liefferink, J. D., P. D. Lowe and A. P. J. Mol (1993b), 'The environment and the European Community: the analysis of political integration', in: J. D. Liefferink, P. D. Lowe and A. P. J. Mol (eds), *European integration and environmental policy*, London, Belhaven Press, 1–13.

Liefferink, J. D., and A. P. J. Mol (1993), 'Environmental policy making in the European Community: an evaluation of theoretical perspectives', in: J. D. Liefferink, P. D. Lowe and A. P. J. Mol (eds), *European integration and environmental policy*, London, Belhaven Press, 99–113.

Lindberg, L. N. (1971), 'Political integration as a multidimensional phenomenon requiring multivariate measurement', in: L. N. Lindberg and S. A. Scheingold (eds), *Regional integration. Theory and research*, Cambridge, MA, Harvard University Press, 45–127.

Lindberg, L. N. and S. A. Scheingold (1970), *Europe's would-be politics. Patterns of change in the European Community*, Englewood Cliffs, NJ, Prentice-Hall.

Lindberg, L. N. and S. A. Scheingold (eds) (1971), *Regional integration. Theory and research*, Cambridge, MA, Harvard University Press.

Lowe, P. D. and J. Goyder (1983), *Environmental groups in politics*, London, Allen and Unwin.

Marsh, D. and R. A. W. Rhodes (1992), 'Policy communities and issue networks: beyond typology', in: D. Marsh and R. A. W. Rhodes (eds), *Policy networks in British government*, Oxford, Clarendon Press, 249–268.

Mazey, S. and J. Richardson, J. (eds) (1993a), *Lobbying in the European Community*, Oxford, Oxford University Press.

Mazey, S. and J. Richardson (1993b), 'Introduction: transference of power, decision rules, and rules of the game', in: S. Mazey and J. Richardson (eds), *Lobbying in the European Community*, Oxford, Oxford University Press, 3–26.

McCormick, J. (1985), *Acid earth, the global threat of acid pollution*, London, Earthscan.

McLaughlin, A. and G. Jordan (1993), 'The rationality of lobbying in Europe: why are Euro-groups so numerous and so weak? Some evidence from the car industry', in: S. Mazey and J. Richardson (eds), *Lobbying in the European Community*, Oxford, Oxford University Press, 122–161.

Mol, A. P. J., and J. D. Liefferink (1993), 'European environmental policy and global interdependence: a review of theoretical approaches', in: J. D. Liefferink, P. D. Lowe and A. P. J. Mol (eds), *European integration and environmental policy*, London, Belhaven Press, 17–35.

Moltke, K. von (1979), 'Europäische Umweltpolitik', *Zeitschrift für Umweltpolitik und Umweltrecht*, 1, 77–92.

Moravcsik, A. (1993), 'Preferences and power in the European Community: a liberal intergovernmentalist approach', *Journal of Common Market Studies*, 31 (4), 473–524.

Morgenthau, H. J. (1948), *Politics among nations: the struggle for power and peace*, New York, Alfred A. Knopf.

Nau, H. R. (1979), 'From integration to interdependence: gains, losses, and continuing gaps', *International Organization*, 33 (1), 119–147.

Nilsson, J. (ed.) (1986), *Critical loads for nitrogen and sulphur*, Copenhagen, Nordisk Ministerraad, Miljø rapport 11.

Nooij, A. T. J. (1990), *Sociale methodiek. Normatieve en beschrijvende methodiek in grondvormen*, Leiden, Stenfert Kroese.

Nugent, N. (1991), *The government and politics of the European Community*, London, Macmillan (2nd ed.).

Nye, J. S. (1971), 'Comparing common markets: a revised neo-functionalist model', in: L. N. Lindberg and S. A. Scheingold (eds), *Regional integration. Theory and research*, Cambridge, MA, Harvard University Press.

OECD (Organisation for Economic Cooperation and Development) (1975), *The polluter pays principle. Definition, analysis, implementation*, Paris, OECD.

OECD (Organisation for Economic Cooperation and Development) (1986), *OECD and the environment*, Paris, OECD.

OECD (Organisation for Economic Cooperation and Development) (1989), *Economic instruments for environmental protection*, Paris, OECD.

Opschoor, J. B. and S. W. F. van der Ploeg (1990), 'Duurzaamheid en kwaliteit: hoofddoelstellingen van milieubeleid', in: Commissie Lange Termijn

Milieubeleid (ed.), *Het milieu: denkbeelden voor de 21ste eeuw*, Zeist, Kerkebosch.

Pehle, H. (forthcoming), 'Germany: national obstacles to an international forerunner', in: M. S. Andersen and J. D. Liefferink (eds), *European environmental policy: the pioneers*, Manchester, Manchester University Press.

Persson, G. (1976), 'Control of sulphur dioxide emissions in Europe', *Ambio*, 5 (5–6), 249–252.

Peterson, J. (1992), 'The European Technology Community: policy networks in a supranational setting', in: D. Marsh and R. A. W. Rhodes (eds), *Policy networks in British government*, Oxford, Clarendon Press, 226–248.

Porter, M. and A. Butt Philip (1993), 'The role of interest groups in EU environmental policy formulation: a case study of the draft packaging directive', *European Environment*, 3 (6), 16–20.

Pridham, G. (1994), 'National environmental policy-making in the European framework: Spain, Greece and Italy in comparison', *Regional Politics and Policy*, 4 (1), 80–101.

Prittwitz, V. (1984), *Umweltaussenpolitik. Grenzüberschreitende Luftverschmutzung in Europa*, Frankfurt, Campus Verlag.

Putnam, R. D. (1988), 'Diplomacy and domestic policies: the logic of two-level games', *International Organization*, 42 (3), 427–460.

Rehbinder, E. and R. Stewart (1985), *Environmental protection policy*, vol. 2 of: M. Cappelletti *et al.* (eds), *Integration through law: Europe and the American federal experience*, Berlin, Walter de Gruyter.

Rhodes, R. A. W. (1981), *Control and power in central–local relations*, Aldershot, Gower.

Rhodes, R. A. W. (1986), *The national world of local government*, London, Allen and Unwin.

Rhodes, R. A. W. (1988), *Beyond Westminster and Whitehall*, London, Unwin-Hyman.

Rhodes, R. A. W. and D. Marsh (1992), 'Policy networks in British politics: a critique of existing approaches', in: D. Marsh and R. A. W. Rhodes (eds), *Policy networks in British government*, Oxford, Clarendon Press, 1–26.

Richardson, J. (ed.) (1982), *Policy styles in Western Europe*, London, George Allen & Unwin.

Richardson, J. J. and A. G. Jordan (1979), *Governing under pressure. The policy process in a post-parliamentary democracy*, Oxford, Martin Robertson.

Rijksplanologische Dienst (1993), *Ruimtelijke verkenningen 1993*, 's-Gravenhage, SDU Uitgeverij Plantijnstraat.

RIVM (Rijksinstituut voor Volksgezondheid en Milieuhygiëne) (1988), *Zorgen voor morgen, nationale milieuverkenning 1985–2010*, Alphen aan den Rijn, Samsom H. D. Tjeenk Willink.

Roqueplo, P. (1988), *Pluies acides: menace pour l'Europe*, Paris, Economica.

Rucht, D. (1993), '"Think globally, act locally?" Needs, forms and problems of cross-national cooperation among environmental groups', in: J. D. Liefferink, P. D. Lowe and A. P. J. Mol (eds), *European integration and environmental policy*, London, Belhaven Press, 75–95.

Scharpf, F. W. (1985), 'Die Politikverflechtungs-Falle: Europäische Integration und deutscher Föderalismus im Vergleich', *Politische Vierteljahresschrift*, 26 (4), 323–356.

Scharpf, F. W. (1988), 'The joint-decision trap: lessons from German federalism and European integration', *Public Administration*, 66, 239–278.

Scheuing, D. H. (1989), 'Umweltschutz auf der Grundlage der Einheitlichen Europäischen Akte', *Europa Recht*, 2, 152–192

Schmitter, P. C. (1971), 'A revised theory of regional integration', in: L. N. Lindberg and S. A. Scheingold (eds), *Regional integration. Theory and research*, Cambridge, MA, Harvard University Press, 232–264.

Schmitter, P. (1974), 'Still the century of corporatism?', *Review of Politics*, 36, 85–131.

Sevenster, H. G. (1989), *De gevolgen van de voltooiing van de interne markt voor het nationaal milieubeleid*, Leiden, Rijksuniversiteit Leiden, Europa Instituut (published under the same title by: 's-Gravenhage, Staatsuitgeverij/DOP, Publikatiereeks Milieubeheer no. 1990/2).

Sevenster, H. G. (1992), *Milieubeleid en Gemeenschapsrecht: het interne juridische kader en de praktijk*, Deventer, Kluwer, Europese Monografieën 38.

Smith, M. J. (1990), *The politics of agricultural support: the development of an agricultural policy community*, Aldershot, Dartmouth.

Smith, M. J. (1993), *Pressure, power and policy. State autonomy and policy networks in Britain and the United States*, New York, Harvester Wheatsheaf.

Smith, G. (1990), *Politics in Western Europe*, Aldershot, Dartmouth (5th ed.).

Van den Bos, J. M. M. (1991), *Dutch EC policy making. A model-guided approach to coordination and negotiation*, Amsterdam, Thesis Publishers.

Van Tatenhove, J. (1993), *Milieubeleid onder dak. Beleidsvoeringsprocessen in het Nederlandse milieubeleid in de periode 1970–1990; nader uitgewerkt voor de Gelderse Vallei*, Wageningen, Pudoc, Wageningse Sociologische Studies no. 35.

Van Tatenhove, J. P. M. and J. D. Liefferink (1992), 'Environmental policy in the Netherlands and in the European Community, a conceptual approach', in: F. von Benda-Beckmann and M. van der Velde (eds), *Law as a resource in agrarian struggles*, Wageningen, Pudoc, Wageningen Studies in Sociology no. 33, 267–293.

Van Waarden, F. (1992), 'Dimensions and types of policy networks', *European Journal of Political Research*, 21, 29–52.

Van Zon, H. (1986), *Een zeer onfrisse geschiedenis, studie over niet-industriële verontreiniging in Nederland 1850–1920*, 's-Gravenhage, SDU.

VROM (Ministerie van Volkshuisvesting, Ruimtelijke Ordening en Milieubeheer) (1988), *Doelgroepdocument Raffinaderijen – basis- en achtergrondinformatie ten aanzien van de bedrijfstak*, 's-Gravenhage, VROM, Publikatiereeks Lucht no. 78.

Wallace, W. (1983a), 'Europe as a condeferation: the Community and the nation-state', in: L. Tsoukalis (ed.), *The European Community. Past, present and future*, Oxford, Basil Blackwell.

Wallace, W. (1983b), 'Less than a federation, more than a regime: the

Community as a political system', in: H. Wallace, W. Wallace and C. Webb (eds), *Policy making in the European Community*, Chicester, John Wiley and Sons (2nd ed.).

Wallace, W. (1990), *The transformation of Western Europe*, London, The Royal Institute of Foreign Affairs/Pinter Publishers.

Wallerstein, I. (1979), *The capitalist world-economy*, Cambridge, Cambridge University Press.

Wallerstein, I. (1984), *The politics of the world-economy. The states, the movements, and the civilizations*, Cambridge, Cambridge University Press.

Webb, C. (1983), 'Theoretical perspectives and problems', in: H. Wallace, W. Wallace and C. Webb (eds), *Policy making in the European Community*, Chicester, John Wiley and Sons (2nd ed.).

Weidner, H. and P. Knoepfel (1981), 'Implementationschancen der EG-Richtlinie zur SO_2-Luftreinhaltepolitik', *Zeitschrift für Umweltpolitik*, 1, 27–68.

Weiler, J. (1982), 'The Community system: the dual character of supranationalism', *Yearbook of European Law*, 1, 267–306.

Weiler, J. H. H. (1991), 'The transformation of Europe', *Yale Law Journal*, 100, 2401–2483.

Weizsäcker, E. U. von and H. Schreiber (1988), 'Luftreinhaltung – der schwierige Konsens', in: L. Gündling and B. Weber (eds), *Dicke Luft in Europa, Aufgaben und Probleme der europäischen Umweltpolitik*, Heidelberg, C. F. Müller, 163–172.

Wetstone, G. S. and A. Rosencranz (1983), *Acid rain in Europe and North America, national responses to an international problem*, Washington, DC, Environmental Law Institute.

WHO (World Health Organization) (1972), *Air quality criteria and objectives for urban air pollutants, report of a WHO expert committee*, Geneva, WHO, Technical Report Series, no. 506.

WHO (World Health Organization) (1979), *Sulfur oxides and suspended particulate matter*, Geneva, WHO, Environmental Health Criteria, no. 8.

Wilks, S. and M. Wright (1987), 'Conclusion: comparing government–industry relations: states, sectors and networks', in: S. Wilks and M. Wright (eds), *Comparative government–industry relations. Western Europe, the United States and Japan*, Oxford, Clarendon Press, 274–313.

Williamson, P. J. (1989), *Corporatism in perspective. An introductory guide to corporatist theory*, London, Sage.

Winsemius, P. (1986), *Gast in eigen huis. Beschouwingen over milieumanagement*, Alphen aan den Rijn, Samsom H. D. Tjeenk Willink.

Yin, R. K. (1984), *Case study research: design and methods*, Beverly Hills, Sage.

Young, O. R. (1986), 'International regimes: toward a new theory of institutions', *World Politics*, 39, 104–122.

Index

Entries appear in their English form, as given in the List of abbreviations, pp. xii–iv.